P9-BBT-586

The Secret Trust of Aspasia Cruvellier Mirault

The Secret Trust of Aspasia Cruvellier Mirault

The Life and Trials of a Free Woman of Color in Antebellum Georgia

Janice L. Sumler-Edmond

The University of Arkansas Press

Fayetteville 2008

ISBN-10: 1-55728-880-1
ISBN-13: 978-1-55728-880-6

12 11 10 09 08 5 4 3 2 1

Text design by Ellen Beeler

The paper used in this publication meets the minimum requirements
of the American National Standard for Permanence of Paper
for Printed Library Materials Z39.48-1984.

Library of Congress Cataloging-in-Publication Data

Sumler-Edmond, Janice.
The secret trust of Aspasia Cruvellier Mirault : a free woman of color
in antebellum Georgia / Janice L. Sumler-Edmond.
p. cm.
Includes bibliographical references and index.
ISBN 978-1-55728-880-6 (cloth : alk. paper)
1. Mirault, Aspasia Cruvellier, d. 1857. 2. Mirault, Aspasia Cruvellier,
d. 1857— Family. 3. African American women—Georgia—Savannah—
Biography. 4. Free African Americans—Georgia—Savannah—Biography.
5. African Americans—Georgia—Savannah—Biography. 6. Widows—Georgia—
Savannah—Biography. 7. Savannah (Ga.)—Biography. 8. Savannah (Ga.)—
History—19th century. 9. Trusts and trustees—Georgia—Savannah—Biography.
10. Savannah (Ga.)—Social life and customs—19th century. 11. Savannah
(Ga.)—Race relations—History—19th century. I. Title.
F294.S2S86 2008
975.8'72403092—dc22
[B]
2008013233

To my family: Steven Edmond, Marilyn S. Jackson,
Lurenda Mosley, and Ida Briggs Baker and to the memory
of my parents, Ernest and Lucille Sumler

Contents

Illustrations

(following page 60)

Acknowledgments

Throughout the seven-year journey of researching and writing this book, I have been the fortunate beneficiary of much guidance, support, and encouragement. Institutional support came in the way of a year-long sabbatical from my teaching and administrative duties at Clark Atlanta University. That sabbatical period, occurring early in the life of this project, gave me the time to conceptualize my ideas about Aspasia Mirault and her nineteenth-century world and to construct a first draft of the manuscript. I am grateful also for two awards received in my current role as a faculty member at Huston-Tillotson University. A Sam Taylor Fellowship Award from the General Board of Higher Education and Ministry of the United Methodist Church provided funding for two visits to archival repositories at the final stages of this project. For the past two Decembers, I received UNCF-Mellon Book/Research Awards from the UNCF-Mellon Programs. These awards were used to purchase photographs and to defray duplicating costs.

I am deeply indebted to my girlhood friends, several relatives, a host of new acquaintances, and a number of very capable archival staff persons, all of whom provided assistance as I completed this work. To these individuals, I offer my gratitude: Virginia A. Batchelor, Tina Bowers-Colman, Bridget Battle-Mullice, Diane Batts Morrow, Gillian Brown, Dale Couch, Kathy DuBose, Vaughnette Goode-Walker, Billy Higgins, Herbert Holmes, Father Charles Hoskins, the Jackson family (Rick, Nicole, Deedee, Pharoah, Damian, Tarike, Maya, and Jada), Richard Jarvis, Kathleen Jennings, Allyson and Monique Keith, the Lawrence family (Fred, Mark, Carolyn, Marla, and Monica), Sharen Lee, Donzella Maupin, Sandra Barber Moore, Dorothy Paul, Ruth L. Rivers, Winona L. Scott, Harriet Peeler Stone, Nathan Stone, Jeff VanDetta, and Jeanne Williams. I would like to thank the University of Arkansas Press's readers for their insightful commentary and suggestions.

Over the years, several sister-historians have served as stellar role models who shared sage advice and experiences as we entered the field of history, first as graduate students and later as professionals. These women have been by my side through this book project. The friendship and support of Rosalyn Terborg-Penn, Alexa Benson Henderson, Adele Logan Alexander, Jacqueline A. Rouse, and Vicki Crawford have proved invaluable.

Along this journey, I have enjoyed the support of family members who nurtured me with a rock solid faith in my ability and in the project at hand. I am lovingly grateful to my husband, Steven Edmond; my sister, Marilyn S. Jackson; my aunt, Lurenda Mosley; and my godmother, Ida Briggs Baker.

Prologue

Aspasia Cruvellier Mirault, a remarkable free woman of color, her children, and her grandchildren lived in Savannah, Georgia, throughout the 1800s. Aspasia's experiences as a matriarch, a businesswoman, and a landowner provide an uncommon glimpse of African American life during the nineteenth century. Her effort to raise a family and to achieve economic stability constituted one swatch of the patchwork quilt that was antebellum Georgia. Aspasia's life story, woven into the fabric of her community, illuminates the African American quest for dignity and financial success within a thriving southern environment during the decades leading up to the Civil War.

Indeed, what was the meaning of life for a free black businesswoman in the South during a period when being male and having white skin were the most valued of human properties? During Aspasia's lifetime, the privileges of citizenship as well as access to power and opportunities, especially economic opportunities, remained primarily the domain of white men. Even the majority of white females lacked many advantages afforded their male counterparts.[1] Thus, Aspasia's experiences and those of her family provide a critique about the limitations placed on people of color in nineteenth-century America. A host of legal, social, and economic roadblocks hindered the progress of free blacks, including entrepreneurs like Aspasia.[2] Although they possessed little power, nonetheless Aspasia and other members of the free black community in Savannah prospered by their industry and intelligence and by turning the system to their favor.

The story of Aspasia's life and labors presents intriguing questions. What were the secrets of her success, and how did she manipulate the constrictions to live a notable life? An émigré from Santo Domingo who eventually operated a bakery business in Savannah, Aspasia took bold steps to shape her own destiny. As she encountered obstacles, Aspasia's determination to create her reality speaks volumes about her character and spirit. What amount of verve is required when an African American woman defies a state statute to buy a piece of property? How does one leverage agency to realize self-advancement? In addition to her own hard work, Aspasia effectively used the power and influence of others to create a good life for herself and her children. She cultivated interracial guardianships, intraracial associations, and religious affiliations that helped her navigate the complexities of antebellum Savannah society. Throughout her life, Aspasia relied upon the support of family members and others within the African American community. White support came from several prominent men, including a Savannah mayor, who served as Aspasia's guardians and partners. Although he risked a one-thousand-dollar penalty, another white man conspired with Aspasia to avoid the biased provisions of a state law. In large measure Aspasia's financial success stemmed from her ability to generate sufficient goodwill among whites and to sustain the support of her family and the African American community.

Aspasia's success mirrored similar achievements by many of her free black neighbors. These African American men and women lived productive lives as a cooperative and interdependent community. Many raised families, made a living, and formed a variety of secular and religious relationships both within the black race and across racial lines. Over the years, Aspasia and her cousin Simon Mirault drew steady patronage from a white clientele who frequented their respective business establishments. When Simon's father, Louis Mirault, died in 1828, his white executors meticulously inventoried the deceased tailor's list of clients, black and white, who had contributed to his prosperity. Some of Aspasia's African American neighbors owned real estate and enslaved property; others, like her, operated businesses, and still others served as community leaders and as liaisons between Savannah's black and white populations.

The chronicling of Aspasia's life is not without its complexities. The historian of the black experience is typically confronted with a paucity of private records for African Americas who lived during the antebellum era. No private papers such as letters, journals, or business records have survived from either Aspasia or the members of her immediate family. Thus, there is no evidence of the recorded thoughts or details of their day-to-day experiences. As a general rule, state laws that prohibited most blacks, even free people of color, from obtaining the rudiments of an education were largely responsible for the dearth of private records penned by antebellum blacks. Yet Aspasia and members of her family were literate with some level of education. She occasionally received and presumably wrote letters, but those documents have not been located.

Public records in the form of federal, state, county, and city documents have been analyzed to reconstruct the lives of Aspasia and her descendants. State statues, court documents, newspaper accounts, tax digests, military records, census data, city directories, and church sacramental registers offer glimpses into the lives of Aspasia's family. The methodology employed has its strengths as well its limitations. Although public records are a rich source of information, these documents are typically devoid of personal details and reminiscences. According to the St. John the Baptist Catholic Church Register, for example, Aspasia and her sister Justine attended and served as witnesses at their brother's wedding in February 1828. While their presence is documented, the record fails to reveal thoughts and emotions of the attendees when the groom, who was a free man of color, married an enslaved woman. The available records do not permit us to tap into the thoughts or hear the voices of the participants. Most public records have the same constraints. Similarly, tax digests provided the details of an individual's annual indebtedness, but do not give the taxpayer's reaction to that indebtedness.

This book chronicles events leading up to and including the litigation to settle a property dispute. Aspasia's family based their ownership claim on the existence of a secret trust agreement. But neither Aspasia nor George Cally, her secret trust partner, memorialized their concurrence in a written document. Without any documentary evidence, the existence of an agreement was called into question. The jury that decided the property dispute in 1878 faced a similar dilemma, but their ability to discern the credibility of several witnesses resolved the matter for the trial court. The court reporter transcribed the sworn testimony which verified a secret trust agreement.

The issue of Aspasia's marital status presented a similar challenge. There are no surviving public or private records detailing the date of the nuptials or the first name of her spouse. Yet, Aspasia, either officially or on her own account, changed her surname from Cruvellier to Mirault, having discarded her maiden name during the middle of the 1820s, according to surviving church records. Aspasia had begun to use the surname of Mirault by the time of her brother's wedding. Chatham County records revealed that Samuel Mirault was the most likely candidate to have been either Aspasia's paramour or her husband. Aspasia and Samuel registered together as free people of color in the Chatham County Court of the Ordinary in 1828. Samuel died in 1831 but evidence of his relationship with Aspasia as well as the birth of two children to that union has survived. In the years following Samuel's death, the names of Aspasia's two daughters, Louisa Mirault and Letitia Mirault, were recorded by county officials alongside their mother's name as a family unit and in the federal census records.

Aspasia's life story has evolved through a spectrum of public records and the scattered reminiscences of those who knew her. The historian of those voiceless persons who have left no private papers must corroborate pieces of information among the various sets of available sources and then evaluate those sources within a contextual framework. What follows is the story of Aspasia Cruvellier Mirault, a free woman of color, and her labors to raise a family and to build a successful life in antebellum Savannah, Georgia.

Chapter One

The Cruvelliers in Savannah

Spring came early to Savannah in 1842. Blossoming trees and the sounds of nesting birds signaled a change of seasons throughout south Georgia. Several months of sunny, warm, and humid weather lay just ahead. For Aspasia Cruvellier Mirault, a widowed matriarch and free black entrepreneur, the agreeable weather very likely matched her mood. About to realize a lifelong dream, Aspasia's optimism probably knew no bounds that year. She planned to purchase a piece of Savannah real estate, the culmination of considerable hard work and sacrifice. Certainly, Aspasia could reflect with satisfaction on her recent accomplishments. Over the previous several years, her popular bakery and confectionary establishment, located on the corner of Bull and Broughton Streets in Savannah, had turned a handsome profit. The ever-thrifty Aspasia had accumulated sufficient money for the down payment on a city lot.[1]

Contemplating her next move, Aspasia's thoughts likely raced with anticipation. First, she would purchase the land as the site for a homestead. A top priority was the relocation of her family, including adolescent-aged sons, Joseph and Robert, her grown daughter and helpmate, Letitia Davis, as well as several grandchildren. They lived in cramped quarters behind her bakery shop. Aspasia wanted to build a structure at the new location capable of housing both her family and the business. She must have been pleased to learn that Savannah mayor W. T. Williams and the city's nine aldermen had voted to open the newly platted Pulaski Ward to public auction, presenting her with a golden opportunity to purchase one of the lots.[2]

Aspasia's plans were not without their vexing complications. A Georgia statute passed several decades earlier in 1818 prohibited blacks, even free-born blacks like Aspasia, from buying land in Savannah. The property law emerged from a hostile racial climate that existed in Georgia, relegating most free African Americans to a lowly servile status. The majority of blacks were enslaved. Free blacks occupied a permanent middle ground in southern society slightly above the enslaved blacks but far below whites.[3] An examination of the first half of the nineteenth century suggests that for the most part African Americans, like whites, went about their lives, trying to do the best they could for their families. While life was by no means easy for the majority of Americans, whether they were black or white, the added burden of racial prejudice hampered black progress. Disenfranchised, frequently denied an education, and subjected to harsh penalties when they did break the law, the majority of free blacks lived restricted lives in America. Like their counterparts in Virginia and South Carolina, Georgia legislators never entertained the concept of black suffrage at any time during the colonial or antebellum eras.[4] In keeping with the sentiment found throughout the nation, Aspasia and other free blacks in Savannah confronted racial prejudice in a variety of forums.[5] This gloomy reality for most black people bore little resemblance to Aspasia's lofty plans for herself and her family.

Perhaps absorbed with the prospect of purchasing real estate, Aspasia may have lost sight of the prohibitions placed on black people. Euphoria, occasioned by her monetary success with the bakery, buoyed Aspasia's perspective about the limitations she faced. Aspasia's temporary good feeling would collide with the realities of race when she discovered the details about the law that denied free blacks the right to purchase land in Savannah. In Aspasia's case, her knowledge of the property ban and her unwillingness to succumb to it were two entirely different matters. Determined to provide her family with some degree of financial security, Aspasia devised a plan to own a piece of real estate in spite of the restrictive legislation to the contrary. She entered into a trust arrangement that allowed her to circumvent the state law.

Discerning businesswoman that she was, Aspasia likely weighed both the benefits and burdens of her decision. On the one hand, she would benefit from landownership, particularly the ability to move her family to more comfortable living quarters and to expand her already thriving bakery business. She would have been able to pass on the land acquisition to her children. On the other hand, creating a trust that was contrary to law must have been a burden on Aspasia's mind and may have delayed her action. In the end, the prospects of landownership won out, and Aspasia proceeded with the secret trust arrangement. Employing the same savvy skill and determination she had garnered over the previous decade in building a successful bakery business, Aspasia set her plan into motion.[6] She was determined to fashion her own destiny.

Aspasia was not alone in her resolve to manage her fate in spite of racism. Confronted with discriminatory laws, many free African Americans, whether they resided in the state of Georgia or elsewhere, realized they had few options other than circumventing the restrictions. It was not unusual for sympathetic whites to help blacks avoid the impact of statutory racism. Aspasia had at least one white comrade, a man by the name of George Cally, who assisted her in securing what would become her prized real estate possession. Cally, a native of Massachusetts and a newcomer to Savannah, helped Aspasia with the land purchase. The long-term repercussions of Aspasia's decision to purchase the property through Cally would add unexpected dimensions to her extraordinary life.[7]

Luckily members of the free black community had allies like Cally because their detractors were plentiful. If southern legislators were so inclined, they had many opportunities to act upon their antiblack sentiments. Throughout the early decades of the nineteenth century, Georgia lawmakers and their counterparts in other states used legislation to control African Americans, both those unfortunate souls who were enslaved as well as those blacks who were nominally free.[8] Members of the Georgia legislature never envisioned black people as independent and productive members of society. Instead, the lawmakers enacted legislation to curb black liberty, take away rights, and keep blacks in a dependant status.[9] The mobility of free blacks was restricted through laws. An 1808 law authorized justices of the peace "to bind out to service" young black males over the age of eight. The act's preamble set out the legislators' primary concern, "Whereas, the permitting of free [N]egroes and persons of color to rove about the country in idleness and dissipation has a dangerous tendency."[10]

As viewed by the Georgia legislature, personal freedom was a condition restricted to whites. By decreeing that slaveholders could not manumit their bondsmen without permission from the legislature, lawmakers made themselves the final arbiters of African American freedom. After December 1801, all applications for manumissions in Georgia had to be reviewed by the legislature. In this effort, Georgia was in accord with the majority of her sister states that mandated legislative or judicial approval before manumission could be effected. Severe penalties attached, including a fine of two hundred dollars, for Georgia slaveholders who attempted to circumvent the manumission law.[11] Nearly two decades later during their 1819 session, legislators provided a rationale and a stiffer penalty for violating the restrictive manumission process. Lawmakers remained convinced that "sound policy" and "the exercise of humanity towards the slave population . . . imperiously require that the number of free persons of color within this state should not be increased by manumission, or by the admission of such persons from other states to reside therein." Beginning that same year, violators faced a larger fine of five hundred dollars for each offense of the manumission law.[12]

Another legislative pronouncement, enacted eight years earlier in 1811, consisted of an elaborate set of criminal procedures to govern slave trials. The statute authorized panels of three justices of the peace to hear evidence and adjudge the guilt or innocence of enslaved persons who were charged with a crime. Obviously pleased with their handiwork, just a few years later and with only minor adjustments, Georgia lawmakers expanded the breadth of the same law to include trials for free persons of color. Blacks, both enslaved and free, were lumped together and meted out the same limited degree of criminal justice in the state. Further, in an attempt to keep a close watch on what was perceived as the criminal inclinations of African Americans, lawmakers during their 1817 legislative session hammered out a statute delineating a list of capital punishment crimes for black offenders. People of color in Georgia would pay with their lives if convicted of certain enumerated crimes, such as inciting a slave insurrection, raping a white woman, poisoning a white person, burglary, or arson. Blacks found guilty of attempting any of the aforementioned crimes suffered the same fate as if their actions had been successfully carried out.[13]

Reinforcing their efforts to place the institution of slavery on a solid legal foundation, Georgia lawmakers designed a set of discriminatory laws specifically targeting the free black population, like Aspasia and her family. Antipathy toward free blacks emerged early in the life of the new republic. Few whites ever contemplated the prospect of blacks living among them as equals. Toward the end of the eighteenth century, some whites tried to prevent free West Indian blacks from migrating to North America.[14] By the 1790s in the wake of the Haitian Revolution, large groups of émigrés, blacks and whites from the Caribbean island, sought refuge in cities and towns along the southeastern coast of the United States. While for the most part, foreign whites were well received by their white American counterparts, black people, on the other hand, were shunned. Foreign blacks, especially those from Santo Domingo, struck terror in the minds of white Americans who suspected those blacks might foment a slave revolt in North America. Because of these fears, the white majority population sought ways to prevent black émigrés from settling among them. Lawmakers were inundated with antiblack petitions, and angry whites staged protests, aimed at denouncing the presence of foreign blacks. In 1793, white citizens of Charleston, South Carolina, held a mass meeting to expel "the French [N]egroes," while in nearby Savannah, many ships arriving from the West Indies were diverted from the harbor.[15] Two years later, whites in Savannah gathered to express their concerns and to demand that officials keep all blacks from the island nations, but particularly enslaved blacks, from entering their city.[16] But sometimes their efforts to keep foreign blacks away from North American shores failed. Aspasia's family, the Cruvelliers from Santo Domingo, would join a sizable group of black émigrés who settled in Savannah.

Given the growth of the free black population, the Georgia legislature imposed a system giving whites the authority to control the legal affairs of blacks.[17] Commencing in December 1808, courts began processing applications from African Americans who, in compliance with the new law, entered into a legal arrangement with a white person residing in the same county. Whites became agents for the blacks. The legislators created a powerful tool for the local control of the day-to-day activities of black people and for limiting their individual liberty. Although free blacks did not occupy the same lowly status in society as enslaved persons, they nonetheless were obliged to answer to a white person whose assent was needed to transact most business and legal affairs.[18] In accordance with the statute,

> Said guardian . . . shall be, and is hereby vested with all the powers and authority of guardians for the management of the persons and estates of infants; and all suits necessary to be brought for and against such free persons of color, shall be in the name of such guardian, in his capacity of guardian.[19]

Although the guardian system was intended to limit black independence, in reality it did not always have a detrimental impact on the free black population. It was not uncommon for a black ward to benefit from his or her relationship with the white guardian. Guardians were frequently in a position to assist their wards in securing property and credit or in helping the ward advance in his or her trade or business venture. Some whites took a personal interest in their wards and interceded on their behalf in legal and economic matters. Farish Carter, a Georgia planter, reportedly served as the guardian for about one hundred free black persons.[20] Sometimes a mutual religious affiliation, such as membership at St. John the Baptist Catholic Church in Savannah, helped to cement a positive relationship between black wards and their white guardians. The Miraults, a free black Catholic family and later Aspasia's in-laws, enjoyed such a relationship with their guardian, Jean Gaudry, a white man and fellow parishioner at St. John's Church.[21]

Aspasia's family the Cruvelliers and scores of other black residents of Savannah complied with the state law mandating the establishment of guardian relationships with whites. Savannah resident James Morrison served as the guardian for the entire Cruvellier family, including Aspasia and several of her siblings. Following her marriage into the Mirault family Aspasia switched guardians. She arranged for James B. Gaudry, a lawyer and bank clerk, to act as the guardian for herself and her children. Gaudry exercised his responsibilities toward Aspasia's family throughout most of the 1830s. By 1840, John E. Ward, a lawyer and one-term mayor of Savannah in 1854, served as Aspasia's guardian. Other members of Aspasia's immediate family selected Lewis D'Lyon, an attorney, to attend to their guardianship needs.[22]

Other restrictions and regulations were leveled on the free black population. An 1810 statute required blacks to register with state authorities within ten days of their arrival in Georgia. A fine of thirty dollars or a jail sentence awaited those who failed to follow the law's strict dictates. Eight years later in 1818, Georgia lawmakers mandated an annual registration requirement for all free black persons. Pursuant to the law, on or before the first Monday in March, subsequently changed to July, all free persons of color were obliged to pay fifty cents to the local court clerk who would in turn register their name, age, place of birth, residence, occupation, and date of arrival in Georgia. The annual registration requirement was a precursor to a work conscription law for free black people over the age of fourteen. The only comparable conscription directed at white Georgians was slave patrol duty, dating back to the colonial era and including both white men and women.[23]

In 1818, likely motivated by their need for cheap labor to maintain public works around the state, legislators targeted free blacks as an available work force. Pursuant to Section VII of Georgia statutes:

> Be it further enacted, that all registered free persons of color, between the ages of fifteen and sixty years, shall be liable to do public work in the counties or corporate towns to which they may reside, under such regulation, and on pain of such penalties for noncompliance, as the justices of the Inferior Courts of the several counties, and the mayor and alderman or intendant and wardens or commissioners of such corporate towns shall prescribe; and it shall be the duty of such justices of the Inferior Court and of such mayor and alderman, intendant and wardens or commissioners, to call out such free persons of color, and employ them in public work within their respective jurisdictions for a term not exceeding twenty days in one year.[24]

Satisfying such public work could be dangerous to one's health. In September 1820, a yellow fever epidemic struck Savannah. City officials recorded news of several cases a few days following the arrival of a sailing vessel from the West Indies. The sickness spread rapidly throughout the city with devastating results. Almost 250 residents became ill, a great many of whom succumbed to the fever, before doctors managed to control the illness two months later. At the height of that emergency, Savannah officials, under the public labor law, conscripted free blacks to work as nurses. No thought was given to the prospect that black people might succumb to the illness while performing their duty. Conventional thinking of the era subscribed to the notion that blacks were naturally immune to such diseases.[25]

A little more than a decade earlier, Benjamin Rush, a leading Philadelphia physician and a founding father of the American republic, had used his considerable influence to recruit local blacks to assist in fighting a particularly virulent epidemic when it struck that northern city in 1793. It was only after blacks began dying at alarming rates that city officials reluctantly conceded that African Americans possessed no natural immunity to the disease.[26] Whether or not they knew that blacks were vulnerable to yellow fever, Savannah officials conscripted black workers for the medical crisis. In succeeding years, the labor requirement remained onerous and time consuming, but usually not life threatening. One year, officials assigned a contingent of free black males as temporary laborers with the city's Street and Lane Committee. The men repaired a fort located on Farm Street.[27]

Being forced to labor for several weeks each year without compensation was just one of several legislative injustices imposed upon the free people of color in Georgia. During the 1818 legislative session, lawmakers did their best to stymie prospects for economic progress among the African American population.[28] Less than three decades after Georgians had ratified the United States Constitution with its stated reverence for individual liberty and private property, the legislators contradicted these ideals by denying black people the right to own real estate. Using the rationale that their actions were necessary to suppress "a class of people equally dangerous to the safety of free citizens of this state," Georgia lawmakers passed Section VIII of the 1818 Code of Laws:

> [N]o free person of colour within this state (Indians in amity with this state excepted) shall be permitted to purchase or acquire any real estate or any slave or slaves, either by direct conveyance to such free persons of colour of the legal title of such real estate or slave or slaves, or by a conveyance to any white person or persons of such legal title, reserving to such free person of colour the beneficial interest therein, by any trust, either written or parol, by any will, testament or deed, or by any contract, agreement or stipulation, either in writing or parol, and securing or attempting to secure to such free person of color the legal title or equitable or beneficial interest therein; but all and singular such real estate, and each and every such slave or slaves, shall be deemed and held to be wholly forfeited.[29]

A subsequent portion of Section VIII authorized official escheators, located in the various Georgia counties, to seize and sell property owned by blacks. These state-appointed escheators profited handsomely from their work, frequently netting 10 percent of the proceeds of the confiscated property. Motivated by easy profits, the escheators worked quickly to identify property that could be confiscated. Many African American property owners became the victims of this discriminatory and patently unfair law before the calloused Georgia legislators realized its abuses and amended the law.

In the 1819 amendment, lawmakers granted blacks the right to retain and to inherit any and all land and slave property already held at the time the 1818 law was enacted. The amendment voided a portion of the offending statute by reinstating African American eligibility to purchase land throughout Georgia, except in the cities of Augusta, Darien, and Savannah. Although the restriction was repealed for Darien in 1839, it remained a fixture of state law for the cities of Savannah and Augusta throughout the antebellum era. The threat of enforcement likely remained a reality for aspiring black real estate owners. Yet, court documents of instances where blacks contested the

1818 statute have survived from the post–Civil War era, but not from the earlier years. Judging from her actions to secure a piece of property, we can assume that Aspasia took the threat of legislative enforcement seriously. There is no way of knowing if her apprehensions about the law and her efforts to circumvent it were misplaced. But we do know that Aspasia and other enterprising black residents of Savannah and Augusta resorted to extralegal measures to become landowners.[30]

Despite the prevalence of racial hostility and legislative obstacles, the free black population increased during the early part of the nineteenth century. The migration of persons from the West Indies added to that growth. Several hundred black persons joined their white West Indian counterparts to make up a steady stream of émigrés arriving in Savannah and other southern cities beginning around 1800 and continuing well into the next decade.[31] With the influx of new arrivals over a relatively short time span, Savannah acquired the largest free black population in Georgia. The city's free African American community grew from 122 persons in 1790 to 224 persons in 1800. Ten years later in 1810, Savannah's black population had grown to 578 persons.[32] Charleston, South Carolina, by comparison, had a larger black population throughout the period, but the city's overall rate of growth lagged behind Savannah. Five hundred and sixty eight free black persons lived in Charleston in 1790. Twenty years later in 1810, the city's free black population had increased to 1,472 residents.[33]

Aspasia Cruvellier Mirault was among this émigré group of new arrivals to a southern city. Sometime during 1800, Aspasia and several members of her immediate family, the Cruvelliers, free mulattoes from Santo Domingo, began their new lives in Savannah. The surviving evidence suggests that Hagar Cruvellier may have been the family matriarch who migrated to the United States with four of her relatives, probably her children, Francis, Peter, Justine, and Aspasia. The Cruvelliers were escaping the civil strife and rebellion then characterizing their Santo Domingo homeland.[34] Beginning in the early 1790s and continuing until around 1810, many whites fled the island leaving behind the military and political turmoil of the Haitian Revolution and its aftermath. Toussaint L'Overture, a former slave turned military general, led a large black army that defeated the French Emperor Napoleon Bonaparte's America-based regiments. Once Toussaint had taken control of the island, he liberated the slave population. As a result of those dramatic events, most Santo Domingo whites and their mulatto allies found themselves at odds with the transformation of their homeland. The mulatto landowners and overseers elected to leave the island, turning themselves into refugees and casting their future with the fledgling United States of America rather than with an island controlled by ex-slaves.[35]

Widespread incidents of war and revolution occurring both in Europe and the European colonies in the Caribbean did not seem to disrupt the flow of traffic along the Atlantic sea channels. Maritime activities were at an all-time high, and shipping lanes between the United States and the islands of the West Indies were filled with vessels carrying cargo and passengers. Between the late 1790s and the early 1800s, many of those passengers were refugees, like Aspasia and her family traveling aboard the *Henry*, or one of its sister vessels that plied the international waters along the Atlanta eastern seaboard from Boston to the Caribbean islands and many seaports in between. Indeed, the *Henry* may have been the sailing vessel that transported the Cruvelliers from Santo Domingo to Savannah. Commanded by Captain Daniel Cheney, the ninety-two-ton sloop made its maiden voyage sometime in late 1799 or early 1800. Agents for the *Henry* placed advertisements in the local Savannah newspapers hoping to attract potential customers. Booking reservations from their Savannah office on the wharf near the Coffee House, the agents publicized information that their ship was available to transport either passengers or freight cargo.[36]

Whether it was the *Henry* or some other vessel that brought the Cruvelliers to Georgia, they would soon encounter the racial divisions that characterized antebellum American society. The Cruvelliers and other free blacks were exposed to a rigid racial stratification, the cornerstone of which was the institution of African American slavery.[37] Yet, it was very likely that free black émigrés were not surprised or even offended by the frequent sight of slave auctions on the streets of Savannah. In their Santo Domingo homeland in the years before the revolution had emancipated the slaves, auctions for the buying and selling of human property had been a common feature of the island. Perhaps the Cruvellier family may have been involved in such transactions in Santo Domingo. As the new black arrivals in America would soon discover, the acquisition of slave property often translated into increased wealth for the owner. Savannah's free black entrepreneurs, especially those with service-oriented businesses, found that their enslaved property provided a useful labor force. As they began to prosper in Savannah, several members of the Cruvellier family, including Hagar, Aspasia, and other free people of color in Savannah and throughout the South, would count slaves among their own property as perhaps they had previously done in Santo Domingo.[38]

Before the passage of legislation in 1818, black people could purchase slaves. Savannah newspapers routinely carried notices that Africans and African American men, women, and children were being sold to the highest bidder. On November 6, 1800, the same year that the Cruvellier family arrived in Savannah, the *Georgia Gazette* carried an advertisement placed there by David Leon, a slave broker. Among the sixteen people he had for sale, Leon praised the attributes of one particular family unit, consisting of a twenty-seven-year-old male, skilled as a carpenter and cooper, the man's twenty-four-year-old wife, described as "a complete house wench" whose skills included washing and ironing, as well as the couple's six-year-old son. In addition to this one family unit, Leon prepared to offer at auction three female house servants and several "young fellows bred to the field."[39]

Slavery coupled with discriminatory legislation did not inhibit the economic progress of all the black population. A sizable portion of Savannah's free people of color, including the Cruvelliers, carved out comfortable livelihoods for themselves. Against considerable odds, many free African Americans prospered, experiencing the joys of family and community as well as a degree of economic success. By the late eighteenth and early nineteenth centuries, the African American population in Savannah had achieved several economic, social, and religious milestones. Many of these milestones would not have been achieved without interracial cooperation. While blacks frequently relied on other black people for assistance, it was not uncommon for blacks and whites to find mutually beneficial common ground. Some free blacks adroitly utilized the legallymandated guardian system, business associations, and religious affiliations to their advantage and for profit. By 1819, approximately twenty years after his arrival in Savannah, Louis Mirault, a free West Indian–born émigré and future in-law of Aspasia, had become a successful tailor with a predominately white clientele. Mirault's property holdings included a house and nine slaves, and he was considered a lay leader within the local Catholic community.[40]

Black spiritual and moral support gatherings that later evolved into African American churches played a significant role in the lives of blacks living in Savannah. These religious groups did much toward fostering strong family and community ties. From its humble beginnings in 1788 and under the able leadership of the Reverend Andrew Bryan, an enslaved minister, the First African Baptist Church of Savannah became a community stalwart and a vital lifeline for its African American members, both slave and free. Once Bryan and the other church leaders managed to convince the white community that they were not a threat to the society, their independent black institution grew and prospered within Savannah. In May 1789 and 1790 respectively, Bryan, who was already an ordained minister by that time, purchased his freedom and a piece of property in the Oglethorpe Ward section of the city. That same lot served as a permanent location for his church. When he died in October 1812 at the age of ninety-six, Bryan had provided nearly twenty-five years of leadership to his religious congregants and to the larger black community.[41]

Black Catholics, including Aspasia's family, experienced the richness of their faith in Savannah. Blacks who belonged to the Catholic faith worshiped alongside their fellow white parishioners. The eclectic Catholic congregation consisted of Santo Domingo expatriates, Irish, English, Minorcans, and Germans, as well as a sizable number of blacks and mulattos with varying degrees of African ancestry. These Catholics found a network of interaction and cooperation. Although racial barriers certainly existed, both in society and within the Catholic Church, people of color benefited from their religious affiliations. Blacks and mulattos, slave and free, took part in the various church rites and rituals. St. John the Baptist Catholic Church's registry, dating from 1796, provides a historical window for viewing church life among the black Catholic faithful. Of the nearly one hundred church entries inscribed, roughly one-half of those entries document marriage or baptisms of black parishioners.[42]

The church registry documents the closely knit character of the black émigré community from Santo Domingo. While their small numbers did not sustain a separate émigré community beyond the first two decades of the nineteenth century, initially the free people of color from the West Indies constituted a distinct subset within Savannah's black community.[43] But by 1820, these émigrés had meshed socially and economically with other free blacks and with the resident enslaved population to lay the foundation for an African American community in Savannah.[44]

Distinct and separate groups of black people lived in Savannah. Between 1800 and 1820, one's birthplace and religious affiliation formed the basis for these distinctions as strong social ties, and even marital bonds among the city's black émigré community were visible. Throughout this period, during which the émigrés considered themselves a separate group, free blacks from the West Indies typically intermarried with others from their homelands. This Caribbean-based community took part in a variety of church-related activities, such as serving as baptismal sponsors and as witnesses for weddings among their West Indian–born compatriots.[45]

In keeping with this tradition, a large group of émigrés gathered on Thursday evening, August 30, 1804, when two free mulattos from Santo Domingo recited their wedding vows before the church rector. Twenty-four-year-old Jean Fromantin took fourteen-year-old Marie Charlotte as his bride.[46] The following year, in February 1805, Alexander Debrofois and Josephine Olive LeRoi, both free mulattos and émigrés from Santo Domingo, were wed. The bride was twenty-two when she became the wife of the thirty-year-old Alexander. Two years later, the Debrofois couple celebrated the birth of their first son. St. John's Church was the location for a ceremony held on March 27, 1807, when the priest offered prayers for the child the couple named Pierre Joseph Debrofois. Possibly due to the child's fragile health, the Debrofois couple had delayed the ceremony for several months after the child was born. Pierre Joseph, born the previous August, was seven months old at the time of his baptism ceremony. The child's godparents, Louis Mirault and his wife, Theresa, both free persons of color, sponsored the baptism ceremony. Over the next six years, Josephine gave birth to four more children, all of whom were baptized at St. John's Church. One of her daughters, Louisa Martha, was baptized in May 1807. Similar ceremonies for the couple's sons, Pierre Alexander, Joseph Etienne, and Jean Baptiste, took place in 1809, in 1811, and in 1813. All five Debrofois children enjoyed the support of a separate set of godparents, selected from their parents' close-knit circle of friends, relatives, and fellow émigrés.[47]

Even though the Debrofois chose black émigrés for their children's godparents, they might have selected American-born blacks, whites, or Native Americans. Catholic Church records provide evidence of interracial cooperation among the parishioners in a variety of religious rites and ceremonies. On Saturday, February 12, 1803, Father Oliver Le Mercier, the rector of St. John's Church, officiated at the marriage of John Crooks and Felicite Alfo, two free blacks. In attendance at the marriage ceremony were Thomas Miller, a white Savannah merchant, and a free black man named Desire, who was the groom's godfather.

The following month, on Sunday, March 6, another white man named Peter Joseph Michael Mirault joined Felina, a free black woman, as godparents for infant Michael Joseph at his baptism. The eight-month-old baby boy was the son of Agatha, a free mulatto woman. Twenty-year-old Pauline, a slave woman from Africa was baptized at St. John's Church on Sunday, October 23, 1804. Her godparents were William Debrux and his wife, Pauline, a prominent white couple, and likely Pauline's owners. Three years later, the June 4 marriage between Renette Michelle, a fifteen-year-old American Indian and twenty-six-year-old Paul Guilliaume Mirault, a free mulatto at St. John's Church, added to the interracial blending of people among the Catholic faithful in Savannah.[48]

St. John the Baptist Catholic Church and the black West Indian émigré community supported Aspasia's early life. The church activities of several Cruvellier family members were recorded for posterity. On July 17, 1803, one of the Cruvellier women, probably Hagar, sponsored the baptism for the infant daughter of Quash Dolly. The newborn was the legitimate offspring of Dolly, a prominent free black man and landowner, and his slave wife, Lucretia Gibbons. Both the complexities of slavery and an intraracial network within the black community were evident in the ceremony. Although Lucretia was married to a free black man, she remained the legal property of John Gibbons, a white Savannah slaveholder.[49] The fact that two free mulattos, a man named Negril and a Cruvellier woman, served as his child's godparents leads to the speculation that Dolly had aspirations to purchase the freedom of his wife and their infant daughter. As further evidence of the growing cohesion among distinct groups within Savannah's African American population, two free mulatto émigrés served as the godparents for the child of a native-born, free black man and his enslaved wife.

Several other members of Aspasia's immediate family participated in the religious life of Savannah's black émigré community. On Sunday, August 4, 1812, Aspasia's brother Francis Cruvellier and his wife, Mary Celeste, brought their eight-month-old son Francis Richard for baptism in the faith. Three years later in January 1815, Francis asked his younger brother Peter to serve as the godfather for his second child and first daughter. Just a year earlier it had been Francis's turn to serve as a godparent when on April 11, 1814, Marie Victoire, a free black woman, sponsored a baptism for her son Francis. At the conclusion of the ceremony, Francis Cruvellier signed the church registry alongside the signature of Father Abbe Antoine Carles, the officiating priest.[50]

Church records contain an entry marking the nuptials for Peter Cruvellier, Aspasia's brother. When Peter selected a wife, he did not follow his elder brother's example. Francis Cruvellier wed Marie Celeste, a free woman of color. On February 27, 1829, Peter, a free man, exchanged vows with Betsy Reding, a slave, before Reverend Joseph Stokes. Peter enjoyed the support of his family in his selection of his bride. The groom's two sisters, Aspasia and Justine, attended the ceremony and served as witnesses.[51]

As demonstrated by their signing of church documents, the Cruvelliers and a substantial number of other individuals in Savannah's black community were literate. Undoubtedly, their ability to read and write in English, and probably in French, placed these African Americans in unique circumstances. Aspasia was literate as were several members of her immediate family. Her brother Francis signed the baptismal certificate in 1812. Aspasia and her sister Justine signed as witnesses at their brother Peter's wedding. Savannah's free blacks used their ability to read and write in various ways. They placed advertisements and notices in the local newspapers, and they sent and received letters. In accordance with the postal practices of the era, Savannah residents, whites as well as blacks, were listed in the newspaper if they had mail awaiting them at the local post office. On numerous occasions, Aspasia's name appeared on the lists of postal patrons who had undelivered mail.[52]

Although lawmakers enacted statutes to curb the mobility of black people within the state, nonetheless some free people of color traveled extensively, seemingly ignoring such restrictions. Such contradictions characterized the lives of free blacks in Savannah and throughout Georgia. Instead of confining their comings and goings to Savannah and its immediate environs, some of the more affluent members of the black community traveled away from their homes sometimes for months at a time. In December 1819, Louis Mirault, one of the city's free black tailors, gave notice in the local newspaper of his extensive travel plans. On that particular occasion, Mirault advised that his upcoming trip would last several months. Ever the consummate businessman, Mirault made arrangements for his clients to collect their garments and to settle their accounts during his absence from the city. Similarly, some years later, a newspaper notice that an A. Mirault had recently arrived in Savannah from Philadelphia on the schooner *Samarits* may have been a reference to Aspasia returning from a trip to the northern states.[53]

Apart from the church records and postal notices in the local newspapers, the surviving Chatham County tax records dating from 1806, provide glimpses of the lives of Savannah's free black population. The Cruvellier family members paid their annual taxes consistently from 1809 through the early 1830s. Francis Cruvellier, who from all appearances was the family patriarch, practiced the tailoring trade in association with Peter and Aspasia, his younger brother and his sister. It is likely that Francis and Peter arranged a business partnership. The two Cruvellier men each paid an annual assessment tax of $10.00 granting them the right to practice their trade while Aspasia's assessment was one-half the amount paid by her brothers. In 1812, young Aspasia, who had not yet reached her teens, worked alongside her brothers supplying customers with finely stitched apparel.[54] Aspasia must have found satisfaction and some level of financial security in her work as a seamstress, for she remained in the occupation for a good many years.

Talented and resourceful members of Savannah's free black community, including the Cruvelliers, labored diligently at their various trades. Tailoring was a popular trade among blacks, and Francis and Peter had plenty of competition for customers. Louis Mirault practiced tailoring as did Jean Baptiste, Ben Wall, and Louis Charles. Free black men pursued a number of other trades as well. Some made their living as carpenters or barbers. Julien Fremintain and Joseph Clark practiced carpentry. Neighbors Ali Debroise, Louis Alexander, and August Jackson were barbers. During 1810 and 1811, Joseph Bullock, a free black, worked as a cooper, making barrels and casks, while Bullock's neighbor, Isaac Sheftal, labored as a butcher. Besides Bullock, other coopers included Jonas Cuthbert and Thomas Crawford, the latter born in Africa. Elijah Jones was a shoemaker, and Pompey Benhem and James Oliver were known as draymen, the nineteenth-century term for teamsters. Draymen made their living by transporting goods in wagons and often owned their teams. Henry Cunningham, a prominent free black landowner and longtime Savannah resident, served as a minister of the Second African Baptist Church for several decades.[55]

Working in tandem with their spouses, free African American women in Savannah contributed to family incomes. After working as seamstresses for a number of years, Aspasia and her sister Justine Cruvellier switched careers to become pastry cooks and established a bakery shop. Others, like Charlotte Reed, remained seamstresses all of their lives. Women worked in shops or became hucksters, the nineteenth-century label for street vendors. Although Hagar Cruvellier labored as a Savannah shopkeeper in 1817, just a few years later she was working as pastry cook. Throughout the 1820s, Susan Campbell worked as a nurse while Rosella Oliver, another free black woman, worked as a huckster. Oliver's work supplemented the income from her husband James Oliver's drayman business. If her experience was typical of her fellow hucksters, Rosella peddled a variety of foods, including fruit or cakes, along Savannah's busy streets or in the market places.[56] The majority of black women labored as washerwomen, laundresses, nurses, and housekeepers, less desirable and less lucrative occupations. Nancy Cox and Rhina Curry earned their living as washerwomen.[57]

Savannah's African American residents worked at a variety of trades and skills to support their families, and some of them accumulated considerable wealth. Yet, their inability to purchase land legally after the passage of the 1818 statute served to diminish black people economically compared to Savannah's white community. As a result, the number of black landowners in the city of Savannah was far less than it might have been without the discriminatory restrictions.

TABLE 1. BLACK TAXPAYERS IN SAVANNAH GEORGIA

Year:	1816	1819	1820
Total black taxpayers	139	248	249
Free black males w/real property	26	12	20
Free black women w/real property	28	25	23
Free blacks without real property	82	212	206
Slaves with property	3*	1**	0

* 2 male slaves, 1 female slave
** 1 female slave

Source: Chatham County Tax Digests, 1816, 1819, 1820, Georgia Historical Society.

Overall, black landownership, though legal in most of the South, was uncommon among African Americans in southern cities during the early decades of the nineteenth century. Although a small number of black people purchased land in areas of the South that had no race-based property restrictions, there were relatively few black property owners in the region.[58] Francis Cruvellier, Aspasia's brother, owned two slaves, but there is no record to suggest that he ever possessed any Savannah real estate. Instead, Francis rented a dwelling located at 9 Jekyll Street in the Darby Ward section of the city.[59]

A few of Francis's black neighbors had purchased land prior to the enactment of the 1818 law. In other instances blacks acquired real estate holdings in Savannah through inheritance. With the notable exceptions of Quash Dolly, who owned a lot on Yamacraw Street, and a small number of other free black landowners, most African Americans paid taxes to practice their trades and not for landownership.[60] Like Dolly, James Oliver, a free black originally from Virginia, was one of the exceptions. During the 1820s, Oliver, the drayman, and his wife paid taxes on two pieces of Savannah real estate. The Olivers owned lot number 26 and the western half of lot number 12, both located in the Oglethorpe Ward of the city.[61] Oliver likely purchased the section of lot 12, but in 1820, he inherited lot 26 and one slave from a female relative named Ann Oliver. Ann, a free woman of color, had paid taxes both on her real estate and the bondsman during the previous year.[62] Free black women in Savannah, like Ann Oliver and others, faired better than their male counterparts when it came to landownership. Not only did these women manage to acquire more valuable property than black males, but correspondingly they paid more state and local taxes as a result of their ownership.[63]

Early in 1820, much of the property and the livelihoods of nearly all Savannah residents, both black and white, were severely threatened by a citywide catastrophe. Residents had just welcomed a new year as well as a new decade when a devastating fire engulfed Savannah. Just after midnight on the evening of Monday, January 10, 1820, a fire broke out at Boone's livery stable on Jefferson Street, near the Baptist church. The Cruvellier family along with hundreds of their neighbors would be profoundly affected by the events of that fateful night. The fire spread rapidly along Bay Street and then on to Broughton Street raging out of control and consuming numerous commercial establishments and rows of tenements before the fire companies could even begin their work.[64]

A steady west by northwest wind carried hot cinders to remote parts of the town destroying the many wooden structures in the fire's path. Then suddenly, the already grim situation took an ugly turn when the fire ignited a large quantity of gunpowder being stored illegally in a house on Market Square and set off two huge explosions. Mindful of the ever-present dangers of fire, Savannah's aldermen had earlier passed an ordinance prohibiting the warehousing of explosives. One resident had chosen to violate the city's law with devastating consequences. A wall of flames raged throughout most of the night, leveling buildings, destroying property, and shattering lives. The fire consumed approximately six square city blocks extending all the way to Abercorn Street. On Tuesday when the sun broke through the dark and smoke-filled sky, much of the city lay in ruin. Savannah's future looked as dim as the charred landscape.[65]

While there are no surviving reports on the number of fatalities and injuries, the record of massive property destruction throughout Savannah astounds the imagination. Few Savannah residents or business establishments were spared. Rows of tenement buildings that had housed several hundred people as well as scores of retail shops went up in flames. Contemporary estimates suggested that the city sustained nearly four million dollars in property losses, a staggering amount for the time. The *Daily Georgian* newspaper, its own offices destroyed by the fire, still managed to report the tragedy, publishing a list of residents who had lost real and personal property.

The fire was no respecter of race, victimizing whites and blacks alike in the citywide calamity. Alfred Cuthbert, who hailed from a politically influential white family, African American tailors Louis Mirault and Aspasia's brother Francis, and scores of other residents sustained heavy losses. Aspasia and Francis along with other family members probably watched in horror as the fire engulfed their tailoring equipment and inventory of cloth. Louis Mirault, who was out of town at the time, would not learn of the tragedy and of his losses for several weeks. The White Bluff Church and the Jewish Synagogue were destroyed by the fire. Theodore Bartow and James Walker, two white men, lost all of their merchandise, as did F. S. Fell, Thomas Longworth, and some fifty or more residents. Andrew Morel, an African American, watched helplessly as his residence and his tailor shop located at number 10 Carpenter Row in Trustee Garden burned.[66]

The Savannah fire changed many lives. The staggering property loss rendered hundreds homeless and without work. Because they had sustained loss like their neighbors, members of the Cruvellier family probably took advantage of a generous bread offer. Beginning on January 14, four days after the fire and continuing for a week thereafter, a baker identified in the local newspaper as Philip Brasch provided free loaves of bread to destitute Savannah residents. Neighbor helped neighbor. Dr. J. E. White led a group of physicians who offered their services while the city aldermen successfully passed a series of resolutions in an effort to relieve the suffering. Herbert Davenport, the city surveyor, formed a committee charged with locating suitable housing for the homeless while the city marshal investigated reports of looting and searched for stolen property in buildings and boats.[67]

To relieve the suffering, Savannah mayor Thomas V. P. Charlton asked for financial assistance from outside the city. In his impassioned "Address to the Citizens and Inhabitants of the United States," printed in the local newspaper, Charlton described the devastation visited upon Savannah. According to the mayor, his city was in ashes. He wrote of once "splendid edifices filled with merchandise and all the products of taste and elegance" that the fire had left in ruins. The mayor estimated that approximately 460 structures, consisting of housing and several three-story buildings had been destroyed. Charlton asked his fellow countrymen for help.[68]

It is likely that Francis Cruvellier sustained a staggering loss to his business and closed his tailoring establishment permanently. Following the fire catastrophe, Francis's name disappeared from the tax rolls. In the Chatham County tax digest for 1821, the year following the fire, the name of Francis's wife, Mary C. (Celeste) Cruvellier, appeared for the first time. Having paid her taxes, Mary was listed alongside the names of other family members, including Peter, Hagar, and Aspasia Cruvellier, but Francis's name was not listed.[69] Did Francis decide to give up the tailoring profession following the fire? Did he succumb to the yellow fever epidemic that struck the city with a death toll of over two hundred during the fall of that same year? The historical record provides no indication, and Francis's fate remains a mystery.[70]

The closing of Francis's tailor shop was only the first in a series of significant changes for members of the Cruvellier household. By 1823, both Aspasia and Hagar had moved away from their Jekyll Street residence. Hagar relocated to lot number 8 in Reynolds Ward where she supported herself by operating a shop.[71] Starting in 1823 and continuing for the next three years, Aspasia worked as a seamstress together with her sister Justine. The two women resided on Bay Lane and probably formed a partnership, reminiscent of their brothers' business arrangement of the previous decade. Such family support would have been a God-send for Justine, who at that time was a widow with three small daughters, Rose, Dorrie, and Polly.[72]

Even though Aspasia may have found sewing a satisfying profession, as fate would have it she was not destined to remain a seamstress. While her brothers Francis and Peter had provided her with the initial impetus to try her hand at sewing, her sister Justine probably introduced Aspasia to the bakery business. By 1825, Justine had left the sewing trade and started baking for a living. Following her sister's example, Aspasia joined Justine the succeeding year in an enterprise with merchandise inventory worth about fifty dollars. Aspasia found her true occupational niche as a pastry cook, and she doubled the value of her merchandise within five years.[73] Their new careers as pastry cooks appealed to both Aspasia and Justine. Having taken up a new livelihood, Justine moved frequently during this time period, perhaps to remain in close proximity to jobs in her new line of work. She vacated the Bay Lane residence in Washington Ward that she had previously shared with Aspasia. Her new home was in Derby Ward, a newly plotted area of the city. The following year, while she continued to perfect her trade, Justine and her daughters moved once again, this time to York Street.[74] Aspasia frequently changed residences as well, but by 1828 she had settled into a permanent location at the corner of Broughton and Bull Streets. There she opened her bakery shop.[75]

Adapting to a new career as a baker and pastry cook was only one of several new aspects of Aspasia's life during the 1820s. Having settled into a livelihood, Aspasia expanded her horizons with a mate and motherhood. She probably became Samuel Mirault's wife, and the couple started a family. Samuel Mirault is the most likely candidate to have wed Aspasia and fathered her children. Although no official documentation survives specifying the date of the nuptials between Aspasia Cruvellier and Samuel Mirault, by 1825 or 1826 the young couple had apparently formed a romantic bond. Together, they presented themselves at the county clerk's office and registered together as free persons of color in 1828. Because several entries in the church registry document the Cruvellier family's connection with St. John's Catholic Church, the absence of Aspasia's nuptials remains a mystery. Was Samuel already married, or did some other circumstance prevent an open declaration of their marriage bond? The dearth of surviving records leaves few details to inform us about the Mirault couple. We know that they were the same age, and that they became the parents of two daughters, Louisa and Letitia, before Samuel's death sometime between 1829 and 1831.

Her affection and devotion to Samuel and their children likely brought Aspasia considerable happiness. As one outward manifestation of her commitment to their relationship, the former Aspasia Cruvellier chose to be known by the Mirault surname for the remainder of her life. Aspasia used her married name in late February 1828 when she and her sister Justine served as witnesses at their brother Peter's wedding to Betsy Reding. Although he was not listed as a witness, Samuel probably attended his brother-in-law's nuptials as a member of the extended wedding party. By means of her union with Samuel, Aspasia began a lifelong association with members of the Mirault family that included patriarch Louis Mirault, who likely assumed the status of her uncle-in-law. For decades to come, Aspasia and her children sustained a familial relationship with Louis Mirault, and later with his children and other kinfolk. In 1841, Louisa, the eldest daughter of Aspasia and Samuel, served as a baptismal sponsor for Jeannette, one of Louis Mirault's granddaughters.[76]

Following Samuel's death, the cause of which was not recorded in the surviving documents, Aspasia Mirault proceeded to carve out a successful livelihood for herself. She remained steadfast in her determination to fashion her own destiny. Having begun her working life as a seamstress in the tradition of the Cruvellier family, Aspasia did not hesitate to switch careers. She became a first-rate pastry cook. Within a relatively short span of time her shop on Bull and Broughton Streets became a popular confectionary that attracted a sizable and most likely a predominately white clientele.[77] A little more than a decade later, by the early 1840s, profits from her thriving business coupled with the needs of a growing family motivated Aspasia to negotiate a land purchase. The primary obstacle to her goal was the discriminatory 1818 statute. To circumvent the law, Aspasia created a secret trust agreement during the spring of 1842.[78]

How are we to gauge the prudence of Aspasia's actions? Did they amount to a clever maneuver to circumvent the legislative designs? Aspasia's secret land transaction was not without its potentially negative implications. By purchasing the property through another person, Aspasia had opened herself and her family to a risk. Was her creation of a secret trust necessary? If the authorities discovered that Aspasia had violated the law, would she be forced to suffer the penalties under the statute? These and other questions remained unanswered. Yet in the spring of 1842, the Mirault household had good reason to celebrate. Aspasia, a free woman of color, was about to become a Savannah landowner.

Chapter Two

A Secret Trust Agreement

For nearly two decades, Aspasia Cruvellier Mirault juggled the demanding roles and responsibilities of a mother, landowner, entrepreneur, slaveholder, and later as the mistress of a well-to-do black man. Ample business profits, a land acquisition, and good family relations characterized Aspasia's life during the 1830s and 1840s. Providence seemed to favor Aspasia as she and George Cally adroitly maneuvered around the prohibition against blacks owning land in Savannah. Aspasia and Cally, an unlikely pair of collaborators, created a secret trust agreement.

Cally attended a Savannah auction on April 29, 1842. After placing a successful bid on lot number 22 in the Pulaski Ward section of the city, he paid $172.20 of Aspasia's money for the down payment. With this purchase, Cally became the owner of the property and holder of the deed. The deed granted to him and his descendants legal title to the lot in fee simple. The terms and conditions of Cally's real estate purchase were straightforward. Following a financial plan comparable to a twenty-year mortgage, Cally was obligated to make annual ground rent payments in the amount of $41.23 until the debt totaling $861 had been retired.[1] Although on paper he held legal title to the lot, in reality, Cally by mutual agreement served as the clandestine trustee for Aspasia and her children. By the means of her agreement with Cally, Aspasia had become the silent owner of a valuable piece of Savannah real estate.

Aspasia's experience with lot number 22 provides evidence that antebellum blacks could acquire land in locales where such purchases were prohibited by law. Typically, extra legal methods were required to effect such land acquisitions. Certainly, Aspasia was not alone in her use of a secret trust agreement to achieve the desired result. While there is no way of knowing the exact number of free people of color in Savannah who engaged in a similar ruse to own land, judicial records reveal instances in which blacks demonstrated their determination to circumvent racially biased laws. An agency borne of interracial cooperation allowed African Americans to avoid the harsh dictates of state or local laws. The complexity of race relations was manifested in several documented Georgia cases. Sympathetic white people, often serving as guardians, defied state and local authorities. As a result, black people acquired land. Without disclosing their true intentions, whites took title to real estate for the use and occupation by African Americans whose money had supplied the purchase price.[2]

As for Aspasia and Cally, the creation of the secret trust and the purchase of a city lot were just two aspects of what amounted to their complex relationship. We can only speculate why these two individuals arranged to buy a piece of real estate. In 1842, Cally was then a twenty-two-year-old white carpenter originally from Salem, Massachusetts. That same year, Aspasia had attained the status of an African American matron in her forties and old enough to be Cally's mother.[3] Yet these two Savannah residents developed a friendship and bond of confidentiality that lasted many years. Aspasia took a leap of faith by trusting Cally. She allowed him to use her money, purchase a Savannah lot, and take legal title to the property. Aspasia's trust was reciprocated, for Cally too assumed an enormous risk by entering into the secret agreement. The Georgia legislature had devised two penalties for violations of the 1818 statute. Individuals would be subject to a substantial monetary fine, and the state was authorized to seize and sell the property. If the authorities had discovered Cally's role in formulating the trust agreement that benefited Aspasia and her heirs, he stood to incur a fine of up to one thousand dollars.[4]

Apart from their involvement in the real estate purchase, Aspasia and Cally became the subject of salacious gossip. Some residents believed that the two were lovers. Many years after the alleged romantic affair was to have taken place and in the midst of the legal battle over Aspasia's property, several trial witnesses testified that Aspasia and Cally had cohabited during the 1840s and 1850s. According to sworn testimony from J. J. Maurice, a contractor hired by Cally to repair Aspasia's roof, the couple "lived in cahoots." Still another witness, James A. Bowen, corroborated Maurice's testimony by relating information that purportedly proved Aspasia and Cally had had an illicit affair.[5]

In spite of the rumors and suspicions, Aspasia and Cally were good friends, but not lovers. Instead, it was likely that Letitia Mirault Davis, Aspasia's twenty-two-year-old daughter, was the true object of Cally's affections. Indeed, a love relationship and an interracial common law marriage sustained the connection between Cally and Aspasia's family in 1842 and continuing for several decades thereafter. It is likely that Cally's romantic liaison with Letitia made him all the more willing to risk entering into an illegal trust agreement with Aspasia. For nearly two decades, Cally, in his role as Aspasia's putative son-in-law, enjoyed a close association with the members of the Mirault household, both in their business dealings and in their personal affairs.[6]

Their trust agreement created a bond between Aspasia and Cally, but that bond did not prevent Cally from sharing their secret with others. As might be expected and in keeping with the clandestine nature of the agreement, the official deed to the property contained no mention of the secret trust. Nonetheless, the Aspasia-Cally arrangement was commonly known and even discussed discreetly in some social circles. On occasion over the course of at least ten years, Cally, when in the company of friends and business associates, admitted that lot number 22 in Pulaski Ward belonged to Aspasia. Cally, who was described by one associate as being loose with his words, told people that he was merely serving as the trustee of the lot for Aspasia and her family.[7]

While we are left to speculate about Aspasia's true motives for entering into a secret trust agreement with Cally, it is clear that the acquisition of a homestead in Savannah may have warranted some degree of risk taking. It is even possible that Aspasia may have considered buying the land without Cally's assistance. Although laws restricting the liberties of free blacks were common place in antebellum Georgia and elsewhere, many such restrictions were selectively enforced. Although Savannah officials passed an ordinance in 1839 prohibiting blacks and whites from teaching black children or from operating a school for blacks, the enforcement of that ordinance was both lackluster and sporadic.[8] If the city lacked the force of will to punish men and women who taught black children, perhaps officials would have permitted a free black pastry cook, like Aspasia, to purchase a city lot.

Considering all the pertinent facts, it is not surprising that Aspasia and other blacks aspired to become Savannah landowners and entrepreneurs. The historical record suggests that the city remained a tolerable habitat for members of the African American population throughout the antebellum era. In spite of the discriminatory designs of the state and municipal lawmakers, the city of Savannah was a reasonably suitable locale for people of color to settle and raise their families. With a population of 11,214 in 1840 that grew to just over 13,500 residents in 1848, including 632 free blacks and some 2,700 enslaved persons, Savannah possessed many of the more urbane trappings of city life, including utility companies, banks, and transportation companies.[9] The city's strategic location for commerce along the Savannah River and its close proximity to the Atlantic Ocean offered residents, both black and white, many opportunities, especially economic opportunities.

City directories for the period showcased Savannah's more salient features, including transportation companies, financial institutions, schools, and churches. Various modes of transportation facilitated travel in and around Savannah and other nearby cities during the nineteenth century. Savannah was home to several steamboat companies whose vessels plied the Savannah River and beyond, transporting people and materials to domestic ports and various international destinations, particularly in the West Indies. Scores of sailing ships departed Savannah daily carrying valuable cargoes of rice, cotton, wheat, copper, wool, beeswax, and lumber. By 1850 these ships carried Savannah's lumber products to a number of foreign ports in Canada and Great Britain.[10]

During the three decades immediately preceding the Civil War, Savannah's industries paralleled its shipping concerns. Following the example of several northern American cities, such as Lowell, Massachusetts, and Philadelphia, Pennsylvania, Savannah factories manufactured textiles. Taking advantage of the numerous seaworthy vessels available to transport products to markets, manufacturing firms constructed their factories and mills close to Savannah's waterways, keeping employment high and the economy booming. Cotton mills, rice mills, and lumber companies employed Savannah residents, whites as well as free and enslaved blacks. Some companies used an integrated work force, but others relied exclusively on African American laborers. In 1848, for example, the Upper Steam Rice Mill's management advertised its desire to employ "[N]egro men, women, boys, and girls" as employees for "liberal wages."[11]

By capitalizing on its navigable waterways, Savannah became a transportation metropolis. The traveling public, consisting mainly of middle- and upper-income white persons, enjoyed the most modern modes of transportation available. The Steam Packet Line offered biweekly passage from Savannah to Augusta, Georgia, a trip of 150 miles. The line's two vessels, the *H. L. Cook* and the *Ivanhoe*, departed from Savannah on Tuesdays and Saturdays at 6:00 P.M. A rival company operating under the name of the Steamboat Company of Georgia advertised the availability of its steamers, the *Cherokee*, the *Tennessee*, and the *Chatham*, the latter advertised as an iron vessel. All three vessels provided service to New York City with an intermediate stop in Augusta.[12] Savannah travelers were not limited to sea passage. Starting in the mid-1830s, railroad companies competed with steamships for their share of passengers. Rail travel was available along two main lines, the Central of Georgia Railroad and the Atlantic Coastline Railroad.[13]

Religious denominations, charitable organizations, and banking concerns complimented Savannah's mid-nineteenth-century cosmopolitan milieu. St. John the Baptist Catholic Church, founded in 1796, welcomed all the Catholic faithful residing in the community.[14] Enslaved blacks participated in church services along with whites and free black parishioners, including Aspasia Cruveiller Mirault who attended St. John's Church all of her life. Although Aspasia remained dedicated to Catholicism in accordance with her family's tradition, the city offered her a variety of religious faiths from which to choose. Several other religious denominations authorized the establishment of racially mixed congregations in the city.

Besides a sizable Catholic congregation, by the late 1840s, two Episcopal churches and one Methodist church also held regular services in the city. Savannah's Episcopalians could boast that they simultaneously represented one of the oldest as well as one of the newest congregations in the area.

Episcopalians first banded together to form Christ Church soon after the colony of Georgia was founded. That early congregation was integrated. Church officials noted that on July 7, 1750, the Reverend Bartholomew Zouberbuhler, Christ Church's rector, baptized a black woman. As Savannah's population grew and new wards for the city were plotted, the faithful organized a second congregation, St. John's Episcopal Church founded in 1840. A third church, St. Stephens, was established in the winter of 1855 for black Episcopalians. Like the Catholic and Episcopal churches, the Methodist denomination grew in Savannah. According to the city directory for 1848, congregants of the First Methodist Church proudly announced the third anniversary of their new sanctuary in the Oglethorpe Ward section that had been dedicated in 1845. The rapid growth of Methodism became apparent. By 1858, Trinity Church in St. James Square and Wesley Chapel on South Broad Street joined First Church in administering to the faithful.[15]

Although the Lutherans and the Presbyterians formed congregations in Savannah, by the early 1840s, the Baptists eclipsed all the other religious denominations in the number of congregations in the city. The segregated Baptist churches consisted of two predominately white congregations and three black congregations. Black Baptists traveled by wagon on Sunday afternoons to the westernmost section of the city where they baptized new converts in the Ogeechee Canal. While not as numerous as their Baptist counterparts, congregants of the Jewish religion rivaled other groups within the city in longevity. The Jewish population established the Synagogue Mickva Israel in 1790.[16]

The characteristics of urban life in Savannah extended beyond an impressive array of church edifices and large congregations. Aspasia and her neighbors enjoyed a considerable degree of personal safety within the city. Although they lived in a rapidly growing urban environment, rife with all the problems and concerns of that era, Savannah officials had adopted measures to keep incidents of crime and violence at a minimum. By the early 1840s, Savannah had a police force consisting of a team of watchmen, armed with muskets and noise-making rattles, which protected city residents and kept a watchful vigil over their property. Individuals arrested for breaching the law were incarcerated in the Guard House, located on the corner of Whitaker and President Streets. Besides a system of watchmen, Savannah residents took pride in other city institutions, including the Metropolitan Fire Company.[17]

The twin themes of modernization and improvement dominated the thinking of Savannah officials. The city authorized the establishment of a gas works facility, erected on an elevated plot of land that the locals labeled Gas House Hill. In 1850, the Savannah City Council negotiated a contract to light the city, and a lighting company was organized. Pipe lines carried gas to iron posts topped with lanterns to illuminate Savannah's main streets. The city's efforts to adopt the trappings of nineteenth-century modern life extended beyond a street lighting system. Around the same time, Savannah instituted its own water works and plumbing system. The combination of cast-iron pipes, a tower, and a reservoir provided many residents with an ample supply of city water.[18]

The growth of Savannah's financial and charitable institutions reflected the city's nineteenth-century milieu. The State Bank of Georgia located on Drayton Street, along with its main competitor, the Planter's Bank, testified to Savannah's prosperity. While we are left to speculate whether Aspasia invested any of her bakery shop profits in one of Savannah's financial institutions, she may have followed the example of Andrew Marshall, an African American minister who owned four shares in the city's Marine and Fire Insurance Bank.[19] Similar to the banking houses, charitable good works in Savannah benefited various segments of the city's population. The fundraising efforts of two white medical doctors, coupled with a large bequest, resulted in the 1832 founding of the Georgia Infirmary. The infirmary provided medical services to disabled and sick persons in the African American community. Like the infirmary, the city's charities were organized around specific racial or ethnic groups. The Irish Union Society came into existence in 1845, while the German Friendly Society of Savannah predated the Irish organization by eight years. Still other groups worked on behalf of seamen, mechanics, and widows residing in Savannah. In 1848, the Widows Society of Savannah exemplified a charitable model of women assisting other women. That same year, the Widows Society, operated by an all-female staff, supported forty women in need.[20]

Judging from her modest prosperity, Aspasia was more likely to have been a contributor rather than a beneficiary of any charitable largess. Remarkably, and in spite of her status as a free woman of color in the antebellum South, the enterprising Aspasia had done quite well for herself. As an émigré from Santo Domingo, Aspasia came to the United States with her family, the Cruvelliers, and by all contemporary indicators she prospered. She led an uncommon life. She was an intelligent woman, a savvy entrepreneur, and a proud family matriarch who possessed both business acumen and skills as a pastry cook. With her talents coupled with a flair for marketing, Aspasia carved out a business niche for herself in Savannah society by cornering a portion of the confectionary market.

During the spring of 1841, just one year before she and George Cally purchased the Savannah lot, Aspasia advertised her business in a local Savannah newspaper with an enticing heading of *ICE CREAM! ICE CREAM!* Aspasia's advertisement provided important clues about her business strategy.

> *This Afternoon and through the Season, corner of Broughton and Bull streets.*
>
> Aspasia Mirault returns her sincere thanks to the Ladies and Gentlemen of Savannah, for their liberal patronage bestowed on her

> Cream last year, and that no pain has been spared on her part to make her establishment agreeable to the Ladies and public in general.[21]

Aspasia promised the Savannah public that her bakery would continue to meet their high expectations of a quality product and a quality service.

Aspasia's 1841 advertisement was an interesting study in contradictions. On the one hand, the advertisement employed both a deferential tone, thanking the public for its patronage. On the other hand, her advertisement managed to convey Aspasia's sense of confidence and pride in her accomplishments. The advertisement showcased a successful Savannah businesswoman.[22] Aspasia and other free African–American tradespersons and business owners in Savannah and elsewhere relied heavily on the patronage of whites to sustain their enterprises. Their ability to attract and satisfy a white clientele often held the key to their business prosperity. Thus, by maintaining a reputation for honest dealings, providing a quality product, and demonstrating business acumen, antebellum-era black entrepreneurs, like Aspasia, could reasonably expect to grow their businesses with black and white customers.[23] Yet at the same time, Aspasia understood the limitations and restrictions as well as the opportunities available to blacks in Savannah. As a baker, she carried out a formula for success and achieved a degree of independence. Her accomplishments in the business arena may help to explain her defiance of a Georgia statute and the purchase of a Savannah lot a year later in 1842.

Aspasia's advertisement in the *Daily Georgian* newspaper cost her $3.50 and ran for six consecutive days, except for Monday when the paper was not published. Her advertisement first appeared on Tuesday, March 23, 1841, and was last seen on the following Tuesday, March 30, where it was fortuitously placed on a page adjacent to an announcement for a local stage production. "The Lady of Lyon," starring a Mr. Abbot in the role of Claude Malentee and a Miss Abbott, who played the heroine Pauline Lyon, was being performed at the Savannah Theatre that same evening. Theatergoers, checking the newspaper to confirm that evening's performance, could not fail to see Aspasia's advertisement for ice cream.[24]

Aspasia's bakery shop, strategically located on a busy Savannah street corner, was well known for its tasty delights. William Harden, a Savannah attorney from a prominent white family, remembered Aspasia from the days of his youth. For Harden, Aspasia exemplified an upstanding and prosperous woman:

> A negro [*sic*] woman named Aspasia Mirault kept a bakery and confectionery for many years at the northeast corner of Bull and Broughton Streets. She was highly respected and conducted herself in a manner which would have done credit to some of our white citizens. She sold delicious ice-cream of the most popular flavors and her business was well patronized by the white people.[25]

In his comments about Aspasia and her bakery shop, Harden made a mistake about her marital status. Harden recalled that Aspasia was married to one Simon Mirault, a competing African American confectioner. But Aspasia was not married to Simon, who was in all likelihood a younger cousin of Samuel Mirault, the father of her two daughters. Harden correctly reported the location of Simon's bakery shop, situated on the western side of Broughton Street near Whitaker, just one short block from Apasia's establishment. In 1850, the census taker recorded that Simon and his wife, Mary Jane, operated their bakery business while raising a family of three boys and two girls. Twelve-year-old Laura was Simon and Mary's oldest child. Laura's siblings were ten-year-old Rose, seven-year-old Louis, five-year-old Francis, and Simon Jr., the three-year-old baby of the Mirault family.[26]

Mirault family members operated two successful bakery establishments in Savannah, but Aspasia was the first to open a confectionary. At the time, Simon was still a boy living at home with his parents. As a young man, Simon first worked as a brick layer while Aspasia was busy perfecting her trade as a pastry cook. Over time, Simon may have become dissatisfied with brick masonry and began to explore other employment options. Simon, who possessed a keen business sense, observed Aspasia's success and decided to copy her entrepreneurial venture. He may have been all the more willing to abandon brick masonry and to try his luck in the confectionary business because his older sister Josephine worked for Aspasia in the mid-1830s.[27]

There is no clear explanation for the fact that two Mirault family members owned bakeries in Savannah, located on the same street only one block apart. What circumstances could have prompted such proximity? These two talented entrepreneurs might have combined their financial resources to forge a confectionary conglomerate in Savannah. Perhaps Simon's bakery was an extension of Aspasia's establishment, and the two business owners may have assisted each other to some extent. Certainly Aspasia had some previous experience in business collaborations. Two decades earlier, she had consolidated her resources with those of her sister Justine Cruvellier, first as seamstresses and later as pastry cooks.

In the overall operation of her bakery establishment, Aspasia elected not to collaborate with her cousin-in-law Simon. Perhaps there was bad blood or an ongoing feud between the different branches of the Mirault family. Conflicting egos and the desire for personal independence may have dictated a need for not only one but two Mirault-owned bakeries in Savannah. Possibly Aspasia with her dogged determination for financial independence never wanted a joint bakery venture with Simon. Sometime in 1835 or 1836 Simon started his bakery business, and by the mid-1840s, Aspasia and Simon were competing for customers. Many individuals, including African Americans, who operated Savannah's confectionery businesses, could expect a good return on their investments. The longevity of their bakery establishments attested to the considerable success that both Aspasia and Simon enjoyed with their respective business ventures.

From an advertisement Simon placed in a local newspaper, we can glean aspects of both the nature and the extent of his business. It is likely that Aspasia's confectionary took on much the same character. Aspasia specialized in ice cream products while Simon's confectionary primarily sold baked goods. Before competitive ice houses opened in Savannah by the late 1840s, Aspasia was obliged to purchase her ice by the pound and at premium prices from Captain Peter Wittberger's Ice House on Drayton and Broughton Streets, a few blocks from her establishment. To attract customers to his shop, Simon invited the public to view his newly acquired variety of toys and confectioneries. He sold cakes, rolls, and bread, all of which were baked daily, and he offered an assortment of macaroons, iced and ornamented cakes, jellies and creams all made to order. Although city patrons made up the bulk of his clientele, Simon assured his customers located in the outlying rural areas that he would take special care in packaging their orders for shipment.[28] The success of Simon's and Aspasia's businesses was duplicated elsewhere in Savannah and in other cities and towns throughout the antebellum South. Suspending the paranoia that had motivated earlier generations of whites to protest the settlement of "French Negroes" into Savannah and other coastal cities, many whites felt a level of comfort in patronizing African American businesses, especially those businesses that catered primarily to a white clientele. The surviving records suggests that sectors of the general public likely paid more attention to good customer service and quality products than to a proprietor's race or skin color.[29]

The visible pockets of interracial integration and cooperation in Savannah provided a sharp contrast to instances of racial bias. Two distinct portraits of race relations emerged in the city. There was a distinction between the official treatment and policies toward blacks and the everyday treatment of blacks by their white guardians, customers, and neighbors. Although some nineteenth-century whites demonstrated that they could be colorblind when it came to patronizing black-owned business establishments, Savannah city officials were less tolerant. The city council imposed a special tax exclusively on black people engaged in businesses and trades. Since the extant record fails to disclose the motivation behind the special tax, we are left to speculate whether the assessment was devised as a means to exert additional controls on enslaved persons and free people of color or whether it was used merely to raise revenue. Both were probably considered. A city ordinance passed in December 1840 obliged African Americans to purchase badges authorizing them to ply their trades within the city. The racially discriminatory ordinance provided for a fee schedule that varied according to the specific trade being taxed.[30]

African American butchers and bakers, like Aspasia and her cousin-in-law Simon Mirault, paid ten dollars annually for their badges while pilots and other boatmen, fishermen, painters, and wood sawyers paid a slightly lower fee of eight dollars each year. The payment schedule included higher fees for blacks in the same profession who worked in Savannah, but lived outside the city. The same badge that cost Aspasia ten dollars would have doubled to twenty dollars if she had resided beyond the city limits. In addition to the higher nonresident fees, all such workers, irrespective of trade, paid a nonresident tax of eleven dollars and twenty-five cents. In a few categories, fees varied according to the worker's gender. Badges for black females who worked as porters or day laborers cost two dollars and fifty cents while their male counterparts paid four dollars for their badges. Nonresident porters paid ten dollars.[31] The city's elaborate schedule favored both Savannah residents and all female workers who paid lower fees than their nonresident and male counterparts. In spite of their apparent need for more revenue, city officials may have tried to strike a balance in distributing the tax burden among various categories of black workers.

Aspasia paid the city tax on her business and still managed to make a profit. During the 1840s and for the greater part of the 1850s, one significant component of her entrepreneurial activities included the ownership of slaves. Aspasia joined a select group of African American slaveholders in Savannah. Throughout the period, the number of free blacks who owned slaves remained small. African Americans in Savannah owned a total of fifty-three enslaved persons in 1820. By 1860, that number had declined to thirteen slaves.[32]

Because ownership of enslaved property was a form of wealth, Georgia legislators with their antiblack biases were loath to permit African Americans to prosper through slave acquisition. The 1818 state statute effectively stripped free black Georgians of their human property. The following year in 1819, the legislature reconsidered their original action and amended the law to allow blacks to retain and to pass on through inheritance any enslaved persons already in their family's possession. It is likely that Aspasia did not purchase human property. As one of the siblings in the Cruvellier family, Aspasia probably shared ownership or inherited enslaved persons from one of her relatives, possibly Justine, Hagar, or Francis.[33]

One can only speculate how much in monetary terms slave ownership contributed to Aspasia's overall wealth. Aspasia's family, the Cruvelliers, and several other more affluent free black families in Savannah were able to support their economic endeavors through the use of slave labor. These free blacks may have been duplicating the same slaveholding enterprises previously followed in their native Santo Domingo. In Savannah, the Cruvelliers, as tailors and as pastry cooks, joined their fellow black urban craftsmen, including carpenters and brick masons, who purchased slave workers.[34] Before the Savannah fire destroyed his tailor shop in 1820, Francis likely used enslaved laborers in his business. Four years earlier, in 1816, Francis, who was at the time the owner of two slaves, paid the tax collector $11.50, a portion of which was the assessment on his human property. Several members of the Cruvellier family continued to own slaves throughout the antebellum era. During the 1830s, Hagar resided in the Reynolds Ward section of Savannah and worked as a shopkeeper. Two enslaved females who resided in Hagar's household more than likely worked in the shop alongside their free black mistress.[35]

Like Hagar, Justine Cruvellier combined her entrepreneurial activities and slave ownership. During the 1830s Justine probably shared her slave property and a bakery shop management with Aspasia. In 1837, Justine owned four slaves and a piece of real estate located in Derby Ward worth four hundred dollars. Justine's tax liability that year was five dollars and fifty cents, of which three dollars and seventy-five cents was the assessment for her enslaved property. Similarly, two years later, in 1839, Aspasia paid a tax of ninety-three cents on her slave holdings and seventy-eight cents on her stock merchandise for the bakery shop.[36] Judging from a July 1839 newspaper notice about her runaway slave, Justine, like her white slaveholding counterparts, had no reason to expect loyalty from her slaves. Justine's notice offered a ten-dollar reward for the apprehension and return of a black woman named Serena who had absented herself from Cruvellier's establishment on Broughton Street two weeks earlier. Serena was described as a "short stout woman with large mouth and eyes, and is well known in the city having long engaged in the confectionary." Eager for the slave's return, Justine inserted a warning in her notice, "All persons are forbid [*sic*] from harboring said slave or removing her from the state under the penalty of prosecution."[37] While no advertisements for runaways belonging to Aspasia have been located, she nonetheless experienced her share of difficulties with slave property. An August 31, 1835, entry of the Savannah Board of Health Department records indicated that an enslaved infant belonging to Aspasia became a mortality statistic. The unfortunate baby died of teething problems, a common cause of death for children during that era.[38]

Over a period of time and with the assistance of enslaved laborers, Aspasia's bakery shop prospered. Aspasia was the matriarch of a nine-person household in 1830. A decade later in 1840, her household had grown from nine to fifteen persons, five of whom were enslaved. Three of the five female slaves were between the ages of ten years old and twenty-four years old. Aspasia owned two girls who had not yet reached their tenth birthday. Aspasia's slaves included mothers and their daughters. Three members of Aspasia's household worked in manufacturing and trades while two others worked in commerce.[39]

Although financial prosperity remained a priority for Aspasia, her goals for a good life extended beyond monetary matters. The overall well-being of her children and the day-to-day issues related to the family probably consumed large portions of her time. Throughout her life, Aspasia experienced both the benefits as well as the challenges associated with close family ties. As a young, unmarried woman, Aspasia lived and worked closely with members of her immediate family. She worked as a seamstress in her elder brother Francis's tailor shop, and later, she began her career as a pastry chef under the guidance of her sister Justine. Before the untimely death of Samuel Mirault, Aspasia experienced a few years of married life. The couple set up housekeeping, and Aspasia bore two children. Samuel's death by 1831 significantly altered Aspasia's life. As Samuel's young widow, Aspasia had to provide for the couple's two small daughters, Louisa and Letitia.[40]

Because she was a relatively young woman when her mate and the father of her two daughters died, it was not long before Aspasia opened herself up to another relationship. During the early 1830s, Aspasia formed a romantic liaison with James Oliver, a married man, and she bore him three sons, two of which lived to become adults. Joseph, born in 1832, was the first child born of Aspasia's union with Oliver. The following year, Aspasia gave birth to their second child, named Robert. A third son, James, died as an infant. Aspasia's paramour was a well-to-do free man of color and a bona fide African American success story. A native of Virginia, James Oliver migrated to Savannah and made his living as a drayman. His wife, Rosella, worked first as a seamstress and later as a huckster. During the 1830s, Oliver became prosperous and brought three lots with houses worth fourteen hundred dollars on St. Gall Street. His 1833 tax indebtedness amounted to forty-three dollars for his three lots, one wagon, and one slave.[41] Whether the enticement was love, money, or a combination of the two, Aspasia became Oliver's mistress and the mother of his children. A romantic triangle evolved with Aspasia, Oliver, and his wife, Rosella. The Olivers had no children of their own, and Aspasia may have fulfilled his need to procreate. Did Rosella resent Aspasia and the children Aspasia bore for her husband, or did she accept Oliver's infidelity as a matter of course? Could Rosella have possibly condoned the union of her husband and his mistress?

Aspasia's sons, Joseph and Robert, took Oliver's surname as their own. Judging from Oliver's economic prosperity, if he had been so inclined, he possessed the means to provide for his children. Years later during the post–Civil War era and long after both Oliver and Aspasia had died, the adult Robert listed the names of both of his parents on a Freedmen's Savings Bank application.[42] Robert Oliver used his parents' names to identify himself to the bank administrators. This identification offered evidence that a parental affiliation between James Oliver and Aspasia's two sons existed.

Romantic relationships outside of marriage, similar to the liaison between Aspasia and James Oliver, were not uncommon in antebellum Savannah society. Within the expanded circle of the Mirault family members and friends, there were several other instances of children born out of wedlock. Charlotte Reed, a seamstress, never wedded Robert Scott with whom she had two sons, Thomas and Duncan. Even though their parents never married, Charlotte's sons took their father's surname. In later years, the eldest son Thomas married

Mary A. Nayle, one of Aspasia's granddaughters. Andrew Morel, a free black tailor, fathered a child by a woman who was not his wife. Married to Ann, a Santo Domingo native, Morel became involved with an American-born free mulatto by the name of Eve Wallace. Eve gave birth to Morel's son.[43]

Although Aspasia became involved in romantic liaisons at least twice during her lifetime, the premature deaths of both partners cut off her chances for long-standing relationships with them. Sometime in 1835, James Oliver met his demise.[44] Similar to the time when her mate Samuel Mirault died, Oliver's death once again shifted the responsibility for Aspasia's survival and the survival of her four children to herself. She spent precious little time lamenting her fate. Instead, Aspasia set about raising her family, building her bakery business, and, all the while, securing their futures. During the remainder of the 1830s and throughout the decade of the 1840s, Apasia's hard work paid off nicely, and she achieved an enviable level of success.

In spite of her widowhood, her race, and her societal status as a free woman of color, Aspasia fashioned her own destiny, creating a moderately prosperous lifestyle for herself and her children. At the beginning of the 1850s, Aspasia looked toward the future with optimism. While there would be good times in the decade ahead for Aspasia and her family, regrettably, the good times would be fleeting. Before the end of the decade, Aspasia would be dead, and her demise would signal the death knell for some of the dreams she had envisioned for her family.

Chapter Three

Hurricanes, Presidents, and the Death of a Matriarch

Oh that the good times might last forever! The decade of the 1850s dawned brightly for Aspasia Mirault and her family. Over the succeeding ten-year period their lives would be punctuated by a host of joyous as well as sorrowful occasions. The happier times included a wedding in the family, the birth of several children, and the continued success of Aspasia's confectionary business. As it is in the lifespan of all families, the Mirault clan would also bear witness to several sorrowful events during the decade, occasioned by the deaths of loved ones and damage to their property in the wake of a forceful hurricane.

A balance sheet of the family's more joyous and sorrowful years would reveal that 1853 turned out to be a good twelve-month period for the Miraults. That year, they embarked upon an important building project and also celebrated a wedding. During the first few months of 1853, Aspasia realized one of her lifelong ambitions when she began a house construction project on her lot in the Pulaski Ward section of Savannah. Later as the winter months turned first to spring and then to summer, the family celebrated the nuptials of Aspasia's son, Robert S. Oliver, and his bride, Diana Johnson.

Aspasia's house construction proceeded like clockwork. She relied on the construction expertise of her friend and secret trust confidant, George Cally, who was a carpenter. It was Cally, and not Aspasia, who hired George H. Ash, a Savannah contractor, to build the house on Aspasia's sixty-by-ninety-foot city lot.[1] Judging from the text of his city directory advertisements, Ash was a confident tradesman. In an advertisement published in the city directory a few years after he completed Aspasia's home, Ash labeled himself a "master builder" who was "prepared to contract for building jobing [sic] work of any description in his line." Taking into account his marketing tilt toward self-promotion, the advertisement demonstrated Ash's assurance about completing jobs and the scope of his business undertakings. Addressing the quality of his work product, the advertisement promised future customers that "all work [would be] done with neatness and dispatch."[2]

Although he hired Ash as a primary contractor, Cally took charge of the building operation by supervising all the details at the construction site. Even though Aspasia paid for the construction costs, totaling nearly one thousand dollars, it was Cally who approved Ash's design for the house, as well as oversaw the day-to-day workmanship.[3] Ash worked quickly and, apparently, in a manner that met with Cally and Aspasia's expectations. In record time the three-story brick home, erected on the southwest corner of Whitaker and Macon Streets, was ready for occupancy.

On what must have been a joyous occasion, Aspasia and her family moved into their new home. Three generations of Miraults would occupied the newly constructed home, including Joseph and Robert Oliver, Aspasia's young adult sons, as well as Letitia Davis, Aspasia's grown daughter, and Letitia's children. In addition, several offspring of Louisa Nayle, Aspasia's deceased daughter, shared the new house with their grandmother and other relatives. Along with the blood relatives who moved into the residence, Aspasia welcomed a white person as a resident in her new home. Cally, who had played a crucial role in Aspasia's acquisition of the lot a decade earlier and who had lent his expertise for the construction of the home, moved in with the Miraults.[4] Cally's residency with a free black family undoubtedly fueled the long-standing rumor of his alleged romantic liaison with one of the Mirault women and demonstrates the occasional laxity of Savannah's racial codes.

Aspasia's home construction project contained a crucial business component. By erecting a small outdoor oven at the rear of the new residence, she was able to relocate her bakery shop to her new home location.[5] Continuing the tradition established at the previous Broughton and Bull Streets location, Aspasia's new bakery remained a family-run operation. Letitia learned the bakery trade from her mother and worked as Aspasia's assistant in the shop for many years.

Once settled into the new Whitaker Street residence, the Miraults then turned their attention to the second major family event of 1853. A summer wedding was planned when twenty-year-old Robert, Aspasia's youngest son by James Oliver, asked Diana Johnson, a free black woman, to be his wife. On August 3, 1853, Robert and Diana recited their wedding vows before the Reverend J. F. Kirby of the St. John the Baptist Catholic Church. The bride was eighteen years old on her wedding day. While there is no surviving list of the complete wedding party, Cyrus C. Crueviller, the groom's cousin, witnessed the signing of the couple's marriage license and the recitation of their wedding vows.[6] Family members and friends probably joined in the festivities, including Aspasia, whose expert culinary skills made her the likely chef for the wedding feast.

As the proud mother of the groom, a successful entrepreneur, and a Savannah homeowner, Aspasia must have been pleased with her accomplishments.

Judged by almost any nineteenth-century measure, Aspasia had excelled as evinced by her acquisition of land and the financing of a house building project. The land she had purchased with Cally's assistance was a wise investment. Her property lay in a mixed commercial and residential area within a short walking distance from one of the most fashionable green spots in all of Savannah.

We are left to speculate whether Aspasia or other members of her family walked the four blocks from their Whitaker Street home to Forsyth Park, a forested area enclosed by an iron railing and an ornate gate. Savannah, like her sister cities of Richmond and Charleston, either allowed blacks limited access to such public places or excluded them altogether.[7] By the middle of the nineteenth century, this Savannah green spot had become a popular recreational area. The park itself was steeped in Georgia history and tradition. In 1851, Savannah officials renamed Hodgson Park in honor of John Forsyth, a Georgia statesman. Besides giving the park a new name, the city hired H. D. Headman, a noted landscape architect, to erect a fountain at its center. Headman modeled his creation after a similar fountain in the Place de la Concorde in Paris, France.[8] The fountain must have been viewed as an architectural marvel in Aspasia's Savannah.[9]

Besides her home's close proximity to Forsyth Park, Aspasia also lived near a newly constructed church, St. John's Episcopal Church, located across Whitaker Street and approximately a half block from Aspasia's residence. In 1840, St. John's vestry contracted to build a church structure near the piece of land that Aspasia would purchase two years later in 1842. Construction proceeded at a snail's pace. The sanctuary was not completed until sometime in May 1853, around the same time contractor George Ash put the finishing touches on Aspasia's new home.

When a hurricane of tremendous force struck Savannah in September 1854, neither St. John's church structure nor Aspasia's home escaped the storm's gale force wind and rain. Both roofs were toppled. While it is likely that Aspasia lost only her roof to the storm, the church sustained more extensive structural damage. St John's parishioners found themselves strapped with repair bills exceeding twenty-five hundred dollars. With huge gaping holes in the roof, the church sanctuary filled with water, rendering the building temporarily uninhabitable.[10] Meanwhile, less than a block away at the Mirault home, Aspasia, with Cally's assistance, set about repairing her roof. Cally suggested that she hire a local tinner by the name of J. J. Maurice, who in relatively short order made the necessary repairs.[11] While the historical record does not reveal the full extent of the storm damage to Aspasia's home, some two decades later, when called to testify in a legal confrontation over Aspasia's estate, Maurice remembered Cally hired him to replace Aspasia's roof.[12]

The hurricane force winds did their share of damage throughout the city of Savannah. Some homes were completely destroyed by the storm of 1854 while the majority of residents, like Aspasia, sustained repairable damage to their residences and businesses. During the next twelve months, renovation projects undertaken throughout the city restored many of the houses to their pre-hurricane condition. As for Aspasia's neighbor St. John's Episcopal Church, the ministry authorized a massive reconstruction project soon after the storm's damage had been assessed. Fourteen months after the storm hit Savannah, St. John's Church dedicated its new bells and displayed its indoor illumination system at a festive rededication service. William Battersy, a wealthy parishioner, had donated gaslights for the sanctuary. Because they routinely worshiped at the local Catholic church, it is unlikely that Aspasia or other members of her family attended St. John's first evening worship service that Christmas Eve night. Yet, one might surmise that the Mirault family could hear St. John's bells and observe the glow of the church's gas lights from their nearby Whitaker Street home.[13]

The proximity of Aspasia's residence to several churches, a city park, and a variety of business establishments made her land a desirable piece of real estate. Her Whitaker Street home attracted the attention of at least one potential buyer. In 1856 or 1857 Hill Gowdy, a prominent Savannah merchant and the owner of an adjacent lot, wanted to expand his real estate holdings. Gowdy offered his neighbor Cally twenty-five hundred dollars for his house and lot. Gowdy's offer may have caught Cally off guard. Without thinking carefully about his response, Cally informed Gowdy that he would be obliged to relay the offer to Aspasia, who was the true owner. Several days later, Cally reported back to Gowdy that Aspasia had declined his offer. She had no interest in selling her property.[14] Armed with knowledge about Aspasia's ownership and possibly details about the secret trust arrangement, Gowdy did not betray his neighbors' confidence. But years later when a court battle ensued over the lot, Gowdy testified about his firsthand knowledge of Aspasia's property.

Aspasia's unwillingness to entertain Gowdy's offer showed her independence and her confidence as a homeowner and entrepreneur. Aspasia may have rejected Gowdy's offer to buy her home and lot because she had achieved a level of financial security. While the surviving documentation indicates that Aspasia was able to meet her financial obligations, nevertheless, the day-to-day expenses of running a household and a business, of making annual ground rent payments on her property, and of paying occasional repair bills must have been costly propositions for her to manage. Her bakery business continued to prosper through the mid-1850s, providing the family with a steady source of income. At the end of the preceding decade, in 1849, Aspasia paid her Chatham County taxes of eight dollars on one slave, a dog, and two hundred dollars' worth of in-stock inventory. She paid four dollars in taxes on the slave, two dollars for her dog, and another two dollars for the inventory.[15] Four years later in 1853, as Aspasia relocated her family and the business to the new residence, the assessed value of her confectionary merchandise had risen to three hundred dollars, an increase of 50 percent over the span of four years.[16] In

1855 and in 1856, the value of her in-stock inventory increased to four hundred dollars. By that time, Aspasia no longer owned the slave, but she had purchased a second dog.[17] Aspasia's business finances are not completely revealed from the tax records. Overall, her tax records provide evidence that Aspasia continued to grow her business through the end of her life as she labored to pass on a successful enterprise to her children.[18]

With the move to the Pulaski Ward location, Aspasia operated her confectionary in a bustling mixed commercial and residential district of Savannah. Whitaker Street, the address of Aspasia's home and business establishment, was a popular area for other persons in the same line of work. Aspasia's bakery was located on the corner of Whitaker and Macon. Three of her competitors maintained their businesses nearby. Confectioner James A. Brown and Company operated a business on Whitaker; similarly, Daniel Duthill welcomed patrons to his bakery located at 26 Whitaker; and James P. Long sold confectionary goods at the corner of Whitaker and Congress Lane.[19] According to the Savannah city directory for 1859, Aspasia's establishment, which was by that year operated by her daughter Letitia Davis, was the only black-owned confectionery in the immediate vicinity and was a smaller operation in comparison to the establishments of her white competitors. Three years earlier in 1855, Brown and Company with an inventory valued at five thousand dollars was Aspasia's single competitor on Whitaker Street. Brown's inventory value declined significantly the following year to eighteen hundred dollars. By 1858, there were four bakery establishments, including Aspasia's on Whitaker Street. The Brown Company's inventory was valued once again at five thousand dollars, while competitor James P. Long's business had accumulated five hundred dollars' worth of inventory. The Duthill business had opened its doors to the public by 1858, but the value of the company's inventory was not recorded in the tax digest for that year.[20]

Throughout the 1850s, bakery establishments like Aspasia's and a variety of other businesses offered their wares and services in Savannah. City officials could boast that Savannah had become one of the premier urban areas in the South with a growing population and a thriving and diverse business economy. Although a few African Americans, like Aspasia and her daughter Letitia, found success in the bakery and confectionary business, the career options for the majority of the free black population were limited. Yet, throughout the antebellum era, whites in Savannah and elsewhere had substantially more avenues and opportunities for making a living.

One of Aspasia's neighbors, a white woman by the name of Mrs. Hastings, opened a bonnet emporium at 145 Congress Street on the corner of Whitaker. In an effort to attract a steady stream of patrons and to distinguish her wares from the competition, Hastings advertised mourning bonnets at fifty cents less that any other establishment in the city. Five doors from Hastings's establishment, a carpet and upholstery warehouse offered hearth rugs, floor-cloth, and window shades at reasonable prices. City directories for the period attest to the fact that Savannah residents could purchase any number of consumer items, including life and fire insurance, men's furnishings, pianos, jewelry, clocks, and perfumes. The proprietors of S. D. Brantley & Company, a white-owned apothecary located on Bull near Broughton Street, supplied retailers and wholesales with perfumes, paints, chemicals, window glass, and medicines.[21]

Many white Savannah tradesmen and craftsmen offered their services. James Oliver, a white man, sold made-to-order boots at his establishment on Whitaker just one block south of Broughton. The James & Stevenson Company, a white-owned establishment, advertised plain and ornamental plastering, while Miller & Ferguson, also a white company, provided their expertise as wheelwrights and blacksmiths. John Nicolson, a white plumber and gas fitter, operated another Savannah business, and J. K. Blyler, a white businessman, operated a store located at 147 Bay Street that sold a selection of both foreign and domestic wines, gins, and cigars.[22]

For the most part, employment opportunities for skilled white workers in Savannah remained adequate throughout the 1850s. Individuals who wanted work, more often than not, could find employment. Even Aspasia's confidant, George Cally, remained gainfully employed as a Savannah carpenter from the 1840s through the early 1870s. Cally rented Aspasia's lot in Pulaski Ward and maintained a carpentry shop at the location until 1853 when the construction on her residence began.[23]

Apart from residing in an African American household, Cally maintained another association within Savannah's black community. He served as a commanding officer for one of the city's fire companies, manned almost exclusively by enslaved men and a small number of free black men. Throughout most of the antebellum era and pursuant to a city ordinance, Savannah entrusted its fire protection to blacks. The city was divided into four fire districts. A watchman stationed in the steeple of the City Exchange Building rang a bell to alert the various fire engine companies when a fired was spotted. The enslaved firemen worked at the behest of their owners and typically responded to a fire alarm quickly and in accordance with the orders of their white officers. Cally served as one of those fire officers, a position of considerable prestige. According to contemporary sources, some of Savannah's finest citizens held those posts.[24]

Even though Cally was a member of the fire company, his reputation and social status remain open to speculation. His complicity in a secret trust agreement with Aspasia may not have been known, but evidence of his long-term residency with a free black family on Whitaker Street would have been public knowledge. Did the information about his private life and activities tarnish his social standing among whites? Revelations about the frequency of interracial socializing, living arrangements, and even a few marriages suggest that Cally's lifestyle may not have been so unusual for his era.[25] Apparently, Cally lived quietly with his black paramour and her family while he served as the commander of a black fire prevention unit. In that role, he rendered an important service to the city. The city hosted an annual parade and water hose competition among the various fire companies, and Cally was an active participant in those festive events. The parade was a crowd pleaser. Scores of residents, including the mayor and aldermen, lined the parade route to applaud the black men who had responded faithfully to the fire alarms during the previous twelve months. The firemen obliged the friendly crowds by donning colorful costumes and decorating their engines as they passed in review along Savannah's streets.[26] For the parade in May 1854, firemen in Cally's unit received honorable mention for their "highly decorated outfits."[27]

The following year, although Cally's group, Hose Cart B, consisting of some thirty men, did not receive the top honors for their costumes, they nonetheless cut an attractive figure dressed in their blue coats, trimmed in red, worn over white-colored pants. Two highlights of the annual celebration in 1855 included a farewell to a retiring black fireman and a first place showing in the water hose competition. Hearty applause and cheers greeted Anthony Wall, the city's oldest black fireman and a recent retiree from his firefighting duties, as he marched with his comrades along the parade route. Then following the parade, the firemen of Engine Number 8, who called themselves the "wildcats," bested the competition to claim the gleaming silver goblet. To earn the prize, the wildcats had thrown their stream of water farther than any other team, a distance of 177 feet.[28] A public display of appreciation for a black unit by Savannah's white citizens, although common place during the antebellum years, became unimaginable in the post–Civil War and Reconstruction era.

Apasia and her family maintained a close association with a handful of white citizens, including John Elliott Ward, a one-term mayor of Savannah and a prominent member of both the state and national units of the Democratic Party. As previously referenced, Ward served as Aspasia's guardian for many years. Ward also served as the godfather for one of Aspasia's grandsons, and he was a participant in the infant's baptismal ceremony in 1857.

His guardianship service for at least one and likely several other African American families was one of many contributions John Elliott Ward provided to his city. Ward was a very powerful man in Savannah circles. By all accounts, Ward earned high marks during his one-year mayoral term in 1854. His administration held the reins of municipal power during one of the most celebrated events as well as during two of the most tragic occasions in the city's history. Ward hosted a festive presidential visit to Savannah, and he marshaled the city's emergency resources in response to both a hurricane and a yellow fever epidemic.[29]

A particularly virulent outbreak of yellow fever plagued the city during Ward's tenure as the city's chief executive. The sickness appeared suddenly in early August of 1854 and then waned by late September, but not before reaching epidemic proportions, wreaking havoc on the population, and resulting in many fatalities. In his report submitted to city officials, Mayor Ward related the grim statistics that a total of 594 Savannah residents had succumbed to the sickness. Ward's figures represented the demise of 580 whites and 14 blacks.[30] At first glance the disproportionate number between the white and the black fatalities, without more information, is hard to reconcile. Yet, one possible explanation may be that the mechanism for reporting as well as the interest in reporting deaths among the black population must have been woefully inadequate in comparison to the mechanism for reporting yellow fever deaths among the white residents.

Even though Ward himself contracted the fever and was confined to his bed for several weeks, he nonetheless kept abreast of the city's efforts to control the epidemic and to limit its spread throughout Savannah's many neighborhoods. One portion of Ward's report contained results of his administration's investigation into the possible causes for the epidemic. Several theories had been considered. Ward and several members of his administration suspected that the June 29 arrival of the brig *Charlotte Hague* from Havana, Cuba, with a crew that included two sick sailors, might have been the initial cause of the city's misfortune. Dr. Mackall, Savannah's port physician, had visited the ship and examined the sick crewmen. Ward also reported the unconfirmed rumor that the sick crewmen had come ashore and later died in the city. Applying the scientific approach to the problem at hand, Ward laid out other possible causes, including the botched disposal of a ton of mud in the dredging of the Savannah River as well as the suspected unhealthy condition of the rice fields adjacent to the city. City officials weighed the pros and cons of the theories, ultimately eliminating each one as the cause of the yellow fever epidemic.[31]

Aspasia lost her roof and nearby St. John's Episcopal Church sustained heavy damage to its sanctuary when hurricane-force winds blew into Savannah. The hurricane struck in September 1854 while Mayor Ward and city administrators continued to struggle with the yellow fever epidemic that had already devastated many lives. The storm swept through the city damaging entire neighborhoods. Once again demonstrating his leadership, Ward met the new challenge and received praise from his constituents for his tireless efforts on their behalf. Apart from offering citizens emergency relief during both the yellow fever epidemic and the hurricane, Ward proved to be an innovative mayor whose administration completed the city's waterworks system, implemented an improved method for cleaning the streets, and instituted a new police force. Catering to his interest in public education, Mayor Ward spearheaded the city's allocation of more land for school construction. All of these notable achievements were completed during Ward's brief one-year term in office.[32]

The capstone event of Ward's term was former president Millard Fillmore's four-day visit to Savannah during the spring of 1854. Following his years as the chief executive of the United States, Fillmore accepted invitations from several mayors to visit their cities. In addition to Savannah, Fillmore's southern tour included cities in Alabama, Florida, and Louisiana.[33] Mayor Ward's predecessor had extended the invitation to Fillmore over a year earlier. But it was not until the spring of 1854 that the former president made his journey to Georgia. By the time Fillmore arrived, Ward had assumed the mayor's post and happily accepted the duties as the official host to the distinguished visitor. It is a fairly safe bet to assume that Aspasia and several members of her family joined the huge crowd of Savannah residents at the railroad depot to welcome President Fillmore to the city. A local newspaper reporter covering the event estimated that practically the entire population of Savannah had assembled to witness the rare spectacle of a presidential visit.[34]

The city put on its very best face to welcome and to entertain President Fillmore. At precisely 5:30 P.M. on Friday evening, April 22, 1854, the waiting crowd heard the first of thirty-one guns fired in a salute. With so many persons in attendance, one wonders if Aspasia was situated close enough to the stage to hear her guardian Mayor Ward extend a hearty greeting. In his brief remarks, the former president, described as tall, handsome, and dignified, expressed his appreciation for the warm welcome while he lavished praise on both the city and its residents. Perhaps members of the Mirault family joined the throng of persons who followed Fillmore's large open carriage, drawn by four horses, transporting him and his entourage along South Broad Street and then to Pulaski House on State Street where he stayed during his visit. Catching a glimpse of Fillmore at the depot or along the makeshift parade route would have been the only two opportunities Aspasia and other Mirault family members would have had to witness such a historic occasion. The remainder of Fillmore's stay in Savannah that included a party at Bonaventure Plantation, a reception at Pulaski House, a boat excursion to Fort Pulaski on the steamer *Seminole*, and a farewell ball at St. Andrew's Hall would have been strictly off limits to free persons of color like the Miraults.[35]

Could Ward have permitted Aspasia access to the presidential party? Such a prospect would have been unlikely. Yet, the Miraults enjoyed a cordial relationship with Ward, extending beyond his year as mayor of Savannah. After leaving the pressures of the mayor's office to resume his law practice, Ward appears to have devoted even more time to Aspasia and her family. In 1857, Robert Oliver, Aspasia's son, asked the recently retired mayor to serve as the godfather to his newborn son. Ward accepted and attended the baptism ceremony at St. John the Baptist Catholic Church. To honor the former mayor and godparent of their infant son, Robert and Diana, his wife, christened their baby boy, Robert Ward Oliver. Elizabeth Bullock, one of Aspasia's relatives, joined Ward and assumed the role as little Robert's godmother.[36]

Advantages, economic, social, or otherwise, may have accrued to Aspasia and her family by virtue of the fact that the mayor was her guardian. Ward, later the first United States minister to China during the James Buchanan administration, was an independent thinker who held liberal views for his era.[37] In July 1857, the same year that Ward consented to serve as the godfather to a black child, he delivered the commencement speech at the Wesleyan Female College, located in Macon, Georgia. In his address to the "Ladies of the Graduating Class," the subject of which he stated was "the influence of women over the world's rulers, and through them, over the world's destinies," Ward extolled the strength, power, and many virtues possessed by women.[38] In spite of the rigid nineteenth-century race and gender conventions that gave advantages to whites over blacks and to males over females, Ward's high position in Savannah circles, his contacts, and his influence made life a little easier for Aspasia and her children. Did he facilitate the rental of her bakery shop at Broughton and Bull? Did he steer customers in her direction? While we may never know for sure, the parameters of the Aspasia-Ward relationship are interesting to ponder. In 1857, he was willing to serve as a godparent to Aspasia's grandson. Later that same year, it is very likely that Ward expressed his condolences to the family and offered his assistance with funeral arrangements when he learned that Aspasia had died.

Aspasia Cruvellier Mirault died on November 13, 1857. Dr. C. W. West reported that her death had been caused by inflammation of the brain. Although the death record listed her age, Aspasia had not reached her sixty-fifth birthday as was reported by Dr. West. Her burial took place in the city's Laurel Grove Cemetery in the section reserved for African Americans. The sudden loss of their beloved family matriarch must have been a terrible blow to the grieving family members.[39] A long list of Aspasia's accomplishments, occurring over several decades, provided a strong testament to her talents and ingenuity. She eclipsed racial and gender barriers of her era to determine her destiny both as a woman and as an entrepreneur. In her personal life, Aspasia had sustained her role as a formidable head of household for many years. Not only had she raised four children, but she had ably provided a home for other relatives, including several grandchildren. She and many other free blacks transcended Savannah's racial restrictions to enjoy a considerable level of business success.

Having succeeded as an entrepreneur and a skillful pastry cook, Aspasia left her family a proud legacy and a financial foundation that they could leverage for their own lives and careers. A childhood reminiscence of one white Savannah resident provides a glimpse of the role Aspasia defined for herself in the antebellum South. Looking back some fifty years and recalling the Savannah of his youth, W. B. Burroughs, a medical doctor, fondly remembered Aspasia and what he perceived as her status in the community. She must have been a favorite of the white neighborhood children. Burroughs also remembered her physical stature and her nickname:

> The great happiness was the free from care days of childhood . . . Soon afterwards, in 1850, in a long, one-story house about sixty feet from the northeast corner of Bull and Broughton, a large free mulatto woman, whom we called Spazzee, opened a shop. She was a pastry cook and was much welcomed by Savannah women.[40]

Aspasia's hard work over many years had paid off handsomely. She had attained an enviable status within the Savannah community that included a rare distinction within the St. John the Baptist Catholic Church. As a parishioner at the church over the course of her life, Aspasia purchased a pew for her family. Although African Americans, including her family members both the Cruvelliers and the Miraults, had been included in the sacraments and ceremonies at St. John the Baptist Catholic Church since the early 1800s, blacks had typically been relegated to seating in the church's gallery section. By purchasing a pew, Aspasia had achieved a unique status in church circles.[41]

Besides a church pew, Aspasia bequeathed to her family a valuable inheritance, consisting of a piece of Savannah real estate as well as a profitable business. Aspasia had violated a state statute by purchasing one of the lots in Pulaski Ward section of the city. Yet her family's hold on that piece of property appeared to be secure at the time of her death. So long as Cally, Aspasia's partner in the land purchase, kept the details of their illegal trust agreement confidential, members of the Mirault family could reasonably expect to occupy their mother's property indefinitely. Census records verify that Aspasia's relatives resided in her Whitaker Street home for nearly a decade after her death.[42] Cally, a longtime resident in the Mirault household, maintained cordial relations with Aspasia's children and grandchildren. In 1858, Aspasia had been dead for one year, and Cally remained a resident in her house on Whitaker Street. Two years later, the 1860 census taker recorded that Cally still resided in the home along with Aspasia's daughter, Letitia, Letitia's children, and yet another Mirault relative, twenty-year-old Charles B. Stiles, the son of the deceased Louisa Nayle. Louisa had been Letitia's older sister.[43]

Letitia assumed the primary responsibilities in maintaining the bakery business for three years following her mother's death. Letitia was the logical choice to replace Aspasia as the head of the family household and as the main proprietor of their business. Revealing the same savvy business acumen that had served both her mother and her cousin, Simon Mirault, well over the years, Letitia likewise understood the profitability of advertising. Aspasia had placed an advertisement for her business in the *Daily Georgian* newspaper while Simon advertised his bakery in the *Savannah Daily News*. Following their examples, Letitia paid for two listings under the name of L. C. Davis in Ferslew's *Business Directory* for 1859. She was one of seven Savannah confectioners listed in the directory that year. Even though Letitia advertised her bakery, we can only speculate about the nature of her business accounts. In comparison to the surviving multiyear tax records covering the time period that Aspasia ran the bakery establishment, there is little evidence to flesh out the details of Letitia's business or her tax liability.[44]

Letitia Davis did not live long enough to establish a solid footing in her own right either as a Savannah confectioner or as the Mirault family matriarch. On December 5, 1860, three years after Aspasia's death, Letitia passed away in her fortieth year. The official cause of death was listed as Peritonitis disease.[45] With the untimely deaths of Aspasia in 1857 and her daughter Letitia in 1860, the Mirault family clan had experienced two devastating losses in a short span of time. Letitia's death marked both the end of the family's bakery dynasty as well as the beginning of a new phase in the Mirault family saga. Although it would not become obvious for some years to come, a legal battle over the ownership and control of Aspasia's estate was in the offing. With the deaths of Aspasia and Letitia, the Mirault heirs had lost their two closest links to George Cally, the man who held the legal title to the Whitaker Street lot. Although it does not appear that they were aware of the changes taking place, with each passing year the Mirault family members' claim to Aspasia's property grew more tenuous. By the mid-1870s, only their resort to legal action would settle the real estate controversy once and for all.

In the meantime the surviving Mirault family members banded together for mutual support. When his older sister Letitia died in the winter of 1860, Robert S. Oliver had taken up the trade of brick masonry to support his wife, Diana, and their growing family. From the start of their marriage in August 1853, the young couple had been keen to start a family of their own. Robert and Diana were overjoyed with the birth of their first son, Joseph, in late January 1855. Then tragedy struck the family. Named for his father's deceased brother, the tiny infant Joseph lived one week before succumbing to a severe case of spasms.[46]

Rebounding from the death of their first born, Robert and Diana subsequently had three more children. As fate would have it, they would grieve over the passing of a second child, this time a daughter named Matilda. After losing two babies, the Olivers had two additional children who survived their infant years. A second boy and a second girl were both born healthy and lived into adulthood. Robert Ward Oliver, the couple's second son, was born on June 21, 1856, and was baptized at St. John the Baptist Catholic Church the following year. As previously referenced, former Savannah mayor John Elliott Ward attended the ceremony and served as the infant's godfather. Eight years later in 1862, Diana gave birth to another daughter, whom they named Aspasia Matilda in memory of both her deceased grandmother as well as the female sibling who had predeceased her.[47]

Demonstrating the close ties that were a hallmark of Aspasia Mirault's extended family, Robert and Diana asked Louisa Williams, Robert's niece, to serve as the infant Aspasia's godmother. Louisa was the youngest child of

Robert's deceased sister, Louisa Nayle. For his daughter's godfather, Robert selected Eugene Truchelet, a free black man and a boyhood friend who would later serve with the elder Robert as a musician in a Confederate army band.[48] Although Robert Ward Oliver never knew his elder brother Joseph, who died as an infant in 1855, young Robert nevertheless acknowledged this filial relationship a decade later on his account application at the Freedmen's Savings Bank in Savannah.[49]

Aspasia Mirault left her family a rich heritage. Over her lifetime, she had become the matriarch of a large and extended family, and she had the common sense to cultivate family relationships. Joyous occasions like weddings and baptisms brought the family members together. Aspasia was born a Cruvellier on Santo Domingo, but relocated to Savannah. Through the years, several members of that family, also émigrés to Savannah, remained in close touch with her and her children. Cyrus C. Crueviller, a cousin, signed as a witness when Robert and Diana Oliver applied for their wedding license in 1853. Decades earlier, Aspasia married into the Mirault family, creating lasting ties with that family grouping as well. Louisa Nayle, Aspasia's oldest daughter, served as the godmother for her cousin Simon Mirault's daughter, Jeannette, in a ceremony at St. John's Church in November 1841. Two years later when Simon's son Louis was born, he asked another cousin, Joseph Crueviller, to be the infant's godfather.[50]

As a family unit, the Miraults encountered challenges and achieved some notable accomplishments during the 1850s. Profits from her successful bakery business gave Aspasia the financial resources to proceed with an impressive building project on her Pulaski Ward lot. With Cally's assistance in selecting the appropriate craftsmen, Aspasia built a new home and business headquarters on the corner of Whitaker and Macon Streets. Her son's wedding day and the birth of several grandchildren were some of the important milestones that Aspasia witnessed before her death in 1857. Four years after she died, the Savannah Aspasia had known, the state of Georgia, and much of the South would be radically transformed by the Civil War. The war ushered in astounding changes, including the abolition of slavery and the granting of citizenship to all black people. Many of the antebellum laws, like the 1818 statute that had restricted the liberty and opportunities of black people both enslaved and free, would by the war's conclusion be repudiated. A dramatically different South was evolving for Aspasia's family and their neighbors. She would have been proud to know that as soldiers, as businesspersons, and as community leaders, her heirs and other family members embraced new opportunities in the years ahead.

Chapter Four

Black Confederates

Among the surviving remnants of the lives that were Aspasia Mirault's children, one particular set of records chronicles the Civil War activities of her son Robert Oliver. Even though the records did not include either his middle name (Stephen) or middle initial, corroborating documents verify that the files belonged to Aspasia's son, a teenaged musician and later a bandsman in the Confederate army. Instead of remaining idle on the sidelines while the war raged around him, Robert volunteered for service. The sectional conflict between the northern and southern states that culminated in four years of civil war provided Robert, a young Savannah brick mason, husband and father, with an income during the lean war years. Falling back on his talent as a musician, Robert enlisted for a six-month tour of duty as a bandsman in the Twenty-fifth Georgia Regiment.[1]

Robert was just one of the many thousands of African Americans who volunteered to serve in one capacity or another during the Civil War. In April 1861, when the Confederates fired on Fort Sumter, South Carolina, igniting the conflict, scores of black men, living both in the North and in the South, immediately recognized the high stakes involved. While a substantially greater number of black men offered to take up arms in support of the Union against the Confederacy, some blacks did offer their services to the Confederacy. Overall, the participation of African Americans in the war effort was staggering. Before the conflict ended in 1865, approximately 186,000 black men fought on the Union side. In comparison, the number of black Confederates likely totaled a few thousand, the vast majority of those serving in noncombat roles.[2]

In the initial stages of the war, neither side wanted to arm black men. Offers by black men to take up arms were routinely and firmly rejected. Political and military leaders, both in the North and in the South, were loath to use black men as soldiers. When a group of approximately sixty black men tried to enlist at a camp in Richmond, Virginia, during the first few months of the conflict, Confederate officers expressed their gratitude but turned the men away.[3]

The Union army eventually reversed its initial position and accepted blacks into its ranks after congressional passage of the Second Confiscation Act and the Militia Act in 1862. Relenting to pressure from a few members of his cabinet and several generals, President Abraham Lincoln permitted blacks to enlist. Commencing that same summer several all-black military units were formed. Yet winning the struggle to enlist turned out to be just one of many hurdles black soldiers would face within the Union ranks. Following their enlistment, blacks confronted discriminatory treatment, including less pay and a smaller clothing allowance than their white counterparts. Some, but not all, of the white officers chosen to command the black troops brought their prejudices to their military assignments, creating yet another hurdle for the blacks to traverse. Other white military officers, including Robert Gould Shaw of the Fifty-fourth Massachusetts Regiment and Thomas Wentworth Higginson of the First South Carolina Volunteers, proudly commanded African American soldiers.[4]

In spite of the obstacles, courageous black military units such as two regiments from Kansas, the First and Second Colored Volunteers, and others including the First South Carolina Volunteers and the Fifty-fourth Massachusetts Infantry distinguished themselves as first-rate Union soldiers, proving the naysayers wrong in the process. Gradually, the top brass of the Union army warmed to the idea of using black soldiers. Besides Massachusetts and Kansas, other states, including Pennsylvania, Illinois, Ohio, Indiana, and Michigan, raised all-black military units for the Union cause. This significant change in official policy permitted the deployment of not only free black troops, but also the thousands of enslaved blacks, labeled contraband of war, who fled from the southern plantations seeking freedom behind Union army lines.[5]

Although the northern army began accepting blacks into their ranks, the Confederates remained steadfast in their policy of not arming blacks. Yet from the very onset of the conflict, southerners utilized black labor to support their massive war effort. Hundreds, perhaps thousands, of enslaved men and women and a substantial number of free black men worked on military fortifications, dug trenches, cooked food, or washed clothes for the Confederate military machine. Still other blacks served the South as personal servants to Confederate officers.[6]

A number of Savannah blacks responded to the Confederate call for workers. Anxious that the city and its harbor might be targets of Union guns, municipal officers devised a project to construct defensive fortifications at nearby Fort Pulaski. Twenty-four free men of color volunteered to supply the back-breaking labor involved in the project. When the arduous task had been completed with the fortifications in place by early July 1861, the *Savannah Morning News* reported that the city owed a debt of gratitude to the black men who been honorably discharged from their labors. Three of Aspasia's relatives worked to fortify the city's defenses. Simon Mirault Jr. and two of Simon's first cousins, Robert Low and George Bulloch, received the well-deserved accolades. Low and Bulloch were half-brothers and the sons of Josephine Mirault. Years earlier, Josephine had found steady employment as a pastry cook in the bakery operated by Aspasia, her cousin through marriage. Other free black laborers on the construction project included George Jones, Adam Dolly, Eugene Truchelet, Alex Gun, and the two Woodhouse brothers, William and Robert. Not long after completing the construction, Low, Jones, Touchelet, and the Woodhouse men would join Aspasia's son Robert as musicians in the Confederate army.[7]

Like their northern black counterparts who volunteered to fight for the Union, many southern black men were willing to do much more than just pick up axes and shovels on behalf of the Confederate cause. Although blacks attempted to enlist in the Confederate fighting corps, they were turned away by the Confederate officers. Even as the war dragged on for years, much longer than anyone had dared to predict, Confederate president Jefferson Davis resisted suggestions from some of his top officers, including Generals Robert E. Lee and Patrick Cleburne, to let blacks take up arms for the southern cause.[8] In a letter to a Confederate senator, Lee pressed the issue of employing slaves as soldiers. Under Lee's reasoning, the South faced dire consequences without black assistance.

> I think we must decide whether slavery shall be extinguished by our enemies, and the slaves used against us, or use them ourselves at the risk of the effects which may be produced upon our social institutions. My own opinion is that we should employ them without delay.[9]

Finally, during the winter of 1864 after confronting the staggering lists of battlefield causalities, President Davis reversed his previous course and agreed to arm blacks. Nevertheless, his order, permitting people of color to defend the South, was discriminatory in both its nature and scope. Acting in accord with the prevailing racial prejudices of the era, Davis accepted enslaved persons into the Confederate fighting ranks, but he adamantly rejected the notion that free black men could serve as soldiers. Ultimately, it appears that the critical need for black combatants to be placed on the battlefields and aboard military ships contravened the orders issued from Richmond. The Confederate navy as well as a number of army units from several southern states, including Tennessee, Virginia, and Georgia, all deployed black fighting men among their ranks.[10]

Even though the Confederates were conflicted over the use of black soldiers, at the same time, the army welcomed talented musicians of color into their auxiliary military units. In 1862, the Confederate congress, fully anticipating the use of African American musicians, even passed legislation that ensured black musicians would receive the same pay as regularly enlisted white musicians.[11] It is within the surviving military band records of two Georgia regiments that the names of Robert Oliver, his cousin Robert Low, and several of his African American neighbors from Savannah appear. The evidence abounds that having honed his musical talent during his boyhood years, Aspasia's son Robert used that same skill to serve the Confederate cause.

Robert and his black colleagues responded to the call for Confederate service after reading a public announcement that appeared continuously in the *Savannah Daily Morning News* throughout the spring and summer months of 1861. Although the primary objective of the call to arms in defense of the South was to recruit fighting men, the printed announcement also detailed the army's critical need for skilled musicians. Volunteers could expect a salary of between $11 and $21 per month, depending on the actual assignment, with an added clothing and food allowance. The advertisement read as follows:

> Wanted 2000 able-bodied men for service of the State of Georgia to serve for three years. Said recruits needed for such defense service as the public security in this and neighboring states may demand . . . Musicians required as above. Apply to recruiting officer at Oglethorpe Barracks, Liberty Street, Savannah.[12]

Although Robert responded to the call for volunteers by enlisting in the Confederate army, at the same time, he left no surviving record of his motivations for taking that action. Did his service as a staff band member simply provide him with a good job opportunity, or was it the case that Robert's motivations were more complicated and more intricately intertwined with the tumultuous events of the era? Regrettably, there is no information to reveal either his political leanings or his opinions about the dramatic events leading up to the Civil War. We do not know whether or not Robert was aware of the activism on the part of his free black counterparts in the northern states, like Martin R. Delany, Robert Purvis, Frederick Douglass, and many others, who recruited their relatives and neighbors to serve in the Union army. Those black Unionists, most of whom were career abolitionists, had earnestly dedicated their labors toward crippling the Confederacy and destroying the institution of slavery.[13]

Did Robert Oliver's Confederate service mean that he supported the southern cause? Was it possible that free black southerners, like him, could have been attracted to the highly publicized state's right issue that undergirded the conflict? Could Robert have been loyal to a stratified society or did he support the institution of slavery? At one time, his mother Aspasia and several other relatives had been slaveholders, and in 1839, his aunt Justine Cruvellier advertised in the local newspaper, offering a monetary award for the return of Serena, her runaway bondswoman.[14] Since he was a southerner by birth and perhaps by temperament, it is conceivable that Robert embraced many aspects of the region's southern culture as well as the basic tenets of the Confederate ideology. It is also possible that his true sentiments may have been more closely aligned with those of a group of free blacks in New Orleans. During the early months of the war, the group had been pressed into a kind of semi-military service, helping to defend their city. After the Union army had routed the Confederates and rode victoriously into New Orleans, General Benjamin Butler sent for the group of blacks to question them about their apparent Confederate loyalty. During the course of the meeting, the group's spokesman tried to explain their awkward position to the Union general. They told Butler that they had no choice in the matter. Under the circumstances, they had not dared to reject the assignment. In their defense, the blacks quickly pointed out that they had refused to evacuate the city along with the departing Confederate troops, and they also assured Butler that their true sympathies were closely tied to the Union cause.[15] Could Aspasia's son have held similar views? We will probably never know whether Robert secretly harbored any pro-Union sentiments. Instead, there is only the fact that he joined the Confederate army, not as a soldier, but as a musician.

On October 1, 1861, Robert Oliver submitted his enlistment papers to Colonel Claudius Wilson at the local Confederate headquarters on Tybee Island, near Savannah. He joined the band unit connected to the Twenty-fifth Regiment of the Georgia Infantry. Initially, Robert enlisted for six months of duty as a staff band member, and he collected his pay, amounting to twelve dollars at the end of each month.[16] But Robert's Confederate service lasted considerably longer than he had originally intended. Just as his duty was about to come to an end, he learned that the band's half-year stint had been extended an additional three months. Then at the conclusion of that three-month extension, Robert reenlisted for more Confederate band service, this time transferring to new military unit for a second tour of duty. Robert re-pledged his allegiance at Fort Bartow, located on Causton's Bluff near the Savannah River on May 31, 1862. This second service commitment was made to the Forty-seventh Georgia Regiment band unit for a three-year period or until the end of the war.

Whatever hardships and inconveniences of army life Robert may have endured during his service as a bandsman in the two separate Georgia regiments, loneliness and a lack of companionship would not have been not among his complaints. Quite to the contrary, his months in the military were spent among several close friends and associates. Even though he was in the army and living apart from his wife and son, Robert enjoyed the daily companionship of a relative and several close friends. Although his enlistment may have included some noncombatant work details, his initial and primary assignment in the regiment consisted of playing a musical instrument in a twenty-five-member integrated band along with his cousin Robert Low and several other African American neighbors from Savannah. White musicians made up the numerical majority of this uniquely constituted band, but the unit was nearly evenly divided along racial lines. There were fifteen white band members and ten African Americans. Besides Robert and his cousin, the eight other blacks included Francis Desverger, Francis Gamble, Brave Golphin, Joe Millen, Eugene Truchelet, William Woodhouse, and two brothers, Charles Jones and George Jones.[17] Probably owing to his exceptional musical talent, Robert Low served as the principal musician and band leader for the integrated band unit.[18]

The black bandsmen held no military rank but were listed only as staff musicians. This was in sharp contrast to the white musicians in the Twenty-fifth Georgia Regiment band all of whom held a military rank. Most of the white soldiers were members of the Regiment's Company E. Three men with the surname of Andrews, L. W. Andrews, R. N. Andrews, and S. J. Andrews, served as privates as well as musicians in the Regiment's First Company E. Five other privates played in the integrated band unit, including John Cole of First Company L, and four other white men whose names were Aaron Odom, George W. Watts, Alexander Gambol, and C. B. Scaff, all from Third Company E. The roster of white musicians who performed with the integrated unit included Joseph S. Spencer, who had attained the rank of fifth sergeant in Company E.

Company D of the Twenty-fifth Georgia Regiment was represented in the integrated band unit by two white soldiers, George M. Cooper and George W. Creech. Cooper served as a private while Creech held the rank of fourth corporal. Branch B. Wilson, a private in Company A, served as a musician, while Robert J. Williams and George W. Wright, who were both privates in First Company G, demonstrated their musical talent and their willingness to cross the professional musician's color line playing alongside the ten free African Americans in the band.[19]

The existence of an integrated military unit, even a band unit within a Confederate regiment, must have been unacceptable to some white southerners. Robert Oliver's biracial military band was dismantled after six months. Theirs was a war waged, in large part, by white men seeking to maintain white supremacy and domination over black people. Those same whites likely found it discomforting to witness white men and black men playing music together in an army band.

After the demise of the Twenty-fifth Georgia Regiment band in May 1862, Robert and his fellow African American musicians were formed into an all-black unit, the Forty-seventh Georgia Regiment band. There were no whites in the Forty-seventh as there had been in the Twenty-fifth. The Forty-seventh Georgia Regiment band consisted of just eleven musicians instead of the twenty-five members who had played with the previous regiment unit. Two new African American musicians, Robert Burke and Robert Woodhouse, William Woodhouse's brother, joined the Forty-seventh Regiment band. With the exception of Francis Gamble, who had played with the Twenty-fifth Regiment band but had been mustered out of the army before the Forty-seventh Regiment band had been assembled, the same black musicians made up the new band. As he had been in the Twenty-fifth, Robert Low was once again listed as the principal musician and leader of the Forty-seventh all-African-American band.[20]

Military bands provided important services to the Civil War effort. There were numerous events in the life of any given regiment that called for musical accompaniment. For example, when he arranged for music to be played at official functions, Colonel Wilson, Confederate commander of the Twenty-fifth Regiment, followed the policies and procedures set forth in the *Rules for the Government of Savannah Artillery*. Published in 1861, the book's rule number eleven "Military Duties of the [Musical] Corps" laid out the circumstances for musical accompaniment at the many parades and drills that comprised essential components of military life. Regiment bands boosted morale among the soldiers, quickened the pulse for battle, and played for all regularly scheduled military parades. Annually on January 19, soldiers paraded, accompanied by music, to commemorate Georgia's secession from the Union. Another military ceremony held in late February honored George Washington's birthday. Confederate bands accompanied drill, and they played for funeral services as well as those occasions when officers received their commissions. Considerable pomp and circumstance accompanied the parades, funerals, and commission ceremonies where each member of the unit, including the musicians, dressed in full military uniform.

Apart from their official musical functions, regiment bands filled another important military-related role. Music provided a measure of comfort from the harsh realities of soldiering and broke up the tedious monotony of military life. While regiments remained in the throes of war, military musicians, such as Robert Oliver and other band members, often serenaded the troops with sentimental ballads and lively tunes. Numbers like "The Stonewall Quickstep" and "You Are Going to the Wars, Willie Boy" inspired soldiers facing battle. Repertoire for Confederate bands included the regional favorite "Dixie" and "Home, Sweet Home," the former written by northerner Dan Emmett for the minstrel stage. Other military favorites included "Lily Dale" and "Just before the Battle, Mother." Homesick soldiers reported that the music temporarily quieted their fears and eased their loneliness as they sat around the evening campfires.[21]

As a battlefield musician, Robert and his fellow African American bandsmen experienced the war first hand. Robert had not been an enlisted bandsman quite a month when he and the entire regiment were forced to make a hasty retreat from their Tybee Island encampment. Although the soldiers were likely not privy to the full details of the events unfolding around them, Brigadier General A. R. Lawton had issued Special Order 336 to Colonel Claudius Wilson, the Twenty-fifth Regiment commander, on November 9, 1861. Lawton ordered Wilson to remove the entire force of men under his command except for two companies, from the island to Savannah. The two exceptions were ordered to Fort Pulaski where the heavy guns would be taken. All soldiers were ordered to embark at Kings Landing and proceed to Savannah. Shortly thereafter, Robert and the rest of the Twenty-fifth Regiment learned that Tybee Island, located a short boat ride from Savannah, had been captured and occupied by Federal troops. Although the Confederates had tried their best to halt the enemy's progress, in the end they lost control of all the areas along the Georgia coast. Before long, the entire group of Georgia Sea Islands suffered the same fate as Tybee, falling into Union hands. Having lost the coastal areas to Union control, the Confederates redirected their efforts toward protecting the city of Savannah and keeping its vital port opened.[22]

Robert Oliver and the other black bandsmen witnessed the Confederates' valiant, but ultimately futile, efforts to construct land defenses and to place obstructions in the Savannah River. General Robert E. Lee, then commander of the coastal defenses, used all the manpower and materials at his disposal, including men from the Twenty-fifth Georgia Regiment, to keep the Union troops from capturing Fort Pulaski, a strategically located fortification just twelve miles down river from Savannah. Those efforts failed. Lee's defensive campaign to protect the fort lasted four months, but by the end of April 1862, the fort surrendered to the Union, forcing the closing of Savannah's port. As might be expected, the blockade caused the Confederates considerable consternation. Rumors spread that an attack on Savannah would be the next step in the Union's strategy. When Robert learned of the Union victory at Fort Pulaski, his thoughts in all likelihood turned to his pregnant wife, Diana, who was living in Savannah with their small son. Of course, Robert and the other Confederates had no way of knowing that the Union generals were not interested in Savannah at that time. From the Union's perspective, their control of the river made the occupation of Savannah unnecessary so early in the war.[23]

Although they served in two separate military units, Robert and his fellow African Americans were not involved in many of the fierce battle engagements with those Confederate regiments. By the summer of 1863, when the Twenty-fifth Georgia Regiment received orders to go to Jackson, Mississippi, Oliver and his friends had already been transferred out of the regimental band. The black musicians had been reassigned to the Forty-seventh Georgia Regiment. Meanwhile, the regularly enlisted soldiers of the Twenty-fifth Georgia Regiment, Robert's former unit, participated in the Mississippi campaign and took part in the fierce fighting that extended all the way from

Chickamauga, Tennessee, to Atlanta, Georgia. Likewise, Robert and the other black musicians missed the military campaigns waged by the Forty-seventh Georgia Regiment. That regiment saw action in Mississippi as well as the campaigns in Atlanta and in North Carolina. The soldiers of the Forty-seventh Regiment also participated in the aborted defense of Savannah.[24] The African American bandsmen from Savannah served the Confederacy as skilled musicians for their regiments, but they were shielded from much of the fierce fighting, injury, and death that characterized the war effort. For the Confederacy, blacks were cast in supporting roles, not in combat roles.

Thousands of Confederate soldiers did not survive the war. Colonel Wilson, the commander who accepted Robert's enlistment papers at Tybee Island in 1861, became one of the many casualties. Cutting short what might have been a significant postwar career, perhaps in either politics or in commerce, Wilson, who had been described as "one of the leading young men of Georgia" died during the Vicksburg Campaign in November 1863. He was only thirty-two years old, and during his relatively short military career, Wilson had commanded several thousand men from at least three Georgia infantry units as well as Georgia's First Battalion Sharpshooters.[25]

Whether they built fortifications to protect the city of Savannah or served in a Confederate regiment band, whatever the specific roles Aspasia's heirs assumed during the course of the four-year-long conflict, they observed the war's final stages. During the winter of 1864, they witnessed the historic occupation of Savannah, engineered by General William T. Sherman. After blazing a trail through the state of Georgia and arriving unchallenged in Savannah, Sherman, one of President Lincoln's hardest fighting generals, set up his headquarters just two blocks from the Mirault homestead. In the days immediately preceding Sherman's arrival, General William J. Hardee, commander of the Confederate forces in Savannah, anxiously monitored Sherman's steady advance toward the city. Rather than surrender, Hardee made what must have been a painful decision and ordered the retreat of his men away from the advancing Union army. On the fateful evening of December 20, 1864, the Confederates, nearly ten thousand strong, evacuated the city of Savannah en masse.[26]

One can only surmise the reactions of Aspasia's family members and other Savannah residents to the sudden and startling changes that had befallen their city. The scene must have been oddly reminiscent of Port au Prince during 1800 when the Aspasia and other members of the Cruvellier family fled their Santo Domingo homeland. Over a half century later, Aspasia's descendants must have been shocked to learn that their Confederate defenders had departed, leaving the residents to work out their own precarious fate with the Union army. Bereft of the military support upon which they had depended, municipal officials strategize to make the best of a humiliating situation. To his credit, Savannah mayor Richard D. Arnold took immediate and decisive action in the face of the crisis. In a bold move, Arnold, along with contingent from the board of aldermen, created his own version of a détente with the enemy. On the morning after the Confederate retreat, Arnold rode by way of a horse-drawn coach at the head of a delegation to a location just outside the city limits where he met with General Sherman.[27]

By all reports, Sherman greeted Mayor Arnold and the rest of the delegation warmly. He was especially pleased to receive confirmation that the Confederate army had left Savannah. Sherman telegraphed President Lincoln with the good news: "I beg to present you as a Christmas gift the city of Savannah, with one hundred and fifty heavy guns and plenty of ammunition, also about twenty-five thousand bales of cotton." Later that same afternoon, Sherman and his soldiers began their occupation of the city.[28]

While Savannah residents were powerless to prevent the Union occupation, a few citizens employed their resources and their influence to ease tensions. One pressing issue for General Sherman was the location of a suitable site for his headquarters. While he might have taken any Savannah house or building that met his fancy, Sherman hesitated to avoid inflaming local passions beyond their already high level. The quick thinking of Charles Green, a British subject and Savannah resident, worked to defuse a potentially explosive situation. Green, in an effort to save his Savannah neighbors the embarrassment of hosting the Yankees in their homes, offered General Sherman the exclusive use of his residence. Having accumulated considerable wealth as a cotton merchant over the years, Green lived in a large, stately mansion on Macon Street, located on the western side of Madison Square. Sherman accepted Green's generous offer. Soon thereafter, the Union general headquartered his military operation across the street from St. John's Episcopal Church, just a half-block from the Mirault homestead on Whitaker and Macon Streets.[29] Throughout the historic occupation of Savannah, Aspasia's family lived nearby one the Union army's most-celebrated generals.

Sherman traveled with a sizable army on his long march across Georgia. Estimates suggest that over sixty thousand Union soldiers took part in the occupation of Savannah. As the occupation progressed, soldiers fanned out through Savannah, living up to their label as a conquering army. Savannah houses were confiscated. General Otis O. Howard, who would head the Freedmen's Bureau in the postbellum era, and his men headquartered at the home of Edmund Molyneux on Bull Street.[30] Such extraordinary circumstances could only portend a decidedly different future. In all probability, Savannah residents, including members of Aspasia's family, realized that they were witnessing the beginning of a new era for their city, for the state of Georgia, and for the entire southern region.

On April 9, 1865, at Appomattox, Virginia, less than four months after Sherman's army marched into Savannah, General Robert E. Lee surrendered to General Ulysses S. Grant ending four long years of war. Lee's surrender meant that residents of Savannah and throughout the Confederacy would have a chance to pick up the pieces of their lives interrupted during the conflict. The Civil War—a great equalizer in its distribution of pain and sacrifices, victories and defeats—had touched and, in some respects, dramatically altered the lives of Robert Oliver, his family, and his circle of friends. Whether they were white or black, formerly enslaved or free people of color, like Oliver and members of the Mirault family, tens of thousands of Americans had shouldered their share of the war.[31] With the defeat of the Confederacy, many blacks dared to hope for a brighter future. Should they hope for an end to the myriad racial inequities that had hampered their progress; should they anticipate a rise in their social and economic status? Should they look forward to enjoying all the rights and privileges previously enjoyed by whites? Many blacks had ambitious hopes for the future, but almost as many feared the reality would be much different.[32]

In his description of a scene that was likely replicated in Savannah, and in Charleston and elsewhere, T. Morris Chester, a black war correspondent, reported the emotions expressed by many African Americans in Virginia at war's end. Chester wrote about the city of Richmond soon after Union troops arrived.

> Nothing can exceed the rejoicing of the [N]egroes since the occupation of this city. They declare that they cannot realize the change; although they have long prayed for it, yet it seems impossible that it has come. Old men and women weep and shout for joy, and praise God for their deliverance through means of the Union army . . . Persons who were insulting all manner of complaints against the respectable colored people who happened to live in their neighborhood have suddenly realized that they were very desirable companions, and possessing social qualities worthy of cultivating. What a wonderful change has come over the spirit of Southern dreams.[33]

For the blacks in Savannah and throughout the region, their southern dreams emphasized access to an education for their children and for themselves. They desired land, paid jobs, and civic equality, including the franchise as well as access to public accommodations. Other social priorities such as securing more humane treatment for the insane, the sick, and even the criminal may have crossed some minds. Collectively, African Americans dreamed of attaining full citizenship rights.[34] The historian Edmund L. Drago delineates different views among blacks in Georgia. A great many desired economic advancement above all else while another group that Drago termed the "black political elite" worked for black economic gains in the Reconstruction era, but their primary focus was on securing the vote and civil rights.[35] Aspasia's descendants and their peers, Savannah's formerly free people of color, likely felt an allegiance to the latter group. Having enjoyed varying degrees of economic stability as tradesmen or shop owners, this sector of the city's black community championed civic and social equality opportunities in the postbellum era. A new era was dawning and a new order was being created. While understandably uncertain about the future, African Americans, including the Mirault family members, seemed willing and eager to embrace it.

Reflecting the collective sentiment of those times, a number of black newspapers emerged in the years following the Civil War. As the publisher of one such newspaper, John H. Deveaux, who like Aspasia's family had been free before the war, assumed a leadership role on behalf of his race. Deveaux believed he could best serve the African American community by publishing a newspaper which he termed "an absolute necessity to the welfare and progress of any class of people." When the *Colored Tribune* (later the *Savannah Tribune*) began publication during the winter of 1875, Deveaux's "Salutatory" editorial outlined the newspaper's primary objective.

> *The Colored Tribune* will, as its name indicates, be devoted to the advancement and elevation of the colored race . . . The character of *The Tribune* will be the defense of the rights of the colored people, and their elevation to the highest plane of citizenship . . . *The Tribune* will be firm in its advocacy of justice to the colored people, . . . while demanding for them all the rights secured to them by the laws of God and of the country . . . We shall endeavor to break down the existing prejudice of race and establish friendly relations between all classes of the community.[36]

Thus, as the postbellum era began and progressed, African Americans in Savannah looked forward to experiencing their full citizenship with all of the rights, responsibilities, and challenges connected to that important status.

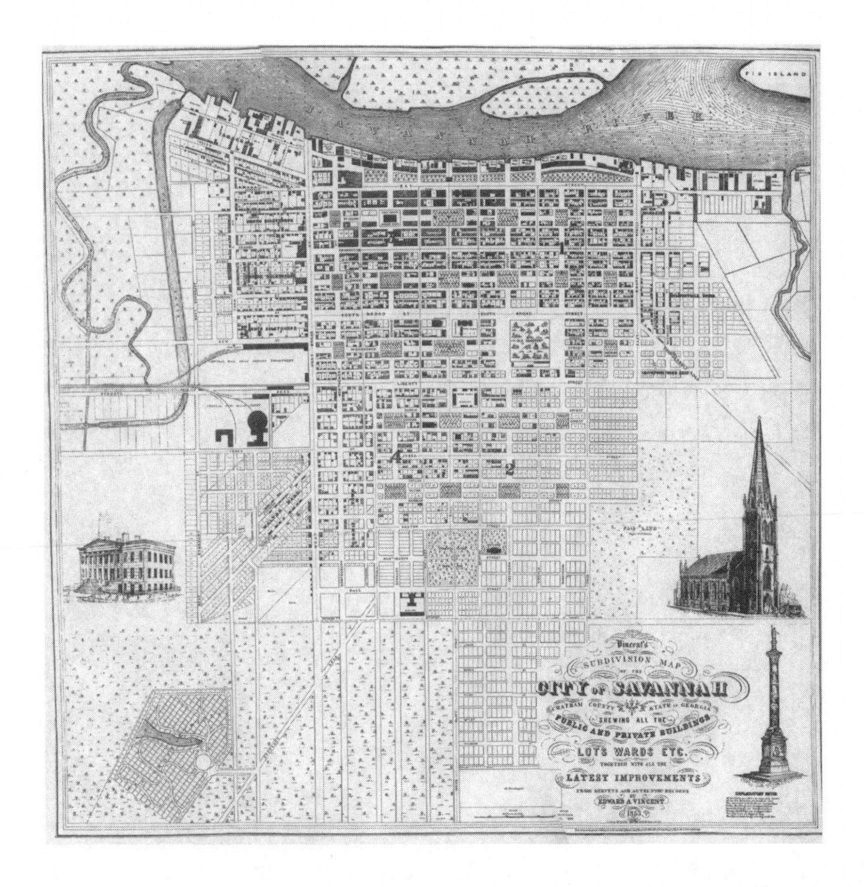

MS 1018, Waring Map Collection, Volume 2, plate 24: Savannah, 1853. *Courtesy of the Georgia Historical Society, Savannah, Georgia.*

African American fireman in Savannah, ca. 1860s.
Fragile Pictures Collection, Manuscript, Archives, and Rare Book Library, Emory University.

Laura Mirault Woodhouse Campfield, b. 1838, was Cyrus Campfield's wife and the daughter of Simon Mirault Sr. *Courtesy of Ruth L. Rivers.*

Henry B. Tompkins, b. 1844, a superior court judge, presided over the *Oliver v. Swoll* case in 1878. *Courtesy of the Probate Court, Chatham County, Georgia.*

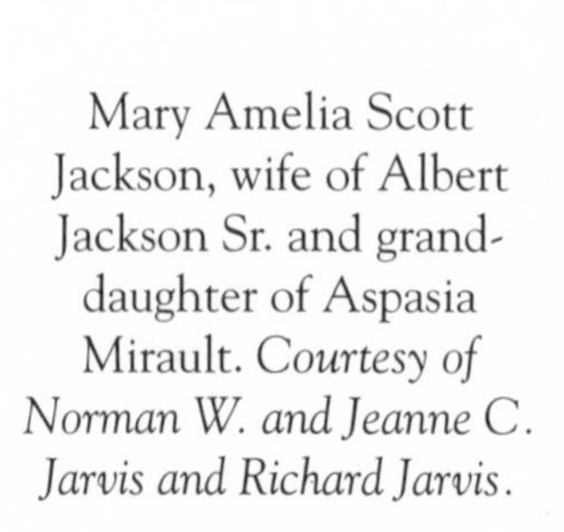

Mary Amelia Scott Jackson, wife of Albert Jackson Sr. and granddaughter of Aspasia Mirault. *Courtesy of Norman W. and Jeanne C. Jarvis and Richard Jarvis.*

Albert Jackson Sr., community leader and partner in the Johnson and Jackson cotton brokerage firm of Savannah. *Courtesy of Norman W. and Jeanne C. Jarvis and Richard Jarvis.*

Sidney M. Jackson, b. 1880, youngest son of Mary and Albert Jackson Sr. *Courtesy of Norman W. and Jeanne C. Jarvis and Richard Jarvis.*

Cecilia May Jackson, great-granddaughter of Aspasia. Known as May, b. 1885, youngest child of Mary and Albert Jackson Sr. *Courtesy of Norman W. and Jeanne C. Jarvis and Richard Jarvis.*

John Joseph "Joe" Millen, the son of Elizabeth Mirault and the stepson of Simon Mirault Sr. Millen was a Confederate bandsman along with his cousins, Robert Oliver and Robert Low. *Courtesy of Ruth L. Rivers.*

Albert Jackson Jr., *far left seated on the ground*, is shown with his fellow Hampton Institute graduates in 1894. *Courtesy of Hampton University Archives.*

Chapter Five

Post–Civil War Savannah

If only the enterprising Aspasia Mirault had lived to see the Reconstruction era, she would have marveled at the changes occurring in Savannah. At its inception the period was alive with many prospects for African American advancement in the economic, social, and civic arenas. Following the Civil War, Georgia legislators ratified a new state constitution and enacted laws that extended citizenship rights irrespective of color.[1] Overall, the African American population—the few slaveholders among them being the likely exceptions—celebrated the triumph of abolition and the granting of citizenship to all black people. Yet, apart from its auspicious beginning, the period was marked by the contrasts of racial cooperation and racial strife. There were instances where blacks experienced the liberties of their newfound citizenship and other instances where the denial of civil rights plagued the black community.

Reports received from Savannah's black community were varied. To avoid racial mixing, the city council took the drastic measure of closing Savannah's parks in 1865. When the parks were reopened the following year, blacks were still denied use unless accompanied by a white child. Street cars became another racial battleground. The Savannah Street Car Company introduced a racially segregated system of seating on their horse-drawn cars in 1869. African American protests that challenged the new seating arrangement coupled with the company's apprehension about a federal civil rights lawsuit eventually brought about a return to integrated seating three years later.[2] Another incident occurred during April 1875, when the African American editors of the *Savannah Tribune* became incensed over a racial slight at a local theater. During a performance, the manager directed black patrons to the balcony for seating where they were separate from white patrons. Many African Americans in attendance became all the more outraged because the concert featured a performance by the all-black Brahms Musical Club.[3] Throughout the Reconstruction era and beyond, Savannah's emerging black leadership consistently articulated the community's hope for equal rights before the law and for the civil and political privileges in accordance with those enjoyed by their white counterparts.[4] Facing challenges as well as opportunities in the postbellum period Savannah blacks, including members of the Mirault family, pursued avenues for their economic and civic advancement.

One unexpected challenge for the Miraults would be their involvement in a lawsuit. By the early 1870s, a cruel twist of fate would thrust the heirs into a legal battle over Aspasia's property. Four members of the Mirault family, including Aspasia's son Robert Oliver and three of her grandchildren, Charles B. Stiles, Mary Amelia Scott Jackson, and Louisa Williams Burton, filed a petition against George Cally in the Chatham County Superior Court. The family discovered that Cally had begun to claim Aspasia's property as his own.[5]

During the time period between the end of the war and his family's involvement in a lawsuit, Robert Oliver resumed his work as a brick mason. Robert was in the prime of his life as a thirty-one-year-old veteran musician of the Confederate army and a family man with a wife and two children.[6] Robert's wife, Diana Johnson Oliver, proved to be a great asset to her husband. Robert and Diana came from similar backgrounds, and there is evidence to suggest that this young couple was well suited. Identical to the prewar experiences of her husband and his family, Diana had always been free, but unlike Robert, she could not read or write. As it turned out, her illiteracy did not prevent Diana from helping to cement their household's economic stability. The ever-thrifty Diana devised a strategy to increase the family's finances. She demonstrated a penchant for saving money. In the years immediately following the Civil War, it was Diana, and not her husband, who became the first member of the Oliver household to open a savings account at the newly incorporated Freedmen's Savings and Trust Company Bank in Savannah. Probably due to her encouragement, Robert followed his wife's lead, opening a bank account in his own name at the same branch two years later in 1869. Saving money soon became a family tradition in the Oliver household. Before long their two children followed in their parents' footsteps. Fourteen-year-old Robert Ward Oliver opened an account in 1869. A year later young Robert's eight-year-old sister Aspasia Matilda Oliver, whose nickname was Aspassy, started saving at the Freedmen's Bank with her own account in August 1870.[7]

At the outset and in the succeeding years, the Freedmen's Bank proved to be successful and popular in Savannah's black community. Besides Robert Oliver and his family, many other individuals and organizations deposited their money in the institution. Saving deposits in the Savannah branch amounted to nearly thirty-one thousand dollars during the month of August 1872.[8] On average, blacks in Savannah deposited between eleven and fourteen dollars in their individual Freedmen's Bank accounts. Although there is no surviving record of the dollar amounts in the four Oliver accounts, the evidence that they and many other African Americans made deposits reflected positively on their financial circumstances.

For the duration of their marriage, Diana Oliver remained the perennial helpmate to her husband. While raising the couple's two children, she found steady employment as a cook with Clara Greenwood, a longtime Savannah resident. Diana put her culinary skills to good use, working at her employer's boardinghouse for young ladies. Typically, Greenwood boarded approximately eight young white women at any given time. The boarders rented rooms and ate their meals, cooked by Diana, at the Greenwood residence located at 52 Bryan Street, near Abercorn.[9] Daily conversation must have been lively for the women sitting around Greenwood's communal dining table. Judging from a list of their national origins, the boardinghouse residents represented a microcosm of Old World Europe meeting New World America. Josephine Galatia, a twenty-three-year-old seamstress from New York City, boarded at Greenwood's along with two sisters from Malouse, France, Justina Collins and Matilda Collins. Twenty-two-year-old Justina and nineteen-year-old Matilda worked as dressmakers. Bella Leonard, another young boarder from Wexford, Ireland, made her living as a seamstress. The city of Stuttgart, Germany, was the birthplace of two Greenwood boarders, Margaret Sinclair, a milliner, fashioned stylish bonnets while Elizabeth Demerest was a dressmaker.[10]

By pooling their resources, including the income from Diana's employment at the Greenwood boardinghouse, the Oliver couple prospered. Their rented residence on the corner of East Broad and South Broad Streets was a testament to their collective labors. Judging from the emphasis Aspasia had placed on hard work and acquiring economic security, there can be little doubt that had she lived, she would have wholeheartedly approved of her son and daughter-in-law's accomplishments. Diana's thrifty nature played a major role in her family's economic well-being. By 1870, the family had accumulated sufficient resources allowing Diana to leave her job as a cook at the boardinghouse and remain at home to keep house for her family. Diana had more free time to enjoy family and friends. Early in March 1870 she accepted William and Frances Woodhouse's invitation to serve as the godmother to their infant daughter Frances Ann. Woodhouse and Diana's husband had been Confederate bandsmen together, and the ties of friendship between the two families remained strong throughout the postwar era.[11]

Like Robert and Diana, other Mirault family members found their own varying levels of prosperity within Savannah's postwar economy. As for Aspasia's grandson Charles B. Stiles, few, if any, of his life experiences prepared him for his participation as a litigant in the family's lawsuit. From his birth in 1840 and extending through the Civil War period, Charles, who was the son of Louisa Mirault Nayle, Aspasia's oldest daughter, spent most of his formative years as a resident in his grandmother's house on Whitaker Street.

Even though Charles was orphaned by the death of his mother sometime in either 1848 or 1849, he found a loving refuge in the Mirault homestead. During the early 1850s, when he was still a youngster, Charles likely emulated the grownup activities of his two teenage uncles, Joseph and Robert Oliver, who also lived in the Mirault home.[12]

A series of family deaths changed the domestic landscape for the Mirault family and Charles bore witness to those changes. Besides his mother Louisa Nayle's untimely demise, Charles lost his uncle Joseph and his grandmother Aspasia, both of whom died during the 1850s. Charles was seventeen years old when his grandmother Aspasia passed away in 1857. Three years later in 1860, the census taker recorded that Charles, who was by that time plying the bricklaying trade, still resided in Aspasia's house with his aunt Letitia Mirault Davis and her children. Before the year ended, the family endured a third death. In early December 1860, Letitia succumbed to peritonitis disease.[13] Years later Charles celebrated the memory of his aunt when he named his infant daughter Geneva Letitia.[14]

In the years following the death of his aunt Letitia, Charles found romance and a home of his own. He married Justina L. Grant, a twenty-year-old mulatto woman, on May 8, 1867. Born in Savannah in 1847, Jessie, as she preferred to be called, was one of five siblings. For several years, as they had begun to raise their family, Jessie's parents, Josiah and Mary Grant, lived in New York City. Perhaps unaccustomed to the northern climate, the Grants and their children migrated back to Georgia when Jessie was four years old. By the mid-1860s, when Charles met and married Jessie, her family had resettled within Savannah's black community. As newlyweds, the income from Charles's occupation as a brick mason and Jessie's work as a dressmaker allowed the couple to set up housekeeping. Three years after the Civil War, Jessie and Charles lived in a rented house on Brownville Street near Price Street.[15]

The young couple was not destined to enjoy a lengthy marriage. Six years after becoming man and wife, Jessie died, probably from complications associated with the birth of the couple's daughter. Charles did not remain a widower very long and within six months of his wife's death, he remarried. On March 4, 1874, the Reverend J. S. Atwell, a black Episcopal minister, presided over the wedding of Charles and Annie B. Smith. Family and friends gathered at a house on Duffie and Lincoln Streets to hear the couple recite their vows.[16] It is likely that Charles's return to the altar so soon after Jessie's death angered his Grant in-laws. Just a month later, on April 6, 1874, Charles signed a *Renunciation of Affiliation for Administration* in the Chatham County Court of the Ordinary. Through his petition, Charles relinquished his right to serve as the primary administrator of his deceased wife's estate. Josiah J. Grant Jr., Jessie's brother, assumed the role as the administrator.[17] The surviving record is silent with regard to the motives behind the actions of the parties to the petition. If the Grant family disapproved of the new marriage, they may have pressured Charles to relinquish his control over his late wife's estate. At the same time, Charles may have voluntarily given up the administrative duties in favor of devoting his full attention to a new marriage and the start of a new chapter of his life.

In the fall of 1874, seven months after signing the court petition, Charles Stiles was summoned to join the family in a legal battle over his grandmother's property. Besides their uncle Robert, Charles and his two sisters, Mary Amelia Scott Jackson and Louisa Williams Burton, would collaborate to reclaim their real estate inheritance. Two years younger than her brother Charles, Mary was a twenty-one-year-old married woman in 1863 when she registered as a free person of color. At that time, Mary resided with her first husband, Thomas R. Scott, in their home on Liberty Street. Duncan S. Scott, Thomas's younger brother, lived with the couple. It appears that at least for a brief period of time, the pooling of three incomes supported the Scott household. While Thomas and Duncan practiced the barbering trade, Mary contributed to the household finances with her salary as a seamstress. She probably learned her trade from her mother, Louisa Mirault Nayle, or from her mother-in-law, Charlotte Reed, both of whom were seamstresses.[18]

As was the case with her uncle Robert and his wife, Diana, Mary and her husband, Thomas Scott, prospered during the postbellum years. To add to their joy as a couple, Mary gave birth to their daughter Mary Louisa in 1865. Four years later in 1869 they became landowners when Thomas purchased lot number 38, located on East McDonough Street near Price Street in the Crawford Ward section of Savannah. The real estate was worth nearly eight hundred dollars. The same year that he became a property owner, Thomas opened a trust account in the local Freedmen's Bank for his young daughter. As fate would have it, Thomas did not live long enough to enjoy the fruits of his labor. He died sometime in 1872 or 1873. Mary did not remain a widow for very long. After a relatively short courtship with a recent widower, she returned to the marriage altar. In the month of June in 1874, Mary wed for a second time, becoming the wife of Albert Jackson, a black entrepreneur.[19]

Their union marked the second marriage for both Mary and Albert. Albert had been previously married to Jeannette Bulloch, the daughter of Josephine Mirault, who was herself a distant cousin of his second wife. Mary, the new Mrs. Albert Jackson, was related to Jeannette through her mother's lineage. Years earlier, Mary's maternal grandmother Aspasia married Samuel Mirault, and, in the process, she acquired numerous Mirault in-laws, including Louis Mirault, the father of Simon and Josephine Mirault. Albert and Jeannette exchanged their wedding vows on January 4, 1869. The couple had two sons. John Wesley was born in June 1870 and Albert Jr. was born during the same month two years later. Within two months of the arrival of baby Albert, Jeannette died, probably from childbirth complications. She left her husband a widower with an infant and a toddler to raise. Albert Jackson and Mary Scott lost their respective spouses around the same time. Then, following a respectable grieving period, they met, married, and began their lives as a couple.[20]

Mary and Albert Jackson enjoyed a considerable degree of economic stability in their marriage. Throughout the decade of the 1870s and for the next thirty-some-odd years, the Jacksons lived well as property owners and entrepreneurs. Mary continued to manage and pay the taxes on the lot in Crawford Ward that she had inherited from her first husband, while Albert increased the couple's real estate holdings through additional purchases of land. In 1875, he purchased a piece of property in the Bartow Ward section of Savannah where he built a house. During their first few years as husband and wife, they resided with their three children—her daughter and his two sons—in Albert's home on Taylor Street.[21]

Examples of economic advancement among blacks were not uncommon during the Reconstruction era. Besides owning several pieces of Savannah real estate, Albert and Mary Jackson demonstrated their entrepreneurial expertise. By the mid-1870s, Albert was well on his way to creating a business empire. He teamed up with John M. Johnson, another black entrepreneur, and the two men opened a cotton brokerage firm. For well over a decade, the firm of Johnson and Jackson, located in the Kelly building at the corner of Bull and Bay Streets, was the only African American–owned business of its type in Savannah. Even though they had considerable competition from white companies, the firm of Johnson and Jackson sustained their partnership for nearly a decade. Because they recognized the positive benefits that advertising had on their business venture, the partners placed yearly advertisements in the city directory.[22]

Like many others in Savannah's black community, Albert and Mary Jackson were civic minded and politically astute. As such they fully embraced the opportunities available to them during the post–Civil War era. In November 1874, Albert along with several hundred of his fellow citizens, both whites and blacks, registered to vote for an upcoming election. Other African American registrants within the couple's circle of family and close friends were Duncan S. Scott, Mary's ex-brother-in-law, as well as her cousin Peter F. Cruvellier.[23] Besides exercising the franchise, the extant record reveals that Albert possessed a charitable character. He served as a founding member and director of the Forest City Benevolent Association. The yellow fever epidemic of the late summer and fall of 1876 took its tragic toll on the city of Savannah. Jackson's seven- year-old son, John Wesley, along with some fifty other persons, succumbed to the illness during one horrendous week in September that year. Undoubtedly grief-stricken over the loss of his son, the elder Jackson still did not hesitate to respond to the crisis. He joined a group that met at First Bryan Baptist Church to organize a society "with a view of relieving the suffering of our distressed people during the prevalence of epidemics and in other emergencies."[24] Ten directors were named to oversee the activities of the newly formed association, including Albert, William H. Woodhouse, a former Confederate bandsman, W. D. Johnson, and the Reverend J. S. Habersham, all of whom pledged "to administer to the sick and destitute" in the black community. Monthly meetings of the Forest City group were held in the First Bryan Baptist Church, and the members coordinated their efforts with the white-run Savannah Benevolent Association of which they were an auxiliary group.[25]

In addition to her sister Mary, her brother Charles, and her uncle Robert, Louisa Williams Burton would become the fourth member of the Mirault clan to join the litigation to reclaim the family's real estate inheritance. As the youngest child of Louisa Mirault Nayle, young Louisa was just a toddler when her mother died. In 1850, she was three years old, residing in her grandmother's home along with several other siblings, including older sister Aspasia Williams, who was then five, and her older brother Charles, who was nine years old that year. After their grandmother died in 1857, Louisa, like her older bother, Charles, probably remained with their aunt Letitia Davis at the family homestead on Whitaker Street. Other arrangements may have been necessary following Letitia's death two years later in 1860. One likely possibility is that during her teen years, Louisa may have lived with her uncle Robert and his wife Diana. Over the years, she enjoyed a close familial relationship with the Olivers. In 1862 while the Union blockade of the Savannah River raged, a quiet ceremony took place at the Mirault family's place of worship, St. John the Baptist Catholic Church. Louisa, who was then fifteen years old, became the godmother to Aspasia Matilda, Robert and Diana's infant daughter.[26]

In later years, as she grew into adulthood, Louisa found a marriage partner in one Tillman Burton. On January 3, 1873, the couple celebrated the New Year by exchanging their wedding vows. Throughout their marriage, Louisa pursued the dressmaking trade while Burton worked as a cotton sampler and merchant. During their courtship, Louisa must have reflected happily that her intended husband possessed many of the characteristics of a good provider. Not only did he have a marketable trade, he also owned some real estate. During the summer of 1871, two years before he asked Louisa to be his wife, Burton purchased a lot on Hall Street from Samuel Grant. By the time of his marriage, he had erected a house on his lot where the couple would reside the whole of their married life. Although there is no record that the couple had children, they lived nearby family and friends and shared happy as well as sad occasions. Louisa and Tillman's Hall Street residence was located near East Broad Street close to the home of her uncle Robert and his family.[27]

Louisa and her husband along with all the other members of Aspasia's family experienced firsthand the many changes that the postwar years brought to Savannah and the rest of the South. The end of the Civil War signaled dramatic transformations accompanied by a host of social, political, and legal changes. Residents, both black and white, were forced to adjust to the new social order of the day. All members of the black community, the ex-slaves as well as those who had been free, held the legal status of citizens. Reconstruction signaled a fleeting opportunity for African Americans to enter the mainstream of national life. To be sure, blacks would encounter stiff resistance to such a marked elevation in their status. Many whites in Savannah and throughout the former Confederacy resented the fact that blacks were exercising their newfound liberty by using public facilities and conveyances, by demanding public education for their children, and by voting. African Americans, including the Mirault family, sought to realize the full range of citizenship benefits and burdens.[28] Little did the family members realize that they would soon rely on the effects of those sweeping changes to reclaim Aspasia's property.

The Radical Republican Reconstruction period was short lived in Savannah and throughout Georgia. Home rule had been restored to Georgia by 1872, thereby shifting the balance of power to the Democratic Party. This power shift occurred in Georgia a full six years before the national compromise between Rutherford B. Hayes Republicans and Samuel Tilden Democrats that sealed the presidency for Hayes and marked the end of Reconstruction. Even though black and white Georgia Republicans would continue to cooperate after their fall from power in 1872, deteriorating race relations and racial separation in everyday life became increasingly more widespread with what the historian C. Vann Woodward termed "redemption" by ex-Confederates.[29] The historian Joel Williamson has characterized this occurrence as "a rising disengagement and alienation of black people" from the mainstream of white society. Increasingly, the black community found itself involuntarily distanced from white citizens physically, politically, socially, and economically. The segregation of the races that historians labeled the Jim Crow era became one outcome of postwar Reconstruction.[30]

Evidence that blacks had become marginalized did not signal a lack of growth or progress within the African American community. The surviving record suggests the opposite view. Many African Americans living in Savannah enjoyed many more opportunities to earn a living and to establish a degree of economic prosperity than ever before.[31] In spite of the growing racial segregation, black people found avenues for building their own communities and for embellishing their own culture. African Americans across the South fashioned institutions, organizations, and enterprises. In Savannah, the contours of a viable African American community took on form as well as substance, and in a relatively short period of time, the black community had assumed many of the cosmopolitan trappings of late-nineteenth-century city life. The wide variety of groups that banded together for a host of different purposes is a testament to the fact that people of color in Savannah and across the South had assumed self-direction and leadership over their own affairs.[32]

The formation of black churches led by many energetic and dedicated black clergymen provided a boon to the fledgling efforts to organize black communities across the South. Often the most well-educated and articulate individuals among their race, black ministers like the Reverend James Lynch who had been the pastor of a Philadelphia church before the war, and the Reverend Henry McNeil Turner, a South Carolinian by birth, urged their fellow blacks to make plans for their collective future. In Savannah, the Reverend James Porter assumed key leadership roles as a state assemblyman representing Chatham County in the Georgia legislature for two terms. Among his many crusades to secure black rights in the postbellum era, Porter championed public education for all children.[33] Besides cultivating a strong religious base, clergymen, like Porter, emphasized the need for black political power. In the political arena, the majority of blacks aligned themselves with the Republican Party although a few black Democrats managed to form political clubs in the city. In addition to their religious and political affiliations, blacks in Savannah organized a variety of literary societies, trade associations, philanthropic mutual-aid groups, as well as organizations with a military orientation and those that promoted a religious theme.[34]

The literate and civic-minded Mirault family members joined their neighbors as participants in these African American community-based groups. While a membership list did not survive, it is very likely that Aspasia's son, Robert, who by the end of the Civil War had been a bricklayer for over a decade, was a member in good standing of the Bricklayers' Union Association of Savannah. This union, with an African American membership, elected Richard Daniels as their president. To support her husband's efforts, Diana probably paid her dues as a member of the Ladies' Bricklaying Union, the women's auxiliary to the men's union. Other tradespersons, besides the bricklayers, found it prudent to unite for mutual support, both in their careers and for social endeavors. A group of blacks who made their living by hauling materials in and around Savannah formed the Wagoneers' Union Association. In 1870, the Wagoneers decided to place their funds in the Savannah branch of the Freedmen's Bank. Unlike the bricklayers, wagoneers, and coopers, all of whom formed trade-specific organizations, the African Americans who founded the Workingman's Friendly Association of Savannah welcomed new members from more than one trade.[35]

African American philanthropic societies that were dedicated to providing mutual aid and assistance for the needy flourished in the city. During her first marriage to Thomas Scott, we might speculate that Mary, Aspasia's granddaughter, found time in her busy schedule to work with the Ladies' Mutual Aid Association. Along with the group's president Anne C. Lafayette and their treasurer Harriet Porter, a Mary Scott is listed as the group's secretary. Even though the association had a duly-elected treasurer, it was only through the authorization of their secretary that funds could be withdrawn from the bank and distributed.[36] Mary sustained her charitable character following her marriage to Albert Jackson and over the ensuing two decades. Her name appeared along with eight others in the *Savannah Tribune* for her donation to the McKane Hospital for Women and Children, a black institution that specialized in training nurses.[37]

It is not hard to imagine that Jessie L. Stiles, Charles's wife, may have joined one of the many African American social clubs that sprang up during the period. Perhaps she was a member of the Girls and Ladies' Friendly Club or the equally popular Social Love and Goodwill Society. At the time, Jessie, who was an accomplished dressmaker and the spouse of a brick mason, might have decided to affiliate with any one of a host of organizations, like the Star Lights of Bethlehem or the United Daughters of Lincoln. Mary Balden served as president of the United Daughters. Charles Stiles may have taken a fancy to the philosophy espoused by the Sons of Africa Society, or perhaps he aspired to join the brotherhood of the Grand Lodge of the Free and Accomplished Masons of Georgia. The Colored Enterprise Association with John Bryan as president and Samuel May as treasurer may have suited Charles's business aspirations. These and many other organizations were available to members of the Mirault family and other black people living in and around Savannah.[38]

A host of circumstances, including marriages between enslaved persons and free blacks throughout the antebellum years, had somewhat obscured the formation of caste lines among Savannah's black population. Thus, during the postbellum era, the class structure in the African American community became less evident.[39] This one-class phenomenon, not evident to the same degree in cities such as Charleston and New Orleans, was demonstrated by the membership diversity among Savannah's organizations. Individuals from a variety of backgrounds and socioeconomic standing worked together within those organizations. While one might expect the children and grandchildren of Aspasia, most of whom were literate tradesmen and tradeswomen, to hold multiple memberships in these groups, many blacks from the lower rungs of the economic ladder also participated fully in the city's organizations. In 1873, forty-one-year-old Pricilla Jordan, a self-employed washerwoman, was elected president of the Ladies' Branch of the Pulaski Circle. Silla, as she was known by her friends and associates, took time away from her busy schedule as a working woman and a wife and mother of four to attend to her civic and social responsibilities through the Pulaski Circle.[40]

Silla Jordan, Aspasia's son Robert, and other African Americans all contributed to Savannah's rapid growth and prosperity, about which Mayor John Screven boasted in his 1873 annual report. The mayor was confident that the city was prepared to meet the era's new challenges. Screven reported that his administration had forged ahead to construct a new marketplace; they had enlarged Laurel Grove Cemetery; and they had also begun work on several street-improvement projects. At the same time, Screven judiciously tempered his praise of the many accomplishments with his candor about the existing budget deficit. Even with the funds from a $500,000 bond initiative, the municipal expenditures had greatly exceeded the projected budget by some $246,000, the mayor informed his constituents. An expansion in street light service, water and gas mains, as well as the establishment of a new city fire alarm system had eaten away at the mayor's cash reserves. His report documented that Savannah was growing, and that the growth had placed a strain on the city's financial coffers.[41]

The annual report unwittingly disclosed the destructive manner in which racial segregation had permeated postwar Savannah. The city maintained a segregated educational system for black students, and according to the report, little progress had been made to find adequate facilities to house the "colored scholars." Mayor Screven lamented that all 220 black students, both males and females, were crowded into one schoolhouse located at the corner of Macon and Lincoln Streets. At the same time, Savannah's white children moved into more spacious quarters, reaping the benefits of the city's financial largess. The mayor reported that "six commodious school rooms have been added to the permanent accommodations of the Public School House, the Massie School House and the Cathedral School House."[42] Any progress that could be noted in the educational conditions for blacks could be credited to local leaders such as Albert Jackson, William Pollard, Louis B. Toomer, and William Cleghorn. These men and a few other prominent African American residents formed an education committee to meet with Mayor Screven and R. D. Arnold, president of the school board, to express their concerns. The blacks remained adamant that city officials should make adequate provisions for the education of their children.[43]

Yet, the educational progress that Jackson and others desired would not be realized in the short term. Gross inequities of opportunity, based on the color of one's skin, mirrored the reality of postwar Savannah. Of the 2,513 children attending school in Savannah, fewer than one-tenth were black. While the board of education hired forty-four teachers for the white scholars, only four were employed to teach the black children. During the previous year, the city had appropriated $40,000 for the public schools, but the bulk of those funds had supported the white schools.[44] These actions foreshadowed the race-based educational inequities prevalent throughout the segregation era. According to Thomas Gamble Jr.'s history of Savannah city government published in 1900, Screven's efforts to provide black children with the benefits of the public school amounted to a good-will effort and a leap of faith on the mayor's part. Gamble detailed how Screven was determined to educate the blacks even though no money had been forthcoming from the state. Assisted by the efforts of Albert Jackson and the other black parents, Screven and the city's board of education proceeded to open a school for African American children while waiting for the state funding to materialize.[45] In his report for that year, the mayor outlined the problems he faced, while gratefully acknowledging the work of Savannah's black community. At the time of his report, Screven had not located a building for the African American students.

> There are no buildings fit for [African American] school houses, but the Board have [*sic*] been actively engaged in endeavoring to obtain buildings which, by proper alterations may answer the purpose. . . . In these [efforts of the Board of Education] it was aided by intelligent and worthy colored citizens, who appreciating the benefits of well-directed instruction, contributed their own earnest efforts to the inauguration of a domestic system of education fitted to assure the community a future class of colored citizens inspired by correct views of their public as well as private duties.[46]

In spite of the problems, Savannah efforts in educating black children eclipsed similar attempts in other southern cities. Although many Republican politicians worked to set up statewide systems of public education throughout the former Confederate states, a variety of obstacles, including the expense of such endeavors, usually resulted in limited success. In 1868, for example, when black and white Republicans crafted a new South Carolina Constitution, the document included a provision for compulsory and racially integrated schools. Yet neither aspect of the provision was enforced by state or local officials.[47]

Beyond the pressing educational issues, other equally important concerns surfaced in Savannah throughout the 1870s. There is no mistaking the fact that the ugly rancor of racial politics caused considerable dissention and distrust in Savannah and in many other cities and towns throughout the South during the Reconstruction Era. Although there is little evidence that the Klu Klux Klan and other night riders terrorized Savannah's black residents as they did in so many other areas of the former Confederate states, nonetheless many whites voiced their opposition toward blacks who exercised the franchise. Yet, in spite of this opposition, African American men in Savannah and elsewhere remained eager and willing to cast their ballots. Several members of the Mirault circle of family and friends demonstrated their desire by registering to vote.[48] These black registrants were in good company. Although he was vilified in the majority press for his activism, Bishop Henry McNeal Turner, a newcomer to Savannah, endorsed the efforts of the black voters.

During the November 1874 election, Turner, who was a respected bishop of the African Methodist Church and the former Union army chaplain of a black regiment, caused quite a stir in the city with his pro-franchise activities. As reported in the *Savannah Daily News*, Turner and two other African Americans, Isaac Seely and Theodore Basch, led a crowd of over three hundred blacks who appeared at the Crawford Ward voting precinct in the Effingham section of the city. In what the paper labeled a "radical maneuver," Turner along with his cohorts demanded that they be allowed to cast their ballots. Confusion broke out when the white precinct managers threatened to close the polls. Finally, cooler heads prevailed, violence was avoided, and the polls remained opened. The large assemblage of blacks voted that evening.[49]

Obviously displeased with the outcome in Crawford Ward, the newspaper reported that the managers had retained a list of the "illegal voters." The next day, a follow-up story made excellent copy. The newspaper's November 5 edition reported that the "radical Negroes," namely Turner and his colleagues, were to appear before a United States grand jury to answer charges for what the periodical claimed were violations of the Enforcement Act. In his 1874 clash with poll officials, Turner relied on the legal authority of the recently ratified Fifteenth Amendment in support of his actions. Yet, Turner's labors to promote the black vote preceded the amendment's enactment in 1870 by at least three years. During the summer of 1867, Turner made numerous speeches, and he prepared announcements for distribution to black churches throughout Georgia, urging "colored citizens of Georgia" to vote in the upcoming elections. As he canvassed parts of South Carolina and Georgia on behalf of the Republican Party, Turner was concerned that blacks, fearing a white backlash, would concentrate on strengthening their economic well-being and leave the political power in the hands of whites. To avoid this outcome, Turner urged a massive registration of blacks in the rural areas as well as the cities. Although black women could not vote, Turner pleaded with them to encourage their menfolk to cast their ballots.[50]

Apparently, Bishop Turner's clashes with poll officials and grand juries in 1874 left him completely disenchanted, not only with Savannah, but with the rest of the American nation as well. In spite of his two important positions as the pastor of St. Phillip's Methodist Church in Savannah and as an elected member of the Georgia Legislature, Turner relinquished his role in the struggle for black civil rights in America. Instead, he set his sights on Africa as the true homeland for African Americans. In December 1874, just one month after his successful attempt to help black voters at the Crawford Ward precinct, Turner issued a call for a back-to-Africa movement. The occasion for Turner's message was the "Convention of Coloured People," a group meeting in Atlanta, Georgia. Although Turner had pressing business and could not be in attendance, he sent his message, espousing black nationalism, to the conventioneers by way of a letter. In his address to "the Coloured People of Georgia," Bishop Turner warned his fellow African Americans that they would eventually need to leave America. He rationalized that there was no other alternative since the "the prejudice against the Negro, now on the rapid increase, North and South, is destined to drive us from this country."[51] Throughout the Reconstruction era and for the next three decades, Turner championed the black emigration cause, working with such groups as the American

Colonization Society and the South Carolina "Liberian Exodus." To further his nationalist ambitions, Turner made several visits to the African continent starting in 1891.[52]

It is open to conjecture what Aspasia's heirs may have thought about Turner's message regarding Africa. In the midst of their own racially charged legal challenges, Aspasia's relatives may have read Turner's message and nodded their heads in agreement. Yet, while they may have contemplated leaving America to place their roots on African soil, such ideas would have to be postponed. First and foremost, there was a legal battle to be waged. Lining up their priorities, Aspasia's son and her three grandchildren garnered their resources to fight for their land here in America.

Apart from debating a permanent homeland for African Americans, Turner and other black residents of Savannah had a number of other pressing concerns. The prospect of financial troubles was paramount. In addition to their struggle for the franchise, many African Americans in Savannah and around the South worried about rumors that the Freedmen's Bank was failing. In the postwar era, the African American response to the bank had been overwhelmingly positive, with depositors flocking to do business with the branches throughout the former Confederate states. There were four branches of the Freedmen's Bank in Georgia alone. Besides the branch in Savannah, additional branches served customers in Atlanta, Macon, and Augusta. Many depositors may have been attracted to the saving institution because the venerable Frederick Douglass, the former slave turned abolitionist and statesman, served as the bank's president. All four members of the Oliver household—Robert, Diana, young Robert, and Aspasia—had opened accounts in the Freedmen's Bank.[53]

In addition to the Oliver family members, a host of their relatives and friends had likewise placed their faith as well as their hard-earned money in the Freedmen's Bank. Jessie Stiles opened an account just before Christmas on December 21, 1868. Thomas R. Scott, Mary's first husband, his brother Duncan J. Scott and his mother, Charlotte Reed, opened savings accounts at the bank. After he opened an account for himself in 1867, Duncan returned to the Freedmen's Bank three years later in June of 1871 to establish a trust account for his fifteen-month-old daughter Margaret.[54]

These individuals were likely among the many depositors in attendance at the mass meeting at St. Phillip's Church on July 10, 1874. Bishop Turner and Louis B. Toomer, a black postal worker who would successfully run for magistrate two years later, called the informational meeting to discuss the bank's troubled state of affairs. Both Turner and Toomer had deposited money in the bank. Their worst fears would be quickly confirmed. The ugly rumors were true; the Freedmen's Bank was about to go out of business. In an effort to stem the tide of despair creeping over the stunned audience, the ever-creative Turner offered several solutions. He urged the gathering to establish their own bank or to deposit their money in one of the many other banks located in Savannah. The bank's failure was a blow to the thousands of depositors, including the Olivers and their relatives and friends.[55] There is no surviving record of how many of these persons lost their savings or who among them managed to withdraw their funds before the bank closed its doors and ceased operations.

As Bishop Turner and others had predicted, the ugly stain of prejudice adversely impacted the lives of many African Americans throughout the post-emancipation era. Aspasia's heirs would confront some of those same obstacles as they entered the legal arena. The issue of race and discriminatory laws would figure prominently in the litigation to control Aspasia's property. The family filed their lawsuit amid the increasingly racially charged atmosphere that was engulfing their city and much of the region. Yet the precursor to their legal woes was the unexpected betrayal of their trust by a former friend and family confidant.

Chapter Six

Betrayal and Litigation

The news that George Cally had betrayed his trust agreement with Aspasia Mirault probably surprised everyone who knew him. After honoring that agreement over many years, with only occasional and discreet disclosures to close friends, Cally had the reputation of a trustworthy man. His deceitful actions toward the Miraults were unexpected. In late 1871, when they first learned that they were about to lose the Whitaker Street property, the Mirault family members must have been baffled trying to determine how they might reverse Cally's actions. It would take time for the family to pool their resources and develop a responsive strategy. By October 1874, they had hired a lawyer and filed a *Bill of Complaint* in the Superior Court of Chatham County. Their court documents set out the family's feelings of betrayal.

> Aspasia Mirault having faith and confidence in the honesty and fair dealing of George Cally of said county (he then and there consenting and accepting a trust for her . . . Aspasia Mirault) did then and there cause to be made to . . . George Cally by the Mayor and Alderman of said city a conditional deed to said lot.[1]

The Mirault heirs were bewildered by Cally's actions. From the inception of the secret trust agreement in 1842 and continuing long after Aspasia's death in 1857, Cally had remained diligent with his trust obligations. Surviving evidence details that he made the needed repairs to the property, collected and shared the rents with the heirs, and for the most part, remained current with the annual ground rent payments. Cally's claims that he was the sole owner of the property as well as his ongoing dispute with the city over the ground rent payments represented dramatic changes in his attitude and actions.[2] In the end, Cally's betrayal of the trust would lead to litigation with the Mirault family.

Nearly the full twelve months of 1871 turned out to be an unusually frustrating period for Cally. His efforts to resolve the ground rent issue consumed an inordinate amount of time and energy. Due to a clerical error, one of Cally's ground rent payment receipts contained the wrong date. The receipt indicated he had paid in full through October 29, 1870, but in reality, Cally had made payments sufficient to cover the ground rent only through October 29, 1869. After Cally succeeded in convincing city officials that they had made the error, he nonetheless failed to secure any monetary relief. The city administrators, all white men like him, still insisted that Cally must pay the entire ground rent bill of $82.86. But Cally, likely focusing on the fact that he had been inconvenienced by the error, had an alternative plan in mind. He wanted to reach a compromise on the amount of ground rent he owed. He stubbornly demanded that they lower his bill in accordance with a dollar-for-dollar proportion to the clerical error. Using his own calculations, Cally owed the city $41, amounting to half of the actual bill.[3]

Over the next several months, Cally devised a strategy to get his bill adjusted downward. He asked for and was granted a meeting to explore the clerical error with Savannah's treasurer John R. Johnson. Together and with a spirit of cooperation, the two men examined the city books covering the period from 1866 forward. Cally's meeting with Johnson, who was also white, did not have the end result Cally had hoped to achieve. Johnson determined that although there had been errors, Cally was obligated to pay the money he owed. Both men realized that there had been more than one bookkeeping error over the years. The city's accounting mechanisms had gone awry more than once. Some of the errors favored Cally by incorrectly indicating that he had paid more than he owed. In other instances, the errors favored the city coffers by failing to credit Cally for the full amount of the payments he made in any given year. In spite of the previous errors, Johnson reported to Cally that for the period in question he owed the city for unpaid ground rent.[4]

Dissatisfied with the outcome of his meeting with Johnson, Cally next made an appointment with George Cornwell, an alderman and chair of the city's finance committee. Early in November of 1871, an undoubtedly frustrated George Cally met with Cornwell at the latter's city hall office. In a subsequent trial deposition, Cornwell recalled their marathon meeting as well as Cally's refusal to listen to reason. Once again, the receipt with the wrong date had caused confusion. Cornwell recalled that "the receipt was explained to him [Cally] to contain a clerical error as to the date. I tried to explain and spent about four hours talking to him about it, but he did not seem to want to understand."[5] Cally left Cornwall's office convinced that the city officials had dealt him a gross injustice.

The issue of the unpaid ground rent taxes threatened Cally's hold on the property. Savannah city officials refused to compromise, and the situation was about to spiral out of control with tragic consequences for both Cally and the Mirault heirs. Faced with his refusal to pay the delinquent ground rent, the city exercised its statutory option to reenter and reclaim the lot in accordance with the municipal code and stipulations in Cally's deed. The codes permitted property to be sold at public auction for nonpayment of past due taxes. The sale of any Savannah property—including Aspasia's lot—to satisfy a tax delinquency followed a series of routine procedures. As one essential component of the process, newspaper announcements provided notice of the various parcels for sale. Following the publication of the announcements, city officials were authorized to auction the property to the highest bidder.[6]

The February 5, 1872, issue of the *Savannah Morning News* reported that George W. Stiles, the city's marshal, would conduct a public auction on the first Tuesday in May. Besides Aspasia's lot number 22 in Pulaski Ward, held by title holder George Cally, several other choice lots were scheduled to be sold on that same day. The other nine delinquent property owners included William Morrell, a white employee of the local rice mill; T. M. Norwood, a lawyer; and Mrs. W. R. Postell, the widow of William Ross Postell, a former sea captain. In a twist of fate, Cally would hire Norwood the following year as his legal counsel to handle the Mirault property litigation. The newspaper advertisement listing Cally and the other delinquent property owners made no mention that Cally was acting as the trustee of lot number 22 on behalf of Aspasia's heirs.[7]

Marshal Stiles conducted a public sale of the property on the courthouse steps on May 7, 1872. Lot 22 was sold to William Swoll, the highest bidder. Swoll, a prominent Savannah landowner and longtime city official, bought the property then valued at about $6,000 for a mere $380.[8] Four days later, on May 11, Swoll went to city hall to take possession of his newly purchased real estate. After paying an additional $806.08, which included the delinquent ground rent, city, county, and state taxes, as well as $150 to insure the buildings on the lot, Swoll received a deed and the title to the property.[9]

Cally, who reportedly attended the auction, must have been astonished to witness the lot being sold, and he petitioned the city's finance committee to reclaim the property. At the city council meeting on September 11, 1872, Mayor John Screven referred a number of petitions, including Cally's, to the Committee on Public Sales and City Lots. For each referral assignment, the mayor summarized the individual requests for relief. In Cally's case, Mayor Screven remarked that the petitioner was disputing the amount listed on the city treasurer's delinquency statement. Cally had rejected the bill of $82.86, amounting to eight quarters of ground rent.[10]

Each petition presented at the council meeting received prompt attention. Just two weeks later, the committee reported its findings on all the requests. While the mayor had initially referred Cally's documents to the Committee on Public Sales, it was the finance committee that reported back to the full council. George Cornwell, chair and spokesman for the finance committee, reported that the city had followed the letter of the law with respect to the sale of Cally's property. Through the committee's investigation of the matter, they discovered that Cally's lot had been sold by public auction in accordance with both the city ordinances and Cally's deed. In addition, the city had properly advertised the lot for sale in the local newspaper. Chairman Cornwell concluded with a recommendation that the council should reject Cally's petition to restore his ownership of the lot.

The mayor's acceptance of the recommendation precluded the committee from further action on Cally's petition. As far as the city was concerned, Cally's claim was effectively closed. Yet, the committee's report did not mention Chairman Cornwell's meeting with Cally several months earlier. If Cornwell is given the benefit of the doubt in this case, then it is likely that he shared details of the meeting with his fellow committee members. While one can only surmise how forthcoming Cornwell may have been about his prior meeting with Cally, there is no evidence that his petition was singled out for negative action. The finance committee members likewise rejected the tax-relief petitions submitted by two other white men, James Lindsay and J. J. Warring, a physician.[11]

The finance committee's decision to deny his petition for relief must have come as a grave disappointment and perhaps a financial blow to Cally. Although he was a carpenter by trade, the surviving record indicates that Cally had encountered his share of difficulties in making a living and accumulating property. The tax digest records for the decade preceding the Civil War reveal that Cally enjoyed a modest income from the rents on a lot located in the Troup Ward section of Savannah. In 1850, Cally paid taxes on Aspasia's property, the Troup Ward lot, and one enslaved person. Eight years later, he had added four horses to his property holdings. Cally may have been less affluent during the postwar years. The disposition of some of his holdings, except in the case of Cally's slave property, is not evident. Following the war, Cally no longer paid taxes on the Troup Ward lot nor on the horses that he had once owned. By the early 1870s, he resided in the Springfield Plantation section of the city while collecting rent from the Mirault property.[12]

Cally was no stranger to controversy. At least two of his business dealings spilled over into the legal arena. In December 1866, Cally brought a lawsuit against Max S. Meyer, a Savannah clothing store owner, for reneging on their contract and for failure to pay Cally the money he was owed. Meyer had hired Cally to build a two-story brick building and to repair a wooden building. The *Cally v. Meyer* litigation extended almost a decade. The parties presented their case to an arbitrator in 1873 and later to a judge and jury in 1875. When the jury awarded Cally a judgment, Meyer refused to concede defeat. His *Motion for a New Trial,* filed in the Chatham County Superior Court on February 11, 1876, was denied, thereby upholding the jury verdict in Cally's favor.[13] Similarly, Cally's legal crusade to reclaim the lot on Whitaker and Macon would include a protracted legal battle.

On October 12, 1872, one month after the city's finance committee rejected his petition for relief on the lot he held in trust for Aspasia's heirs,

Cally took his grievance to a court of law. Having fully exhausted all available administrative avenues to recover the property, Cally filed a lawsuit alleging wrongdoing by the mayor and other city officials. Cally's *Complaint* requested that the deed to William Swoll should be declared null and void. Although no action that Cally had taken up to that point had restored the property to him, he was not ready to give up. Legal action remained a viable option. Cally's court documents made no mention of Aspasia as the true property owner, nor did his lawsuit provide any details of their secret trust agreement. Under penalty of perjury, Cally swore that he was the sole owner of the property. Although he was mistaken about the date of purchase (Cally's documents listed 1843, not 1842), his court documents claimed he had purchased the lot and that he had made all the improvements to the property over the ensuing years.[14]

Cally's bold assertions concerning his ownership of Aspasia's property are difficult to reconcile in the postwar era that had just undergone dramatic changes. Those changes included a much improved legal standing for blacks and the reversal of many discriminatory laws like the 1818 statute.[15] The Miraults and all other blacks had been granted their citizenship by the Fourteenth Amendment ratified in 1868, and they were entitled to a host of accompanying rights, privileges, and responsibilities. Taking into account the changes of that era, one wonders if Cally imagined that the Mirault family would simply permit him to take their property without challenging his claims of ownership.

Sometime during 1870 or 1871, Cally he had begun to consider himself the sole owner of lot number 22 in Pulaski Ward. His motives for abandoning the long-standing trust agreement with Aspasia remain a mystery. In April 1842, Cally became the legal titleholder of lot number 22, but the source of the purchase money was a contested issue. As the parties prepared to litigate the property issue in the 1870s, the Mirault heirs contended that Aspasia had supplied Cally with the money to purchase the lot and to construct the residence. Cally had not owned any real property prior to the purchase of lot number 22. In 1842, Cally paid only his $2 poll tax while James B. Gaudry, Aspasia Mirault's white guardian, paid the $1.20 that Aspasia owed Chatham County for her bakery merchandise and inventory.[16]

The following year in 1843, Gaudry once again paid Aspasia's taxes. That year, her tax indebtedness included not only an assessment of merchandise inventory, but also the additional assessments on a dog, lot number 22, and the building improvements located on the lot. Cally, however, was not listed on the tax rolls for 1843 even though he had taken legal title to lot number 22 the previous year.[17] The fact that her white guardian paid Aspasia's taxes on the lot is persuasive evidence that she was the true owner of the property. It is likely that Aspasia told Gaudry about the purchase and her arrangement with Cally. In turn, Gaudry acted in accordance with his role as her guardian. He ensured that her tax bill on the lot and her business inventory had been paid for that year. Yet 1843 would be the only year that Aspasia was listed as the owner and taxpayer for lot number 22.

Beginning in 1844 the tax digests listed Cally as the only Savannah resident responsible for paying the property taxes on the lot. That year, Cally paid the property tax bill for lot number 22, and Gaudry paid Aspasia's taxes for lot number 23, an adjoining lot. There is no clear explanation for these two payments in 1844. Perhaps the tax clerk simply made a recording error. Aspasia may have intended to pay the property tax on lot number 22, but the clerk entered lot 23 in his record book. Whatever may have been the source of the payment mix-up in 1844, by the following year the property tax payments had been corrected. For 1845, Gaudry, as Aspasia's guardian, resumed his role of submitting the tax payment for her bakery inventory only.[18]

In the subsequent litigation for ownership of the Mirault property, Aspasia's heirs failed to reference Gaudry's tax payments on Aspasia's behalf in 1843 and 1844 in spite of the fact that the information supported their claims to the property. A lawyer by profession and a teller at the Mechanics Savings Bank on Bull Street in Savannah, Gaudry was likely aware of the 1818 statute and its prohibitions against free blacks owning land in Savannah. By paying Aspasia's taxes on lot number 22 in 1843 and the taxes on lot number 23 in 1844, Gaudry was violating that law. Was he complicit in the trust agreement between Aspasia and Cally, or was he willing to take a risk that the law would not be enforced? There is no way of knowing Gaudry's mindset with respect to the property. Gaudry paid property taxes on Aspasia's behalf for two years before Cally assumed the tax liabilities for lot number 22. In many respects Gaudry's actions point to the possibility that he knew about the secret trust agreement and that he concurred with it. The heirs remained adamant throughout the litigation proceedings that a trust agreement had been created in 1842. Beginning in 1844 and continuing until the start of his dispute with the city during the early 1870s, Cally remained the taxpayer of record for the lot.[19]

Finances, those associated with the property and other related money matters, constituted a strong lilnk connecting Cally with members of the Mirault family. Those monetary links provide one possible motive for Cally's actions in disregarding the trust agreement and claiming the property as his own. On several occasions over the years, Cally boasted to friends and associates that he had loaned money to Aspasia and to her daughter Letitia. According to Cally's version of the story, from time to time the two women needed his help to pay their taxes. The Chatham County records support some of Cally's claims. On four separate occasions, first in 1852, and then for three consecutive years beginning in 1856, Cally paid the merchandise and poll taxes for Aspasia and her daughter. Perhaps in later years, Cally may have rationalized that his previous payments on behalf of the two women justified his claim to their property.[20]

Although the tax digests lend support to Cally's claims about loaning money to the Mirault women, these same records raise as many questions about the lot and the Cally/Aspasia/Letitia relationship as they answer. Cally may have indeed played the Good Samaritan and loaned or simply gave the two women money for their taxes. It is also possible that Aspasia and Letitia may have provided him with the funds to make the payments on their behalf. The specific years that Cally paid the taxes for Letitia coincide with the years of her mother's declining health in 1856 and then her death in 1857. Letitia may have just been too busy to take time away from caring for her own children and her ailing mother as well as the running the family bakery to tend to the task of paying her taxes. Savannah residents paid taxes in two locations. The annual ground rent for real property and other municipal fees were collected at the treasurer's office at city hall located in the Exchange building on Bay Street across from Bull Street while Chatham County taxes were paid at the courthouse on Bull and York Streets.[21]

By the early 1870s, the ground rent dispute on lot number 22 had escalated into a multiparty lawsuit. In 1872, Thomas Mason Norwood, Cally's attorney, drafted his client's *Complaint and Bill for Equitable Relief* against the co-defendants Swoll, the mayor, and other city officials. The Mirault heirs would not join the litigation for another two years. Cally's complaint laid out his version of the property issue, including details of his alleged purchased of lot number 22 with his own money thirty years earlier. Since that time, Cally claimed that he had dutifully paid all ground rent and taxes and that he had also born the cost of erecting a brick house on the premises. Cally also recounted his version of the clerical error in the city treasury's accounting records that, he believed, had cost him the title and ownership of his property. While one section of the complaint extended an olive branch to city officials, expressing Cally's willingness to settle the matter, in another section of the document Cally expressed his displeasure and annoyance over the situation. The document characterized the May 1872 auction as "contrary to law, manifestly wrong and tend[ing] to the injury of this complainant (Cally)."[22]

The Mirault heirs acknowledged that they had no warning about Cally's selfish intentions toward the property. The heirs had been under the mistaken belief that he was still honoring the trust agreement and managing the property in their best interest. The news of Cally's actions presented the heirs with multiple concerns, and they realized that to recover the property, they too would be forced to seek relief through the courts. The heirs' legal action began during the fall of 1874. Their *Bill of Complaint* laid out the family's grievances while setting forth their requests for relief. The heirs alleged that Cally had betrayed that trust, and they saw it as their obligation to offer proof of those allegations. The heirs knew that in order to support their claims, they must convince the court that Aspasia had exercised complete control and management over the property. Thus, their court documents detailed Aspasia's expenses as well as the ways she had used the lot through the years. The heirs claimed that "Aspasia Mirault entered upon [the] lot and took absolute control and management of the same and ever after and up to the time of her death with her own means paid into the treasury . . . the annual ground rent . . . and also paid all taxes due." The heirs also alleged that Aspasia had paid for all the construction on the lot, rented out portions of the lot, and collected and "reserved for her own use and benefits the rents and profits arising" from the property.[23]

In their court documents the heirs emphasized that Cally had assented to all of Aspasia's actions with respect to the property. According to the heirs, "George Cally had full knowledge of all these things and acquiesced therein and recognized the claim and equitable right of Aspasia Mirault." The heirs found it prudent to relate Cally's previous acknowledgment about Aspasia's ownership of the property. Their *Bill of Complaint* explained how Cally, before losing his title to the lot, had faithfully honored his agreement first with Aspasia and later with her heirs for nearly three decades until 1872.

> [George Cally] repeatedly acknowledged that whilst the title to said property was in him, nevertheless he held it for the sole use and benefit of Aspasia Mirault and continued to do so until long after the death of Aspasia Mirault, and after her death continued to treat said property as the property of the lawful heirs of Aspasia Mirault until sometime in the year 1872 when [the heirs] learned that George Cally pretended to set up a claim to said property.[24]

Once the Mirault heirs filed their court documents, Cally was obligated to respond. As might be expected, he professed his innocence of any wrongdoing. In his *Plea in Defense of the Complaint* filed in June 1875, Cally reiterated some of the statements made in his 1872 court documents, primarily the assertion that he was the sole owner of lot number 22. He denied that the heirs had any valid claim to the property, and instead he began relying on the discriminatory statute that had forced Aspasia to create the trust agreement years earlier. Cally argued that since the late Aspasia Mirault had been a free person of color and a resident of Savannah, the 1818 state statute rendered her incapable of owning any real estate. By virtue of this statutory disability, Cally claimed that the Mirault heirs should be barred from suing him.[25]

George Cally did not live long enough to sign the third and final set of court pleadings filled on his behalf to reclaim lot number 22. Cally died in February 1876; he was fifty-six years old. His younger brother Samuel Cally traveled from their birthplace in Salem, Massachusetts, to attend the funeral and represent Cally's interests in the ongoing litigation. Although Samuel took the initial steps to serve as the administrator of his late brother's estate, it is likely that Norwood offered Samuel a more viable alternative. Norwood advised Samuel that the estate would be better served if Joseph A. Cronk, a Savannah attorney and a colleague of Norwood, assumed the complicated role of administrator for Cally's estate. Since the Mirault property litigation was pending at the time of George Cally's death, Norwood likely realized that hiring an administrator with some legal expertise would be a wise choice under the circumstances.[26]

Samuel Cally heeded Norwood's advice. During the month of April in 1876, the court appointed Cronk, who immediately began managing the outstanding matters for Cally's estate. In February 1878, as Norwood and Cronk prepared for the trial that would decide the ownership rights to the property, Cronk filed an answer to the heir's complaint. On behalf of the estate, Cronk reiterated the assertion that the mayor and other city officials had been unreasonable in refusing to accept Cally's version of the ground rent issue. Cronk returned to Cally's argument that the 1818 state statute had rendered Aspasia incapable of holding any interest in Savannah property.[27]

Having received notice of the voluminous court pleadings filed by Cally's estate and by the Mirault heirs, William Swoll, the lot's new owner, may have regretted his purchase. He would spend the next six years making court appearances, filing documents, and authorizing appeals on his behalf to secure his title to the property. When the trial to settle the property dispute got underway during the winter of 1878, there was every indication that Swoll's auction bid of $308 would cost him a great deal more in legal fees. Swoll was a defendant in two lawsuits. Cally sued him to reclaim the property, and in a second lawsuit, four members of the Mirault family, Robert Oliver, his nephew, and two nieces, all of whom claimed entitlement to the lot as Aspasia's heirs, named Swoll as a defendant party in their court documents.

For his defensive pleadings, Swoll denied that Cally and the heirs had any viable claims to his property. In a series of two *demurrers*, legal pleadings rejecting the legal sufficiency of the petitioners' allegations, Swoll asked the court to dismiss both complaints that he characterized as having no viable legal or equitable basis.[28] To defend himself from Cally's charges, Swoll argued that Cally had forfeited the property by failing to pay the annual ground rent. He argued that the public auction and his city-issued deed to the property were both legally valid, and that city officials had followed the letter of the law when Marshal Stiles reentered the property.[29]

Although Swoll produced ready answers to Cally's claims on the property, he may have found the allegations raised by Aspasia's family members more challenging to rebut. The heirs accused Swoll of using his prior knowledge about the property to his advantage and to their detriment. They alleged that prior to making the purchase at the auction, Swoll "well knew" of the claims of Aspasia Mirault and her family and "if it had not been for this cloud upon the title of George Cally which was known to many persons present at [the] sale, [the] property would have sold for a much larger sum—

for a sum approximating its real value."[30] Some of Swoll's actions leading up to his acquisition of the property were suspect and through the course of the litigation Swoll made statements that fueled the heirs' suspicions. In his pretrial deposition, Swoll admitted under oath that he had accompanied city Marshal George Stiles when Stiles posted the official notice of reentry on the property. According to Swoll, he himself drove the marshal to the lot in his buggy and assisted him in nailing the notice to a tree. Swoll also disclosed that he routinely accompanied Stiles on his rounds.[31]

Were the Mirault heirs' suspicions correct about Swoll? Was it just a coincidence that Swoll accompanied the marshal to the same lot that he later purchased, and what role, if any, did he play in the city's attempt to repossess the property? In Swoll's response to the complaint filed by Aspasia's family, he insisted that he was merely an innocent and good faith purchaser of the property. He claimed that he did not know Robert Oliver or any of the other Mirault heirs. Swoll was equally emphatic in his dismissal of suggestions that he possessed prior knowledge of the heirs' claims of ownership through Aspasia. His responsive pleadings called upon the court to hold the Mirault family strictly accountable to the proof of their allegations against him.[32]

The legal maneuvers by the attorneys for Swoll and the estate of George Cally that would have stripped a black family of their property reflected the political climate of the era. Blacks in Savannah and elsewhere had already begun to see an erosion of their citizenship rights five years earlier and before Reconstruction officially ended. In Savannah and throughout the state of Georgia, the Democrats and their Redeemer governments were rapidly displacing the interracial coalitions and circumstances that had raised black expectations about their future in the postwar South.[33] Still the Mirault heirs believed they could find justice in a Savannah courtroom. Certainly, such hopeful prospects were dimmed by the fact that no African American had ever served on a Savannah jury. Black leaders called attention to that issue. In a letter to the editor of the *Colored Tribune*, a citizen, calling himself a taxpayer, pointed to the omission of blacks on juries and demanded a change. "Notwithstanding the laws provide that we shall serve upon the juries, we have been constantly denied that privilege." The writer was disappointed that for the previous eight years "the names of colored men have been in the jury box . . . and not one colored man's name has ever been drawn . . . *Justice and the advancement of the age* Demand *it*."[34]

The Reconstruction government in Georgia had long since been replaced by Democratic Redeemers when Mirault family and the other litigants met in a Savannah courtroom in 1878 to determine the ownership rights to Aspasia's property. By that time William Swoll, a key defendant in the case, had acquired considerable political influence in the city. Years earlier, he had chosen Savannah as his adopted home. Swoll had immigrated to the United States from his native Germany, and then labored diligently to make his mark in his new country. Swoll's home life included his wife, Maria, an immigrant from Mayo, Ireland, who supplemented the family income by working as a dressmaker during the early years of their marriage. The couple had five children, four girls and a boy, three of whom lived to reach adulthood.[35] A man of many talents, Swoll had a special skill for profitable real estate deals. By the 1850s, following the death of William Thorne, a well-to-do bookseller and an original member of the Georgia Historical Society, Swoll purchased Thorne's impressive home, located on the southwest corner of Perry and Bernard Streets.[36] Over the next several decades, Swoll purchased other pieces of Savannah property. In addition to his successful real estate ventures, Swoll worked for the city in a variety of positions, including street contractor, city scavenger, and chief engineer of the fire committee. [37]

Facing the prospect of a protracted litigation battle over the Mirault property, Swoll hired two attorneys, William D. Harden and Rufus E. Lester, to represent his interests in the case. Beginning in 1866, Harden's advertisements in the city directory attracted a steady stream of clients to his law practice, located on the corner of Liberty and Lincoln Streets in Savannah.[38] Although he moved his offices over the years, first to Bay Street and then to the Commerce Building, Harden, who was a solo practitioner for the bulk of his career, remained a respected member of Savannah's legal community. Concerning the Mirault property litigation, Harden's legal services extended not only to Swoll, but also to the city to which he provided legal counsel. The city of Savannah was named by George Cally as a co-defendant in the lawsuit.

Rufus Ezekiel Lester joined William Harden as co-counsel for Swoll. In 1877, Attorney Lester was a solo practitioner with an office located at number three Whitaker Street. Two years earlier in 1875, Lester had won a degree of notoriety within Savannah's black community. Eschewing the two major parties, Lester ran for mayor as an independent candidate. In his bid for municipal office, Lester secured endorsements from several prominent African Americans. For one, James Simms, an ordained minister who held the offices of clerk and deacon at the First African Baptist Church, threw his considerable clout behind Lester. Other blacks followed Simms's lead and supported Lester.[39] It appears that political expediency provided the foundation for Lester's support from the local black electorate. His sudden popularity among blacks in Savannah may have had more to do with the waning confidence in the Republican Party and a desire to select an independent board of aldermen than with the candidate's platform.[40]

African American support for Lester's first mayoral bid was, for the most part, misplaced. Perhaps the black Savannah electorate was unaware that as a state senator during the years immediately following the Civil War, Lester had been instrumental in ousting the black elected officials from the legislature. In one speech, Democrat Lester cajoled his white Republican counterparts into turning against the black Republicans. Lester reminded the whites that

Abraham Lincoln and the Republican Party had advocated excluding black people from settling in the territories in favor of white laborers. Lester applied Lincoln's racial bias to the contemporary situation they confronted in Reconstruction-era Georgia. According to Senator Lester, "Democrats here and the Conservative Republicans here and law loving men everywhere, are unwilling that he (African Americans), in his present state, shall be allowed to make laws for the country." Arguments and political maneuvering by Lester and other Democrats proved to be effective. In September 1868, a sufficient number of Republicans joined forces with the Democrats to expel the forty-nine black politicians from the Georgia legislature. Fortunately, the black lawmakers were reinstated in time for the 1870 legislative session.[41]

In addition to providing legal counsel for William Swoll against the Mirault heirs, Lester represented Swoll on several occasions. Following the case involving the Aspasia's property, Swoll was embroiled in yet another lawsuit, likely involving land. Obviously pleased with Lester's previous legal services, Swoll retained him again in the spring of 1880 to handle a matter against a defendant named Swift.[42]

While the attorneys Harden and Lester represented the interests of Swoll in the lawsuit, another Savannah lawyer used his legal expertise on behalf of Aspasia's family. Alfred B. Smith, a white attorney, represented Robert Oliver and the other Mirault heirs. One can only speculate whether Aspasia's heirs ever contemplated hiring an African American attorney to reclaim their property interests. There were several black lawyers who practiced in Savannah city during the post-Reconstruction era. One of the black lawyers, John H. Kinckle, was reputed to have enjoyed a successful law practice from his office at 110 Bryan Street, a predominantly African American residential area of the city.[43] Alfred Smith agreed to serve as the Mirault family's legal representative. As a busy lawyer with numerous clients, Smith maintained his law office at the corner of Bull and Bay Streets while at the same time serving as solicitor general for the Eastern Judicial Circuit.[44]

Thomas Mason Norwood completed the list of five lawyers who matched their courtroom wits and strategies over Aspasia's property during the winter of 1878. Together Norwood and Joseph A. Cronk represented the Cally estate. Born in Talbot County, Georgia, Norwood brought almost twenty years of legal expertise to the Mirault property litigation. As the trial got underway during the winter of 1878, Norwood was a forty-eight-year-old Savannah resident with a wife and family.[45] In later years, Norwood would be elevated to a coveted judgeship on the Savannah City Court from which he would retire with distinction.[46]

With the legal issues clearly defined and with the attorneys hired and prepared to represent their clients, all parties were poised to begin the trial. Cally's betrayal of his trust obligations as well as his mismanagement of the ground rent issue had produced two lawsuits. Looking backward from the winter of 1878 over a span of thirty-six years to the spring of 1842, no one could have imagined that a secret trust agreement between a matronly free woman of color and a young white man had the potential to create such a legal quagmire. The two persons who initiated the agreement, Aspasia and Cally, were both dead. Yet the issues surrounding the land in question, and more important, the ownership of a valuable piece of real estate, remained very much alive. All those years ago, Aspasia had labored to build a secure nest egg for her children and grandchildren. Lot number 22 in Pulaski Ward was her primary legacy to those she had left behind. If it required a barrage of judicial procedures as well as a full-blown trial to resolve the property ownership issue, Aspasia's heirs and their opposing litigants were prepared to meet the challenge.

Chapter Seven

A Trial Indeed

In February 1878 someone needed to boost the Mirault family's spirits as they prepared for one of the greatest challenges of their lives. Robert Oliver, a skillful musician by avocation, a moderately successful brick mason by trade, and head of the family since the death of his mother and older sister Letitia, probably rose to the occasion and helped his relatives remain positive. Robert, then forty-seven years old, garnered the family's financial and emotional reserves to reclaim Aspasia's property. As lead petitioner for their *Bill of Complaint*, Robert clearly set an example of strength and determination for his family. In many ways, Robert was well suited for the role of legal protagonist. Had he not inherited some of his mother's grit? The fortitude required to file the lawsuit challenging the actions of whites was similar to the resolve Aspasia herself had mustered in 1842 when she bypassed a state statute to purchase a city lot. Certainly, Robert was made of the same stern stuff and could leverage his interest in Savannah's stratified society. He was, after all, a veteran of the late war, having served the Confederate cause as one of a handful of black musicians in two Georgia regiments. To endure through the lean war years, Robert had seized an opportunity to serve his southern homeland and provide for his family.[1]

A decade after the war ended, Robert and his family faced an equally difficult test of faith and endurance. Aspasia's heirs held fast to the belief that justice would prevail in their case if only the court could understand the facts as they knew them. Theirs was a wise decision to seek redress of the property issue through the judicial system. Although the Miraults were probably unaware of the fact, Reconstruction-era trial courts, as opposed to appellate courts, meted out a fair amount of justice to African American litigants. Having lived through the postwar years, the Miraults would have witnessed dramatic changes occurring in their city and throughout the region. Many of the antebellum laws that had discriminated against the former slaves and the free people of color, like themselves, had been repudiated with the defeat of the

Confederacy and with the ratification of a new state constitution in 1865. The heirs must have realized that they had the right to own property without the previous legislative restrictions. Empowered by the radical political and social changes, the Mirault heirs pressed forward with their lawsuit. Their *Bill of Complaint* filed in 1874 challenged George Cally's and William Swoll's claims to the property. Yet, as the heirs filed their petition, the brief period of Reconstruction under liberal Republican rule in Georgia had already given way to a more conservative Democratic Redeemer government. Just as black participation in Georgia politics steadily declined, the Mirault heirs were entering the courtroom phase of their litigation.[2] Theirs would be an uphill legal battle, but the Mirault family had everything to lose and everything to gain. An unusually valuable piece of property and a legacy of hard work and achievement Aspasia had intended to bequeath to her son and grandchildren lay in the balance.

The tri-party litigation of *Robert Oliver et al. v. George Cally v. William Swoll et al.* began in earnest as the attorneys for the three sets of litigants assembled their evidence in preparation for trial. The principals in this extraordinary civil case remained aware that the procedural wheels of Georgia justice turned slowly. Cally had fired the first legal volley in 1872, and the Miraults responded with their own legal action two years later. In early January 1875, E. H. Pottle, the presiding judge of the Chatham County Superior Court, entered a ruling acknowledging that the Mirault heirs had legal standing and could intervene as litigants in Cally's lawsuit. Yet even after the judge's favorable ruling, several years passed before the trial began.[3]

The case finally entered the courtroom phase in February 1878. The complicated matter to decide who owned Aspasia's property involved two separate lawsuits. Cally had sued William Swoll and several Savannah officials over his loss of the property. The second lawsuit pitted Robert and his relatives against Cally and Swoll, as co-defendants. The heirs argued that neither defendant had a viable claim to the property. For the sake of expediency and with the consent of counsel, the two lawsuits were consolidated into a single trial to be heard in the Superior Court of Chatham County. Over three days, Judge Henry Tompkins and twelve white jurors listened to the legal arguments and gauged the credibility of the witnesses.[4]

Henry Bethune Tompkins, the man who presided over the Mirault property case, was a relative newcomer to the Superior Court bench. Born in Barbour County, Alabama, in 1844, Tompkins saw Civil War action first as a Confederate adjunct and later as a captain in the Thirty-ninth Regiment of the Alabama Volunteers. Tompkins's soldiering was cut short when he was wounded during the Battle of Atlanta. Tompkins studied law and was admitted to the bar in Tennessee in 1866 before moving to Savannah. Shortly thereafter, Tompkins set his sights on a judgeship.[5] Initially appointed by Georgia governor James M. Smith in January 1875 to a two-year stint on the court, Tompkins had just begun his second term as a judge when the Mirault property trial began in 1878. Three years earlier, Tompkins, an attorney with a law practice in Savannah, had been a good choice to fill the vacancy in the state's Eastern Judicial Circuit, occasioned by the retirement of Judge William Schley. Schley resigned in early January 1875. Tompkins not only knew Schley, but he had apparently followed the senior jurist's distinguished career and had appeared in Schley's courtroom on behalf of his clients. Before his appointment to the Superior Court, Tompkins worked as a solo practitioner from his law office at 111 Bay Street in Savannah.[6]

As it would become evident during the course of the Mirault property trial, Tompkins made an easy transition from the position of lawyer to judge, acquiring a balanced judicial temperament in the process. The litigation provides evidence that Judge Tompkins remained open minded, studious, and fair to all parties in this interracial property dispute. From the outset of his legal career, Tompkins possessed the earmarking of an ambitious lawyer who had designs on winning a judgeship. His rapid assent to the judicial bench would be marked by careful strategy and planning on his part as well as some serendipitous good fortune. Seeking to distinguish himself from other judicial candidates, Tompkins cultivated key political connections that were bound to net a judgeship in due course. One bright feather in Tompkins's cap was his acquaintance with Governor James M. Smith, a Georgia native who had served as a colonel and regiment commander in the Confederate army. Tompkins knew that Smith, a powerful and influential man, could help him realize his ambition.

Good fortune paved Smith's path to the governorship of Georgia. After the votes were counted in the special election held in December 1871, Smith filled the unexpired term of Republican governor Bullock. Because he feared that the legislature would impeach him, Bullock had abruptly resigned and fled the state two months earlier. For the general election in 1872, Smith, who was a Redeemer Democrat, won reelection to a four-year term by decisively trouncing Dawson A. Walker, his Republican challenger, by sixty thousand votes. The Smith-Dawson contest was characterized by considerable political maneuvering including accusations of vote fraud and Ku Klux Klan violence. With Smith sitting in the governor's office, Tompkins may have sensed that his chance to secure a judgeship was close at hand.[7]

On July 7, 1874, having just returned home to Savannah from a trip to Atlanta, Tompkins penned a letter to Governor Smith. While in Atlanta, Tompkins had paid a courtesy call on the governor. Tompkins's letter confirmed the rumor that he and Smith had previously discussed during their meeting. Judge Schley of the Eastern Circuit had just announced his pending retirement to be effective at the end of the term. Schley's resignation signaled a big break for Tompkins; the chance to fill a judicial vacancy was well within his grasp. If Tompkins's streak of good fortune would only hold a bit longer, the governor might soon have an opportunity to nominate him to the Superior Court bench.[8]

Schley's resignation was Tompkins's second opportunity to secure a judgeship. In January 1873, Tompkins's appointment by way of an executive order had suddenly been withdrawn. Tompkins persevered and on his second attempt became a judge. While Tompkins, as an acquaintance of the governor, had the inside track with respect to the judgeship, ultimately his confirmation by the Georgia senate took the conventional route. Besides Tompkins, other applicants for Schley's position included William B. Fleming and William D. Harden, both well-respected Savannah attorneys. As luck would have it, Tompkins seemed to have a virtual lock on the position. Governor Smith asked the group of practicing attorneys in Savannah for their assessment of Tompkins's suitability and fitness for the judgeship, and they responded favorably to his inquiry. The Savannah bar members, all white men, thought highly of Tompkins, describing him as "respected" and "competent to discharge the responsibilities." Another colleague reported that Tompkins's appointment "will give satisfaction to the bar and the community." With such endorsements, it is not surprising that the thirty-eight white members of the Georgia Senate voted unanimously to confirm Tompkins's appointment to the Superior Court bench. Governor Smith signed Tompkins's commission on January 19, 1875. Three years later, the case of *Oliver v. Cally v. Swoll* would be tried in Tompkins's Savannah courtroom.[9]

The jurors selected for the Aspasia Mirault property case were a diverse group of Savannah's white male citizens. In 1878, there was little chance that an African American would have served on the jury. It was a disappointment to many in the black community that no African Americans had been called for jury duty.[10] Drawn from a pool of thirty-six white male residents, the twelve men represented a broad segment of Savannah society. The white jurors selected to decide the Mirault property case were engaged in nine occupations, ranging from clerks and merchants to businessmen and skilled tradesmen. Judging from their different occupations, it is likely that their individual life experiences were similarly varied. Jurors John D. Hill, Joseph M. Foreman, Frank Winter, and D. F. Maxwell were employed as clerks at the time of the Mirault property trial. The business owners among the jury included William G. Morrell, a well-to-do rice broker and a partner in the firm of Pritchard & Morrell. Another juror, George S. Marshall, was part owner in a family business. Marshall and his younger brother, Theodore, operated a ship brokerage and commission firm. George J. Mills, who was elected as the jury's foreman, held the position of money broker at the city's Planters Bank. The tradesmen on the jury included Frank Campbell, a tinner (roofer); Thomas Turner, a piano tuner; and D. Lopez Cohen, a carpenter. Florence Joseph Morris owned a retail grocery store, while James Garrett worked as a conductor on the Savannah Skidway & Seaboard Railway.[11]

The impaneled members of the jury recited the oath on Thursday afternoon, February 14, 1878. After they selected Mills as their foreman, the jury proceeded to hear the first sworn testimony in the case. Pursing a rigorous schedule, Judge Tompkins kept the court in session throughout the remainder of the day and well into the evening hours. Just before 8:00 P.M. Tompkins struck the gavel, adjourning the day's session and dismissing the litigants and their attorneys. Before leaving the courtroom, the parties were obliged to listen to the judge's final instructions, including the announcement that the trial would resume the following morning promptly at ten.[12]

The Mirault property case extended over three full days, including a weekend session that consumed the greater part of Saturday, February 16. With so much at stake in the trial, the first rows of the courtroom were probably reserved for the principal litigants and members of their families. The Mirault heirs must have taken up several front-row benches. Since he was a principal litigant in the lawsuit, Robert Oliver probably attended each court session along with his wife, Diana, and their children, Robert Ward and young Aspasia, named for her grandmother. Charles B. Stiles, another litigant and the elder Robert's nephew, took off from his work as a brick mason to attend. Similarly, Charles's two sisters Mary A. Jackson and Louisa Burton laid aside all their routine activities to be present in the courtroom. Albert Jackson, Mary's husband and a successful African American cotton broker, took an active interest in the lawsuit and supported Mary's participation as a litigant. The same is probably true about Tillman Burton, a cotton merchant and the husband of Louisa, who had much to gain by endorsing his wife's bid to reclaim her grandmother's real estate.[13]

On the defendants' side of the courtroom, William Swoll, a city employee and real estate investor probably sat with his wife, Maria, and their three daughters, Margaret, Sarah, and Wilhelmina. The other principal defendant was conspicuous by his absence from the courtroom. As discussed earlier, Cally, a co-creator of the secret trust agreement and a key player in the lawsuit, had died two years earlier in 1876 at the age of fifty-six. Samuel Cally, George's younger brother, was managing the affairs of the late Cally's estate. Up until his death, Cally had steadfastly maintained that he was the owner of the property in question. As a result and whether he wanted to or not, Samuel must have felt obligated to see through to the end the litigation that had been initiated by his brother.[14]

The legal drama played out in the courtroom was rich with colorful testimony. The jury heard statements about a secret trust agreement and an interracial romance. An early witness at the trial was John R. Johnson, Savannah's treasurer, who testified about Cally's legal title to the property and his delinquency on the ground rent payments. Johnson established that while he had known Cally over the years, he was not familiar with the Mirault family.[15]

Edward Lovell, a sixty-two-year-old man, testified at the trial. It was disclosed that Lovell and Cally, both of whom had relocated to Savannah from Massachusetts, maintained a close friendship through the years. Unlike city treasurer Johnson, who knew Cally but not the Miraults, Lovell testified that he did know several members of the Mirault family and that he had been well acquainted with Aspasia. A former alderman and vice chairman of the Savannah City Council, Lovell recollected back some thirty-odd years to 1842 when Cally purchased the lot. At that time, Lovell remembered that Cally took Lovell into his confidence by candidly admitting that "when he [Cally] bought the lot . . . from the city, he said it was for Aspasia." As Lovell recalled, Cally had stopped short of disclosing the actual source of the purchase money. Although he might have easily pressed Cally for more specific details about the matter, Lovell told the jury that he let the matter drop.[16] Because the historical record is silent, there is no way of knowing whether Lovell knew whose money—Cally's or Aspasia's—had been used to purchase the lot. Yet, both the longevity and the apparent closeness of the Cally-Lovell friendship tend to cloud Lovell's claims of ignorance about the matter.

Even though they were confidants, Lovell nevertheless divulged one of Cally's more negative personality traits. Lovell admitted that Cally had been "a loose man with his statements." According to Lovell, Cally shared details about the property, not only with him, but with several other acquaintances. While Cally may have been in the habit of disclosing personal matters, there is no hard evidence that he acted recklessly with Aspasia's secret. Lovell testified that Cally was sometimes "loose" with his statements, but he also pointed out that, for the most part, Cally had exercised some discretion and that Cally had never been so careless as to divulge details about the secret trust agreement to any other city officials.[17]

Lovell's testimony provided the jury with information about the way Aspasia and Cally had used the lot during the 1840s and the early 1850s. For the first decade or so after they had purchased the Pulaski Ward property, Aspasia erected a building on the premises that Cally used as his carpentry shop. Aspasia, in the meantime, continued to maintain her bakery shop on Broughton Street. Lovell testified that Cally may have paid her rent for the use of the carpentry shop before the building was destroyed by a fire. That fire may have provided the impetus for Aspasia to find alternative uses for the property. Construction on Aspasia's residence began shortly thereafter. Lovell recalled that "Cally had a carpenter shop on the lot prior to 1852. When it burnt, Cally built the present house."[18]

From the list of witnesses and a review of their testimony, it is possible to glean aspects of Norwood's trial strategy. Beyond establishing that Cally had been the legal titleholder and taxpayer, Norwood wanted to prove that his late client had taken actual possession of the property. Through the testimonies of Lovell and George H. Ash, it was established that Cally had occupied the lot. Ash testified about the interracial living arrangement within Aspasia's household. Ash stated that during 1853, Cally hired him to construct Aspasia's three-story residence in the Pulaski Ward section of the city.[19] Ash described the building of Aspasia's home and his interactions with Cally and the Mirault family. He recalled that for a number of years Aspasia had been the proprietor of a bakeshop on Broughton Street. He was aware that Robert Oliver was Aspasia's son. Although Ash never learned how Cally, whom he described as "an unmonied man," managed to finance the construction, Ash did recall Cally telling him that the house was being built for Aspasia. Upon his completion of the project, Ash remembered, "When I finished she moved in [and] Cally lived there also. I saw him there sometimes." Ash also observed some of the day-to-day interactions between Cally and Aspasia. With respect to the management of the family bakery business and the household affairs, Ash observed that "she [Aspasia] seemed to have entire control."[20]

Corroborating testimony concerning Aspasia's control of the property came from John J. Maurice, who had been hired to replace her roof after a hurricane struck Savannah in 1854. Two decades later when he testified at the trial it was obvious that the intervening years had been good to Maurice, and that he had prospered. By the late 1870s, Maurice had expanded his business to include his son William. The two men were established Savannah coppersmiths with a shop located on Barnard Street near York. At the trial, Maurice disputed Cally's claims of exclusive ownership to the property by giving testimony that was harmful to Cally's interests in the case. According to Maurice, Cally had candidly admitted to him that the property as well as the house belonged to the "old lady [Aspasia]." Maurice knew that it was Aspasia, not Cally, who paid him for the roofing job. "When I applied to him [Cally] for pay for putting on the roof, he said he would try and get the money from her and pay me, which he did," Maurice explained. Maurice had gathered the lion's share of his knowledge about the Aspasia-Cally relationship during one lengthy discussion when Cally admitted that Aspasia owned the property. Cally explained that he was merely the trustee for the property. Maurice told the jury that he had remained curious about the true nature of the Aspasia-Cally relationship. Maurice guessed that they were an interracial couple, romantically involved and living in "cahoots."[21]

The testimony of witness W. H. May might have confused the jury. May, a white man and longtime Savannah resident, testified that he was familiar with the property at issue in the case and that he had known Aspasia and Cally. Yet, May's recollections were disjointed and riddled with inconsistencies. At one point May called the deceased woman Aspasia. Later, he referred to her as Letia. Aspasia and Letia were two different women, and with respect to the latter individual, May was probably referring to Letitia Davis, the younger of Aspasia's two daughters. Toward the end of his testimony, May misspoke about Louisa Nayle, another Mirault family member. He mistakenly identified Louisa as Letia's daughter. Louisa had been Aspasia's daughter and Letitia's older sister.[22]

But it was May's clear recollection of the family's insolvency that threatened to discredit the heirs' principal argument. The heirs argued that Cally had used Aspasia's money to purchase the lot and to build the house and make all the repairs. May's testimony raised doubt that Aspasia had been the primary source for financing the property and improvements. Had Cally provided the down payment for the Mirault lot? Had he paid for the property maintenance over the years? According to May, there had been frequent transfers of money between Cally and various members of the family. From May's testimony, the jury learned that Cally was in the habit of lending "Letia" money, sometimes as much as twenty-five dollars, to pay her taxes.[23]

As the trial continued, the Mirault heirs must have been pleased with the statements made by witness James Russell. In what amounted to the most succinct sworn testimony given during the trial, Russell's statements did much to bolster the heirs' arguments. Russell, a Savannah tradesman, recalled that Cally had approached him to do some needed work on Aspasia's Whitaker Street residence. While it is unclear whether the two men ever reached an agreement about Russell's employment, nonetheless, Cally did tell Russell that the property belonged to Aspasia. Cally made it clear to Russell that although Cally was initiating the work order for the property "it was the old lady's and she would pay for it." Russell remembered his conversation with Cally occurred sometime in 1859.[24] But Russell was mistaken about the date. Since Cally promised Russell he would receive payment from the "old lady," the conversation would have occurred sometime before Aspasia's death in December 1857.

Like Russell and Maurice's statements to the jury, the testimony of Hill Gowdy, a successful merchant, added more credence to the heirs' argument that Aspasia, not George Cally, had been the true owner of the lot and residence on Whitaker Street. Gowdy, a native of Hartford, Connecticut, had moved to Savannah as a young man and with the passage of time became a prominent citizen. Gowdy, an acquaintance of Cally, gave the jury his impressions of the property dispute based on his firsthand knowledge. Gowdy was the Miraults and Cally's next-door neighbor. In 1855, Hill Gowdy purchased lot number 21, the property directly adjacent to Aspasia's lot. For the next twelve years, Gowdy lived there with his wife, Mary, their five children, and three white servants.[25] When Gowdy asked Cally if he wanted to sell what Gowdy had presumed was Cally's property, Cally admitted that Aspasia was the owner of the lot. According to Gowdy, Cally acknowledged that he held the property in trust for Aspasia and her heirs.[26]

The evidence for the jury's consideration in the Mirault property trial mounted steadily. On Friday, February 15, the second day of the trial, Judge Tompkins started the proceedings promptly at ten A.M. Remarkably, the trial then continued unabated—except for a noon recess—for the next ten hours. Late that same evening after two full days of testimony and vigorous cross-examination by opposing counsel, Judge Tompkins requested that attorneys present their closing arguments. Under the illumination of the room's gaslights, the first of the four attorneys explained the merits of the case to the jury. Following their summations, the judge adjourned the session for the evening.[27]

Even though the next day was Saturday, Tompkins, apparently eager to bring the matter to a conclusion, ordered the litigants to appear in his courtroom at the customary starting time, ten A.M., to conclude the trial phase of the case. Tompkins charged the jury with instructions and then permitted them to retire to a separate room for their deliberations. The jury wasted no time, proceeding immediately to dispose of the task before them. The jurors reached a consensus on the evidence rather quickly. Before the judge even called for a noon meal recess, the jury foreman, George J. Mills, sent word to Tompkins that he and his fellow jurors had arrived at a decision in the case.[28] After the jury filed back into the courtroom and with the litigants and their attorneys seated, Miller arose for the reading of the verdict. He said,

> We, [the jury] further find that the money paid by George Cally to the city for said lot was the money of Aspasia Mirault, and that Cally agreed with said Aspasia Mirault that he would take the deed in his own name, but in trust for the use and benefit of said Aspasia Mirault and her lawful heirs, and that after said purchase by Cally, said Aspasia Mirault did possess, control and enjoy said lot with the knowledge and consent of Cally, and that she did pay, or cause to be paid, the taxes, ground-rent, and other duties upon said lot, with her own money.[29]

Thus, in a unanimous verdict, the jury concluded that the property belonged to Aspasia's son and her grandchildren. In order for them to award the property to the African American heirs, the jurors were obliged to maneuver around several legal hurdles. Although the facts seemed to favor the Mirault family, the antebellum law stood against them. Their decision for the heirs meant that the jury totally disregarded Georgia's 1818 statute, expressly prohibiting African Americans from owning land in Savannah. Both defendants, Cally and Swoll, had argued the statute's merits, but the jury found that its provisions had no direct bearing on the case before them.[30] From the jury's standpoint, the Civil War had brought about significant changes to the constitution and the laws of Georgia.

The jury's verdict defeated William Swoll's title to the land. As a bona fide purchaser of the lot for value, Swoll had presented considerable evidence during the course of the trial, and he very likely felt secure in his legal claim to the property. In spite of the apparent logic of Swoll's arguments, the jury flatly rejected his claim. Instead, the jury determined that because the city had not legally reentered or reclaimed the property prior to the auction, Swoll's deed was defective. If, as the jury concluded, city officials had failed to acquire title to the land in accordance with the municipal ordinance, then Swoll's deed was null and void.[31]

Having decided the principal legal issue—whether Swoll had a legal claim to the property—in favor of the Mirault heirs, the jury then tackled a second major hurdle. The twelve white Savannah citizens had to determine whether an Aspasia-Cally agreement had ever existed? If they believed there had been a meeting of the minds, the jury was obligated to make findings of fact regarding the nature of that agreement. Once again, the jurors concluded that the evidence supported the heirs' version of the facts. They believed the testimony that Aspasia and Cally had created a valid trust agreement. In all likelihood, the members of the jury found much of the sworn testimony persuasive. On more than one occasion and to more than one of the trial witnesses, Cally had acknowledged that his relationship to the property was not as the owner of the property, but instead as a trustee for Aspasia and her heirs.[32]

In support of the heirs' claim to the property, the jurors determined that the Aspasia-Cally agreement was still valid and binding on the administrator of the late George Cally's estate. The jury also found that Aspasia, without any additional funds from Cally, had used her own money to purchase the land and make the improvements. Having found Aspasia to be the true owner of the property, the jury concluded that Cally, as her trustee, had violated his fiduciary duty to Aspasia and her heirs by falling behind in the ground rent payments. The jury concluded that the heirs should not be held liable for Cally's negligence, and thus the property belonged to them free and clear. Because of this turn of events, Robert Oliver, his nephew, and two nieces emerged from the trial victorious. The verdict allowed Aspasia's family to reclaim their inheritance.[33]

On May 13, 1878, three months after the courtroom drama had ended, Judge Tompkins instructed his clerk to announce his final decree in the Mirault property litigation. Based on the jury's findings of facts in the matter, the deed issued by the city to William Swoll was declared null and void and was to be delivered up for cancellation. Tompkins's decree established that lot number 22 in Pulaski Ward belonged to the heirs of Aspasia Mirault in fee simple. Tompkins called for the original 1842 deed to be reformed by replacing Cally's name with the names of the four Mirault heirs. Lastly, the court issued an order stating that the costs of the protracted litigation were to be borne by the co-defendants, William Swoll and George Cally.[34]

The Mirault family celebrated upon learning they had prevailed in the lawsuit. Their prayers had been answered. The protracted and contentious legal battle, having commenced for the family in October 1874 with the filing of their *Bill of Complaint,* had ultimately restored Aspasia's property to them. At what must have been a jubilant family gathering, probably at Robert and Diana Oliver's residence on the corner of South Broad and East Broad Streets, the Mirault heirs marveled at their good fortune. In the spring of 1878, a courtroom victory was certainly no small achievement for an African American family living in an increasingly segregated southern city. Now, the family members could begin to enjoy the fruits of Aspasia's labors as she had intended them to do.[35] But as the heirs celebrated their legal victory, a host of problems were already looming on the horizon. The defendants filed separate motions for a new trial almost immediately, seeking to overturn the verdict. If the prospect of a new trial was not enough of a concern, there were other vexing issues to be resolved. The heirs faced the deplorable state of the property and a sizable amount of past-due rent.

During the course of the litigation, the heirs had become the victims of foul play from an unexpected source. While Robert Oliver and his relatives were engaged in the legal battle of their lives, Henry Roggenstein, their tenant, had taken unfair advantage of the legal quagmire by refusing to pay rent. The heirs had become painfully aware of Roggenstein's dishonesty during the fall of 1874 when they filed their *Bill of Complaint*. Acting on that knowledge, they had wisely named Roggenstein as a defendant party in their legal documents. Through their court documents, the heirs alerted the court that Roggenstein owed them a considerable amount of back rent.[36]

What had begun as an amicable tenancy was over time transformed into a nightmare for the Mirault family. Roggenstein withheld payment while he benefited from the property. The three-story brick residence on Whitaker Street with a sturdy brick oven in the rear was ideal for Roggenstein, who, like Aspasia, was in the bakery business. Roggenstein probably left his native Mecklenburg, Germany, already well versed in the bakery trade. There is every indication that he worked hard to perfect his skill, thereby realizing a modicum of success in Savannah. Roggenstein was a family man. While he practiced his trade, he supported his German-born wife, Amelia, and their daughter, Caroline.[37]

During the course of the *Oliver v. Cally v. Swoll* litigation, Judge Tompkins attended to the delinquent rent issue. When called upon to give an accounting for his actions and in spite of the substantial evidence that he was delinquent with the rent, Roggenstein nevertheless proffered an explanation for the lack of payments. Roggenstein assumed the position of an innocent party. Under oath, Roggenstein told the court that from the beginning of his tenancy in 1866, he had made regular and timely rent payments to George Cally. That situation, according to Roggenstein, changed drastically when Cally fell behind in his ground rent payments. Roggenstein recalled how during the spring of 1872, he saw the city marshal post a delinquency notice on the property. A few weeks later, Swoll paid Roggenstein a visit. He introduced himself as the new owner, and he told Roggenstein to submit all future rent payments to him. Although he had been prepared to follow Swoll's instructions, Roggenstein faced a difficult dilemma when Cally also paid him a visit. Cally warned Roggenstein to disregard Swoll's statements. Instead, he insisted that Roggenstein should continue to pay the rent to him.[38]

Faced with the untenable situation of having to pay rent to two individuals Roggenstein wasted no time in consulting a lawyer. Toward the end of

1872, he hired the attorney William Saussy, who devised a novel solution for his bewildered client. Saussy advised him to withhold payment from both parties. What had begun as a tug of war over rent payments with Roggenstein in the middle evolved into a windfall situation for the tenant. For four years from the spring of 1872 until the spring of 1876, Henry Roggenstein followed the dubious advice of his legal counsel and paid neither Swoll nor Cally. Liberated from the burden of rental payments, Roggenstein was the tenant of record, but to the consternation of all the litigants, he refused to pay any rent.[39]

Understandably, after learning the details of Roggenstein's delinquency, the court was sympathetic to the heirs' request to recover the back rent. But it would take considerable time and effort before Roggenstein was made to satisfy his debt and account for his wayward actions. By March 1876, John C. Rowland had been appointed receiver with the authority to collect and to hold all rent money recovered from the property. Yet, the parties remained at a stalemate because Rowland's repeated efforts to collect from Roggenstein went unanswered, his solicitations seemingly having fallen on deaf ears. After nearly twelve months of trying to persuade Roggenstein to pay, Rowland, who was by that time near his wits' end over the delinquency, took stronger measures to secure the rent payments. On March 24, he petitioned the court for relief. Judge Tompkins issued an order for Roggenstein to appear before him the next day to explain his refusal to pay. To further ensure Roggenstein's court appearance, the judge ordered the Chatham County sheriff to serve *rule nisi* documents on the delinquent tenant. The legal maneuvering captured Roggenstein's attention. By early April, Rowland reported the tenant "has paid but a small portion of said rent and there is a large balance due by him which he refuses to pay." Based on Rowland's report, the judge issued an *order* directing the receiver to collect the rent through the use of a warrant or a similar legal device.[40]

Periodically, the court returned to the delinquent rent issue. After a substantial amount of the back rent had been recovered, Tompkins authorized Rowland to use a portion of those same funds for property maintenance. The judge signed an order on June 1, 1878, authorizing Rowland to make any needed repairs. To his credit, Judge Tompkins was determined that the Mirault house and surrounding land would remain "in good tenable condition." In his petition, Rowland informed the judge about the deplorable state of the premises. During Roggenstein's tenancy the house had fallen into disrepair. Rowland provided Tompkins with a long list of items requiring immediate attention. The roof and the gutters needed repair and the walls required plastering. The window blinds were in such poor condition that they would need to be replaced. The front pavement as well as the surrounding fence required mending.[41] By the time the trial concluded in 1878, Roggenstein must have paid nearly all the back rent. With an apparent reference to the amount already collected, Judge Tompkins advised the heirs that their share of the $860 they owed to Swoll for having paid the city taxes could be taken from the Roggenstein rent money held by the receiver.[42]

With the rent delinquency matter settled, Judge Tompkins still had to resolve one remaining issue, this time involving Rowland. On February 26, 1879, the judge issued an order giving Rowland just two days to provide the court with a detailed accounting of all receipts and disbursements. Without mincing any words, Tompkins's order called for "a full, distinct, specific and detailed statement and account of his receipts and disbursements accompanied by proper vouchers from the time of his appointment to this date." Was the judge's order merely a routine proceeding in such cases or was this a reprimand? It is left to conjecture whether Rowland during his four-year stint as a receiver for the Mirault property had been completely honest and forthcoming in his accounts of all the money collected. He may very well have been an honest man. Nevertheless, Tompkins's order for an accounting raises some questions about Rowland and the exact nature of his dealings. First, from the misdeeds of a delinquent tenant and perhaps later from the actions of the receiver, Judge Tompkins had considerably more than courtroom drama to contend with as he presided over the Mirault property case.[43]

As the winter of 1878 gave way to the first signs of spring, the Mirault heirs could place two key victories on their side of the legal ledger. With a favorable jury verdict and with substantial resolution of the delinquent rent issue, they had ample reason for celebration. Under the leadership of Robert Oliver, the family's principal litigant, and with the able counsel of their attorney, Alfred B. Smith, the heirs had reclaimed Aspasia's property. More legal battles, however, lay ahead. The arrival of the news that the defendants had filed motions for a new trial and appealed the case for review by the Georgia Supreme Court dampened the joyful atmosphere at the Oliver household. Perhaps Providence would permit them one more triumph as they entered the next stage of the litigation. Whatever the outcome, the heirs, as a family unit, remained committed to the struggle before them. They owed that commitment both to themselves and to the memory of their deceased matriarch, Aspasia Mirault.

Chapter Eight

Reversal of Fortune

In his final decree for the *Oliver v. Swoll* litigation, Judge Henry Tompkins crafted a document that simultaneously concurred with the jury and placed the verdict on a solid legal footing. On the first of five handwritten, legal-size pages, Tompkins meticulously laid out the writing task before him. Closely following the jury's findings of fact, Tompkins addressed the legal issues. One major issue remained unresolved. Because the verdict rendered the city's sale to William Swoll null and void, Tompkins had to determine whether the Mirault heirs or the estate of George Cally should take the property. Tompkins agreed with the jury's verdict, and his analysis demonstrated that the property belonged to the heirs. Following a succinct summary of the procedural history as well as the verdict, the decree detailed the case law that supported the outcome.[1]

Contrary to the argument proffered by the defendants, Tompkins rejected the assertion that the heirs faced any legal disabilities stemming from the 1818 law. The judge ruled that the statute, which had been repealed at the start of the Reconstruction period, could not block their claim to the property. According to Judge Tompkins,

> The change in the laws, wrought by the results of the late war, and the adoption of the Constitution of Georgia of 1865, repealed the whole of the Act of 1818; and the rights and liabilities of parties stood as if the Act had never been passed where the courts had taken no action.[2]

The defendants had hoped to win their claim by aligning the 1818 statue with a specific set of laws. Those laws prohibited a recovery where persons had lost money or other property while engaged in an illegal enterprise. The Mirault heirs could not recover the property if Aspasia and Cally had purchased the real estate through an illegal trust agreement. If the judge had used the defendant's theory, the heirs, laboring under such a legal liability, would have been barred from prevailing in the litigation.[3]

But Tompkins ruled that those laws had no bearing on the case. Typically, a recovery would be prohibited, as the defendants proposed, only if the law in question were still in effect at the time that the recovery was being sought. Tompkins determined that "the illegal contract or transaction, upon which recovery is sought, must still be illegal when the action is tried." By the time the Mirault property case was tried in 1878, a new state constitution was in place, and the 1818 statute prohibiting black ownership of land in Savannah had been repealed. Thus, Tompkins concluded that the Aspasia-Cally trust agreement, although illegal when created in 1842, had effectively lost its illegal character by the time the heirs litigated the property issue.[4]

Judge Tompkins also cited two United States Supreme Court cases, *Clarke v. Bazadone* (1803) and *Church v. Hubbart* (1804), as precedent. He wrote that "the repeal of an Act inflicting a forfeiture or penalty takes away the right to collect or enforce such forfeiture, even though the repeal was made pending the suit for enforcement."[5] The prohibitive 1818 statute, largely ignored at the time, had been repealed. As the law stood in 1878 at the time of the *Oliver v. Cally v. Swoll* litigation, no additional legal impediments existed to prohibit or nullify the secret trust agreement.

Scholarly and analytical, Tompkins's final decree reflected aspects of postwar Republicanism. Although he was a Democrat and a former Confederate soldier, his decree used Reconstruction-era logic. For a brief time following the Civil War, Georgia and the other former Confederate states had repudiated discriminatory legislation such as the 1818 statute. Both enslaved blacks and free people of color, either those who had fallen victim to or those who had managed to circumvent the racial effects of such statutes, were now free of those laws as if they had never been enacted. With his understanding of the political landscape, Judge Tompkins "considered, ordered, adjudged, and decreed" a stunning legal victory for the Mirault heirs.[6]

Tompkins reasoned that things would have been much different if Aspasia had not died in 1857 but had lived to see the postbellum era. A key point for the judge was the fact that Aspasia's heirs had been in possession of the property until after the war:

> If she had lived until after the changes in the law in 1865; and Cally had continued to hold as her Trustee, there seems no doubt that her right would have been complete as against him. Her heirs having been in actual possession up to 1866, under the same conditions as it had been held by Aspasia Mirault, the heirs took the entire estate in fee simple.[7]

But Aspasia had died, and Tompkins stated that her heirs, as her legal representatives, were entitled to prevail in the lawsuit. Liberated from their antebellum legal disabilities, Aspasia's family now had legal standing to assert their claim for the property.[8]

Judge Tompkins detailed how the state legislators in 1818 had devised just two penalties for a violation of the law's provisions. During the period from 1818 to 1865 when the statute was in effect, Georgia officials had the options of imposing a fine or initiating forfeiture and repossession proceedings. In the matter of the Mirault property, the state had failed to exercise either option against Aspasia or Cally. According to Tompkins, the defendants could have increased their chances of victory by notifying the court of the statutory penalties, but neither defendant had provided any details about the remedies legally available to them. Tompkins concluded that with the repeal of the 1818 law, the state had forever waived its opportunity to enforce either of the explicitly prescribed statutory penalties.[9] In drafting his decree, it is likely that Tompkins may have researched the judicial records for evidence of any enforcement proceeding under the antebellum law. There is no indication from Tompkins's document that he found any such proceedings. Similarly, no surviving record of enforcement proceedings or the levying of penalties under the statue has been identified.

In his analysis, Tompkins reasoned that Cally's claim to the property was tenuous at best. If Aspasia Mirault had at any time attempted to set aside the trust and assert her rights as an owner before 1865, she would have failed and forfeited the property. But her failure would not have occurred because of the secret trust agreement with Cally. Instead, according to the judge, the explicit provisions of the statute of 1818, prohibiting blacks from owning property in the city of Savannah, would have defeated Aspasia's claim. At the same time, Aspasia's potential loss of her property did not translate into a victory for Cally. If Aspasia had been threatened with the forfeiture of the property, the law would have also prevented Cally from asserting a claim. Cally, as the trustee holder of an illegal trust agreement, would have been deemed culpable for purchasing a piece of real estate on behalf of a free woman of color. Such an action was in the violation of the law. Cally would have been liable for a fine of up to $1,000 and the property would have been forfeited to the state by escheat.[10] Whether he had been persuaded by the sworn testimony or if the legal precedents had influenced his decision, Judge Tompkins supported the verdict favoring the Mirault heirs. He could discern no provision in the 1818 statute that declared trusts invalid and void as between the trustee (Cally) and the *cestui que* trust (Aspasia).

Having determined that the Mirault-Cally trust agreement was still enforceable, Tompkins then set about determining the final disposition of the property. He first examined an argument suggesting that since the state, by its inaction, had forfeited the escheat option, the title remained vested in Cally. Under that argument, the administrator for Cally's estate would have still been obligated to carry out the provisions of the secret trust agreement. Although Tompkins's initial argument favored the heirs, he chose a second legal argument that he labeled "the more correct view" with respect to the property. Tompkins reasoned that the state's failure to act before 1865 meant that the title to lot 22 in Pulaski Ward was left in abeyance. Once the 1818 statute had been repealed, the judge decreed that the state had lost its inchoate rights to the land. The title then vested in Cally, but subject to the equitable rights of Aspasia's heirs.[11] By applying a legal analysis that took into consideration some of the recent political changes within the state, Tompkins decreed that the property rightfully belonged to the Mirault heirs.[12]

In spite of Judge Tompkins's ruling in their favor, the legal victory for Robert Oliver and his relatives would be short lived. In late May 1878, soon after learning of the jury's verdict, the two defendants filed their motions requesting a new trial. Tompkins provided a rapid response, denying both motions on June 11, 1878. In turn, the defendants lost no time in appealing Tompkins' ruling to the Supreme Court of Georgia. This time their request was granted. The defendants had secured one more opportunity to claim Aspasia's property.[13]

With the state's highest court reviewing their property case, there was a very real possibility that the Mirault heirs might experience a reversal of fortune and lose the property. During its August 1878 term, the justices of the state's highest tribunal agreed to hear the Mirault property case. Rufus E. Lester, one of Swoll's attorneys, traveled from Savannah to Atlanta, a distance of over two hundred miles, to present his arguments in person before the high court.[14]

Just three men comprised the Supreme Court of Georgia in 1878. Hiram Warner presided as the chief justice. He was assisted by two associate justices, Logan E. Bleckley and James Jackson. Organized in 1845, the state's highest tribunal maintained a tradition of attracting highly qualified jurists to the bench and of issuing judicious opinions in accordance with the law. The Warner court that heard the Mirault property case was no exception. Appointed to the chief justice post in 1867, Warner returned to the high court that year for a second time. His previous service as an associate justice had extended from 1845 to 1849 with reelection to another term from 1849 through 1853. Born in Massachusetts in 1802, Warner migrated to Georgia in 1821 at the age of nineteen. He was admitted to the bar in 1824 and spent the rest of his career working as a lawyer, a legislator, a congressman representing Georgia in the nation's capital, and a justice on the Georgia Supreme Court. His congressional service began in 1855 and lasted for the next five years until 1860 when Warner joined the Secession Convention. Warner, who owned a plantation with over one hundred slaves, opposed secession but decided to concede to the majority vote of his colleagues.[15]

James Jackson had been a member of the state's highest court for three years when he heard the appeal in the Mirault property case. Governor Smith appointed Jackson in 1875 to fill the vacancy occasioned by the resignation of

Justice Robert P. Trippe. Jackson was a native of Georgia, born in Jefferson County in 1819. His grandfather and namesake fought in the American Revolutionary War and later served as the governor of Georgia. Young Jackson earned a degree at the University of Georgia and soon thereafter embarked upon his law studies. Once he had been admitted to the bar, Jackson entered the political arena as the representative from Walton County to the Georgia General Assembly during the 1840s. Before the end of that decade and throughout the 1850s, Jackson held several judicial posts. Then during the Civil War, Confederate president Jefferson Davis appointed Jackson as a military judge. Two years after the conclusion of the Mirault case in 1880, Jackson would be elevated to chief justice of the Georgia Supreme Court to replace the retiring Warner.[16]

Logan Edwin Bleckley was the third supreme court justice to render a decision on the Mirault property case. Bleckley, who served as an associate justice, had a long history on the state's highest tribunal. Bleckley began practicing law when he was just nineteen years old. In 1852, he was elected as the solicitor-general for Coweta County, Georgia, and he served in that post until 1861 when he joined the Confederate army. After his discharge for medical reasons, Bleckley continued to serve the Confederacy in a legal capacity for the duration of the war. In the postwar years, Bleckley sat on the supreme court on two separate occasions. Like his judicial colleague Justice James Jackson, Bleckley was first appointed to the high court as an associate justice in 1875, and he served a four-year term. Bleckley resigned and subsequently returned to the bench eight years later as the court's chief justice. Bleckley retired from the bench in 1894.[17]

Following oral arguments and a review of the supporting documentation, the justices reversed the jury verdict in favor of the Mirault heirs. The high court chose to disregard most of the well-reasoned analysis in Judge Tompkins's final decree. That decree had meticulously cited a host of legal precedents from a number of state courts, including cases from New Jersey, New York, and Pennsylvania, as well as United States Supreme Court cases. Those cases stood for the legal proposition that "the repeal of a statute prohibiting certain acts and inflicting penalties puts the parties in the position they would have occupied if the prohibitory statute had never been in existence."[18] But eschewing the considerable legal reasoning to the contrary, the justices ruled that the 1818 state statute, in spite of the fact that it had been repealed in 1865, remained a controlling factor with a direct bearing on the Mirault property litigation.[19]

From the viewpoint of the Supreme Court of Georgia, the 1818 statute rendered the trust agreement between Aspasia and Cally null and void. That statute, which had been the extant law in 1842 when Cally—using Aspasia's money—purchased the lot, precluded Aspasia and her heirs from enforcing the trust agreement.[20] While the jury in Savannah had determined the ownership of the property from among all three litigants—Oliver, Cally, and Swoll—the Supreme Court of Georgia never even considered the Mirault heirs. Crucial to the high court's reasoning was the fact that Aspasia had been a free person of color. Because the 1818 statute had excluded blacks from owning land in Savannah, the Supreme Court of Georgia summarily dismissed the Mirault family's claim to the property.

Having eliminated the heirs, the high court then set about determining which of the two remaining litigants, either William Swoll's or George Cally's estate, possessed the most viable claim to the Savannah lot. That determination was relatively easy for the high court to make since the justices concluded that the jury had misinterpreted the facts of the case. In contrast to the jury findings, the Supreme Court of Georgia ruled that the city of Savannah had lawfully reclaimed the property. This conclusion boded well for William Swoll. His purchase of the lot through a city auction in 1872 gave Swoll a strong legal claim to the property. The high court reversed Judge Tompkins's ruling, overturned the verdict in favor of the heirs, and remanded the proceedings back to the Chatham County Superior Court for retrial.[21]

On January 13, 1879, Tompkins followed directions from the high court by reporting all of the recent developments in the Mirault property case. Tompkins announced that the Supreme Court of Georgia had reversed his previous ruling. He issued an order for the Mirault property case to stand for retrial. In addition, Tompkins announced that Swoll was entitled to collect a judgment in the amount of $144.90 from the heirs as reimbursement for the expenses in appealing the case to the state's highest court.[22]

A full-blown retrial, as had been envisioned by the state's highest court, never materialized. Instead, just two months later on March 29, 1879, the *Savannah Morning News* reported that the two consolidated cases of *Oliver et al. v. Cally* and *Cally v. Swoll* had been presented for rehearing before the superior court judge William B. Fleming. But the parties made quick work of their second court appearance. Probably realizing the futility of further proceedings, both the Mirault heirs and Joseph Cronk, Cally's administrator, consented to a verdict for Swoll.[23] The litigants, bowing to the tremendous pressure stemming from the Supreme Court of Georgia's opinion, agreed to relinquish the property to Swoll. The unfortunate reversal for the Mirault heirs was complete. Swoll, who had purchased the lot and buildings for less than one-tenth of their actual worth, claimed his prize.

The victory for Swoll, as the end product of the Aspasia Mirault–George Cally trust agreement, provides insight into the legal realities as they existed for many nineteenth-century black Georgians. A retelling of the struggle for ownership over Aspasia's property supports the proposition that the burden of racial discrimination frequently thwarted African American progress. For the most part, throughout the antebellum decades, Aspasia and other free people of color failed to realize a secure place within the nation's social, political, or economic matrix. Even the political changes that extended the mantle of civil rights in the postwar years frequently did not translate into equitable and just solutions for many African Americans, including Aspasia's family. As was evident in the litigation brought by the Mirault heirs, an attempt by blacks to purchase land could have disastrous results.

Notably, Aspasia managed to live more of the exception to the typical African American experience than the rule. She found a measure of economic success as a pastry cook and bakery shop owner. This enterprising African American woman used business and personal ties with a white man to procure a piece of Savannah real estate. Aspasia and Cally devised an extralegal measure to circumvent a racist law. Nevertheless, even the advent of legal and constitutional changes brought about by the Civil War and the Reconstruction era did not prevent an injustice in the Mirault property case. By its 1878 ruling in *Oliver v. Swoll*, the Supreme Court of Georgia stripped Aspasia's heirs of their inheritance, thereby demonstrating the dominance of state law over local wisdom.

Details surrounding the secret trust agreement and the heirs' failure to exercise prudent oversight of the property after Aspasia's death raise more perplexing questions than they provide answers. There is no clear explanation as to why, after nearly thirty years of faithfully honoring his agreement with Aspasia, that Cally abandoned those obligations. Whatever his underlying motives may have been, his actions proved to be detrimental to himself and to Aspasia's heirs. At the same time, the heirs cannot be absolved from their responsibilities. Logic defies their failure to claim the real estate inheritance years before the recourse to litigation became a necessity. Their delay turned out to be fatal to their legitimate interests in the property.

Aspasia died in 1857. As the subsequent rulings from the Supreme Court of Georgia detailed, Aspasia's son and grandchildren had been remiss in their failure to exert some measure of ownership over the real estate. Taking into account their legal liabilities as free people of color during the antebellum period, it is understandable that the Mirault family members may have been reluctant to exert their ownership rights until sometime after the Civil War. The shift toward black civil rights during the brief Reconstruction era should have encouraged the family's resolve to claim their legal title to Aspasia's property. Had they acted expeditiously, they might have been the beneficiaries of the 1865 Georgia state constitution that repudiated many discriminatory laws.[24] The Mirault heirs waited until Cally had lost his title to the property before taking action. At that time, the heirs had precious little legal leverage to use in the ensuing litigation against Cally and Swoll.

The sharp dichotomy between the jury verdict that favored the heirs and the reversal of that verdict by the Supreme Court of Georgia raises questions of equity and fairness in late-nineteenth-century Georgia. After evaluating the credibility of the witnesses, an all-white jury determined that the property belonged to the heirs. In his final decree, Judge Tompkins reinforced the jury verdict with his legal reasoning and supporting legal precedents. He rationalized that so long as the heirs had possessed the property for a period of time following the repeal of the 1818 law, then they stood on solid legal ground to defeat Cally.[25]

Yet, the justices of the Supreme Court of Georgia interpreted the legal issues in the Mirault litigation very differently. For the high court, an essential component of the case was Aspasia Mirault's death in 1857, nearly a decade before the discriminatory statute was repealed. In two later judicial opinions, both with fact patterns similar to the Mirault case, the justices adhered to the identical prohibitions against black ownership of land, and they consistently upheld the provisions of the 1818 statute. Adding to the misfortune of people like the Mirault family, the high court ruled that the statute remained enforceable with respect to all wills, trusts, deeds, and other such legal instruments contracted from 1818 through 1865. The justices ruled that prewar bequests, contracts, or agreements that involved the ownership of land by free people of color were deemed null and void. Thus, the Aspasia-Cally secret trust agreement, created in 1842, could not be enforced under the dictates of the high court's ruling. Having no legal basis for invoking federal jurisdiction over their property claim, the heirs could not appeal to the federal courts and were forced to accept the Georgia Supreme Court's unfavorable decision.

Just five years later, the high court issued a similar judicial opinion in the 1882 case of *The Planters' Loan and Savings Bank v. Johnson*, involving an African American family from Augusta. In that litigation, the children of the deceased Peter Johnson brought a suit against Martha A. Johnson, their mother and the widow of Peter. The Johnson children objected that Martha had sold a piece of property to W. M. Wilkerson in June 1878. In their lawsuit, they argued that the land, an inheritance from their father, should be returned to them. The children in the *Planters'* case sought recovery of three-fourths of the lot located in Augusta.

Sometime in either 1858 or 1859, a white resident by the name of Richard Maher purchased the property in question. Maher had secretly bought the land on behalf of Peter Johnson. Maher, like George Cally in the Mirault property case, had agreed to take legal title to the lot but, at the same time, to hold the property in trust for Peter Johnson and his family. In their ruling in the *Planters'* litigation, the state's high court recounted how the 1819 amendment to the 1818 state law had retained the restriction against landownership by free blacks in Augusta and their counterparts in Savannah and Darien. Pursuant to the state statute, blacks residing in the three named Georgia cities could neither purchase land nor could they hold a legal or an equitable interest in any real estate. Unlike the Mirault heirs who lost their Savannah real estate to William Swoll, Martha Johnson of Augusta prevailed in the litigation filed by her children.[26] The justices emphasized the fact that Martha had remained in possession of the land until 1878. Aspasia's heirs moved to another Savannah location in 1866, allowing Henry Roggenstein to rent the property and allowing Cally to collect the rent. According to the Supreme Court of Georgia, evidence that Martha Johnson had taken action to protect her interest in the Augusta property distinguished her from the Mirault heirs. During October 1866, Martha secured a deed to the property from Maher, the titleholder, and she recorded the deed in her name. Later, in June 1878, Martha sold the property to W. M. Wilkerson, and, in spite of the fact that her children objected to the sale, the high court took into account Martha's previous actions to claim the property as her own.[27]

In their judicial opinion that rejected the children's claim to the Johnson property, the justices of Supreme Court of Georgia referenced the 1818 statute. From the court's standpoint Martha Johnson had overcome any disabilities that might have accrued to her from the statutory scheme by securing a deed to the property. Identical to the Aspasia-Cally secret trust, the pre–Civil War property arrangement between Maher and Peter Johnson was null and void. Only Martha Johnson's actions following the statute's repeal had protected her claim to the property. As the new legal titleholder, Martha Johnson's entitlement to the property was good against all claimants, including her children.[28]

During the 1884 September court term, two years after issuing their ruling in the *Planters'* case, the justices of the Supreme Court of Georgia once again revisited the issue of prewar trust agreements involving free people of color. In *Beatty v. Benton*, an 1854 deed conveyed an Augusta lot to one Robertson, a white man, for use by a free black family. Like the Aspasia-Cally agreement in Savannah and the Johnson-Maher arrangement in Augusta, Robertson held legal title to the property in trust for a group of African Americans. Thomas Gardner and his wife, Fanny, both free blacks, supplied the money for the lot purchased by Robertson. Following Thomas Gardner's death, Fanny and Frances Beatty, who was Thomas's daughter by a previous marriage, exchanged legal barbs over their respective rights to the property. Frances, who was already in possession of one-half of the lot, claimed her stepmother's half as well.[29]

In the *Beatty* case, the court ruled that pursuant to the 1818 statute, the 1854 deed as well as the underlying agreement between Robertson and Gardner were both void. However, Fanny Gardner and Frances Beatty were more fortunate than the Mirault heirs had been with their litigation six years earlier. The court awarded the women ownership of their respective one-half shares of the property. The court reached that result owing to the fact that both women had remained in possession of the lot since 1854. In addition, because the state had never escheated the property in the period before the Civil War, the women's respective one-half portions of the lot were deemed by the court to be good against the claims of all others.[30]

Unlike the Mirault property case where Cally, the trustee, lost the property that was later purchased by Swoll, the *Beatty* litigation involved no *bona fide* purchaser with a valid claim to the lot. The *Beatty* matter pitted one family member against another. Even the state of Georgia had neglected to exercise its escheat powers under the 1818 statute. By the time of the 1884 trial in the *Beatty* case, litigants Gardner and Beatty had successfully survived all potential disabilities under the repealed statute. The court was confident that it had rendered a just solution in the *Beatty* case. The court noted that cases with fact patterns similar to *Beatty* "should be adjudicated under broad views of natural equity."[31]

Yet, six years earlier in 1878, the Mirault heirs had not been as fortunate during the course of their litigation. The high court's failure to ensure a just resolution to the Mirault case provided a sorrowful epitaph to the life and labors of one resourceful Savannah woman. Beginning in the 1820s, a young enterprising pastry cook had aspired to own a business and to purchase a piece of real estate. Over the years, Aspasia worked hard to secure a future for herself and her children. Even the occurrence of her widowhood did not impede Aspasia's determination to get ahead. In due time, she built a thriving bakery business. Scores of patrons frequented her establishment on the corner of Broughton and Bull Streets. Aspasia earned a reputation as a well-respected business person and a welcomed member of the Savannah community. Beyond her business accomplishments, Aspasia raised a family of two sons and two daughters. Toward the end of her life, Aspasia provided a home for her orphaned grandchildren. The family residence, a three-story brick house on the corner of Whitaker and Macon Streets in the Pulaski Ward section of the city, served as a structural testament to Aspasia's hard work and sacrifice.

Aspasia Cruvellier Mirault, a proud family matriarch and a successful Savannah entrepreneur, had done much to define her own reality within nineteenth-century southern society. In the years before her death in 1857, she probably looked back on her work with considerable pride and satisfaction. Little did she realize that the burdens and disabilities attached to race in America would undermine substantial portions of her labor. To their credit, Aspasia's heirs tried to preserve her legacy. By filing their *Bill of Complaint* in October 1874 with the clerk of the Superior Court of Chatham County, her son and three of her grandchildren launched a valiant effort to reclaim the fruits of Aspasia's lifelong labors. Several years later the justices of the Supreme Court of Georgia stripped Aspasia's family of their property. In the final analysis, an unexpected betrayal by a once-trusted confidant coupled with the discriminatory designs of Georgia lawmakers had effectively defeated Aspasia's efforts to pass on a valuable inheritance to her children. Nonetheless, the activities of Aspasia and other Cruvellier and Mirault family members, all those decades ago, still provide important lessons through the retelling of their story.

Epilogue

The question remains, what notable events transpired in the lives of the litigants and their families in the years following the *Oliver v. Swoll* trial? Defendant William Swoll appears to have taken his legal triumph in stride. Fresh from his victory over the Mirault heirs and the estate of George Cally, Swoll wasted little time in disposing of what by that time he must have considered a troublesome piece of property. In 1880, soon after the court awarded him the property, Swoll found a willing buyer for lot 22 in Pulaski Ward. For the sum of $4,000, Adam and Anna Kessel, a white couple, purchased the property and residence that Aspasia and her family had once called home. The Kessels, bakers by profession, would operate a business at the location for many years. By the time that the Kessels purchased the property, the lot had already been the location of two bakeries for nearly three decades. The first bakery was operated by Aspasia and the second by Henry Roggenstein. The selling price of the Mirault house and lot netted Swoll a profit of $2,800. Eight years earlier in 1872, Swoll's bid at the city auction combined with his payments for back taxes and insurance had totaled nearly $1,200. His perseverance through the litigation and appeal to the Supreme Court of Georgia paid off handsomely with a profitable sale.[1]

Because the Kessels could not afford to pay the full purchase price, they contracted an indenture agreement with Savannah resident Jacob Quint, who loaned them the money they needed. On August 6, 1880, Adam Kessel and Quint signed the contract, giving Quint temporary title to the lot and also setting up a repayment schedule. Over the succeeding four years, the Kessels retired the loan with annual payments of $1,250 at a 7 percent rate of interest. The Kessel-Quint contract was subject to a recently enacted state law in 1871, setting forth strict guidelines for parties contracting real estate loans. In order for such agreements to be enforceable against a married couple, the contract required approval from both the husband and his wife. Anna Kessel was interviewed separately from her husband to ascertain her approval of the loan. Ironically, William D. Harden, one of Swoll's attorneys in the *Oliver v. Swoll* litigation and the presiding judge of the Savannah City Court, conducted Anna's interview and notarized her signature. On August 16 she fixed her signature to a document that read:

> I, Anna Kessel, wife of Adam Kessel, do hereby consent, ratify, and approve, the foregoing deed which is given to secure the payment of money borrowed and expended in paying for the above premises.[2]

The Kessels repaid the loan and took title to the property. Over a decade later during the late 1890s, the Kessels still lived at the residence, listed as 321 Whitaker Street.[3]

His victory in the Mirault property litigation was just one in a series of fortunate experiences for Swoll. Over the succeeding decade, he continued to accumulate considerable wealth, social status, and influence. On an evening in mid-April 1879, Swoll and other stockholders of the Chatham Mutual Loan Association held their fourth annual meeting to elect officers for the ensuing year. As a director of the association, Swoll managed the election process along with co-directors D. C. Bacon, Herman Myers, F. J. Ruckner, J. W. Fretwell, and Thomas Daniels. It is very likely that Swoll's initial affiliation with Chatham Mutual may have been at the behest of his friend and former attorney William D. Harden, who served as the group's secretary and solicitor.[4]

Coupled with his financial good fortune, Swoll became a fixture within Savannah's more influential circles. He was an active member of Georgia's Democratic Party. During the summer of 1876, just months before the nation went to the polls to elect a new chief executive, Swoll worked with the local executive committee supporting the party's national ticket with candidates Samuel J. Tilden from New York for president and Thomas A. Hendricks from Indiana for vice president.[5] Apart from his political activities, Swoll's day-to-day responsibilities as a Savannah city official were extensive. When a few horses developed the debilitating and ultimately fatal glanders disease, Swoll, as the contractor and representative for the city, investigated the illness together with three veterinarians, D. M. Demison, William Wallace, and B. Ferrier. In late August 1874, Swoll and the other investigators presented their findings to the city marshal. They recommended that two sick animals should be removed from the city before they contaminated other horses.[6] On another occasion, demonstrating his civic and Irish pride, Swoll joined the Hibernian Society. He attended a special meeting held at the Metropolitan Hall on January 9, 1878, when the group planned Savannah's upcoming St. Patrick's Day celebration.[7]

When William Swoll died on June 4, 1887, he left his widow, Maria, and their three daughters a substantial inheritance. In accordance with Swoll's will, Maria received her dower interest, a life estate in all the real estate owned by her husband. The estate, consisting of twenty parcels of land as well as a cemetery plot, made Maria Swoll a wealthy woman. The holdings included valuable lots located in four Savannah wards, including Choctaw, Washington, Anson, and Springhill. At the time of Swoll's death, only two of the lots were encumbered with outstanding mortgages. Maria inherited the couple's residence on Barnard Street, their house furnishings, and a considerable amount of personal property, including horses, mules, wagons, tools, and cash money.[8] Maria survived her husband by fourteen years, and at her death in February 1901, the estate passed to her daughters, Margaret A. Winn, Sarah Francis Cheatham, and Wilhelmina Sawyer.[9]

Although Swoll remained a Savannah resident until the end of his life, Judge Henry Tompkins eventually relocated to another Georgia city. But before leaving Savannah, Tompkins completed a seven-year-long tenure on the Chatham County Superior Court bench. Following his issuance of the final decree in the *Oliver v. Swoll* case in May 1878, Tompkins concluded the final year of his inaugural four-year term as a trial judge. The next year in 1879, he secured a reappointment for three additional years. But in 1882 amidst the statewide post–Reconstruction-era political turmoil that culminated in the election of Alexander H. Stephens as governor, Tompkins relinquished his judgeship to A. Pratt Adams. Judge Adams remained on the bench for six years until 1889.[10] Tompkins was no longer a judge, but he nonetheless enjoyed a distinguished career as an attorney and respected member of the Georgia Bar Association. One might wonder if Tompkins saw relinquishing his judicial post as the incentive he needed to pull up his roots in Savannah and move to Atlanta. Tompkins was thirty-seven years of age and still in the prime of his life when he relinquished his judgeship.[11]

During the summer of 1885, Tompkins, by that time an Atlanta resident, attended the Second Annual Meeting of the Georgia Bar Association. The conclave of lawyers met on August 5 and 6 in the city's Fulton County courtroom.[12] Attorneys traveled to Atlanta from many parts of the state to attend the series of meetings. The bar association president, W. M. Reese, a resident of Washington, Georgia, called the opening session to order. Savannah attorneys were well represented at the convention. The several delegates from Savannah included Rufus E. Lester, who along with William D. Harden had represented Swoll in the *Oliver v. Swoll* case. Back in 1878, Lester laid his other business aside and traveled from Savannah to Atlanta where he presented Swoll's arguments to the high court. Besides his law practice, Lester's career included several stints in the political arena. He served as a state senator in the Georgia legislature during the Reconstruction era, and he was a three-term mayor of Savannah. Lester's three terms as mayor ran consecutively from 1883 through 1889; each individual term lasted two years. Among a number of other well-known delegates to the Georgia Bar Association in 1885 was Hoke Smith, an Atlanta resident, who would serve two terms as Georgia's governor during the early part of the twentieth century.[13]

Tompkins's judicial experience coupled with his stellar reputation among his peers netted him a coveted position on the bar association's prestigious Committee for Judicial Administration and Remedial Procedure. Besides

Tompkins, the other committee members included bar association president Reese; Henry Jackson and John Milledge, both from Atlanta; and J. W. Atkins, a resident of Cartersville.[14] Apart from his committee work, Tompkins more than likely also voiced his opinion during the association's general meeting sessions. During one such session, the delegates debated the pros and cons of raising the standards for admission to the practice of law. While there were dissenters, the bulk of the delegates conceded that the time had come for Georgia to follow the lead of many of her sister states by including a written examination as part of the entry process.[15] Tompkins maintained his attendance at the Georgia Bar Association meetings over the years. While there is no record that the group met in 1887, membership rosters of the annual conventions for the years of 1888 through 1891, all provide evidence of Tompkins's sustained loyalty to this professional organization.[16]

William D. Harden, one of Swoll's attorneys, also prospered in the years following the Mirault property litigation. Although he had lost his bid to become a judge on the Chatham County Superior Court in 1875 to Henry Tompkins, the victorious candidate, Harden was ultimately successful in securing an appointment to the bench. For many years, he served with distinction as the judge of the City Court of Savannah. During the Mirault case in 1878, Harden maintained a hectic schedule, working simultaneously as a member of Swoll's legal team and as the city's presiding judge.

On May 14, 1878, the same day that Tompkins announced his final degree in the Mirault case, Harden was obliged to leave Tompkins's courtroom and go directly to his judicial chambers at the city court. Later that afternoon, Harden, in his capacity as judge, presided over two criminal cases. In the matter of the city's prosecution of Joseph Stephens, a black man accused of larceny and the theft of fourteen dollars, Harden ruled that Stephens was innocent. The second criminal defendant to appear before Harden that afternoon was not quite as fortunate. Harden found George Lowe, a white man, guilty of stealing three turkeys from Dr. Joseph Reed as well as four chickens from Jett T. Howard. Harden sentenced Lowe to eight months in jail and a fine of twenty dollars.[17]

In spite of losing their property to William Swoll, Aspasia's heirs prospered in the years following the litigation. Mary A. Scott Jackson, Aspasia's granddaughter, and her husband, Albert Jackson, would undoubtedly be considered a nineteenth-century African American success story. Jackson plied his considerable skills first as a bookkeeper and by 1877 as a partner in the Jackson and Johnson cotton brokerage firm. Although his 1901 obituary that appeared in the *Savannah Tribune* referenced his studies at the Harvard Institute in Boston, Massachusetts, no surviving evidence has surfaced to verify either his matriculation or his graduation. But with or without a formal education, the Jackson family members found financial good fortune. Over the years following the Mirault property trial and appeal to the Georgia Supreme Court, the Jackson couple accumulated valuable real estate holdings while, at the same time, they operated their business.

Over the years, the Jackson family moved numerous times, on each successive occasion to a larger home within the city of Savannah. The couple began their married life in Albert's house on Taylor Street. By 1877 a year before the trial began, Mary and Albert Jackson resided on Price Street at the corner of Harris. Five years later, in 1882, they had moved to a larger house at 59 Charlton Street, only a few blocks from Aspasia's property on Whitaker and Macon Streets.[18] These residential moves coincided with the growth of their family unit. Mary brought a daughter and Albert brought two sons from their respective former marriages to their marital union in 1874. Their marriage produced three additional offspring: Joseph, Sidney, and May joined their half-siblings, Mary Louisa Scott, John Wesley Jackson, and Albert Jackson Jr., to round out the Jackson family circle.[19]

Their growing family mirrored the growth of their business venture and for Albert the growth of his civic involvement. The cotton brokerage firm of Johnson and Jackson sustained itself within the Savannah business environment at its Bay Street location near the Savannah wharf. Albert Jackson found a stalwart and upstanding business partner in John M. Johnson. Although there is some evidence that Johnson may have been a slave, logic dictates that Johnson was probably a free black man. W. W. Lincoln was very likely Johnson's guardian, not his owner. Whatever his status during the antebellum years, Johnson's rise from a porter to an entrepreneur within five short years demonstrated his skill and his ambition. In 1865, Johnson was a forty-nine-year-old laborer with a wife named Mary Anne and eight children. That year Johnson opened a savings account at the Freedmen's Bank while working as a porter at W. W. Lincoln's Drug Store. The 1870 census lists Johnson's occupation as a junk dealer, but the city directory indicates that he had formed what must have been an unusual interracial business arrangement with David J. Deas, a white commission merchant for cotton farmers. Perhaps Johnson held two jobs for a time. Deas and Johnson paid for a quarter-page advertisement in the city directory for 1870. Their ad announced that they were cotton factors and commission merchants with an establishment located at 206 Bay Street between Barnard and Jefferson Streets.[20]

Sometime in 1871 or 1872, Albert Jackson brought his bookkeeping skills to the Deas and Johnson establishment. Then when Deas died sometime in 1873, Johnson and Jackson formed a partnership and launched their own cotton brokerage in Savannah.[21] The Johnson and Jackson firm, the only African American establishment of its kind in the city, found a niche in that competitive but lucrative market. To be sure, cotton was big business in Savannah at the end of the nineteenth century. Besides Johnson and Jackson, ten other cotton-buying firms were listed in the city directory for 1882. The following year, two additional firms made their appearance, bringing the number of Savannah's cotton brokerage houses to thirteen.[22]

Although its business records did not survive, it is likely that the Johnson and Jackson firm did the bulk of its business with black farmers. In the postwar South, agriculture, and especially cotton production, took on added importance as a means for reviving the southern economy. Yet the rancor of racial politics under the Democrat- Redeemer state governments did not lend itself to the support of black entrepreneurial efforts either in agriculture or agricultural support establishments like cotton brokers, such as the Jackson and Johnson firm. White planters with farms in the black belt of Georgia and other states pressured lawmakers to pass lien laws and other pieces of antilabor legislation to control their black labor force.[23] Growing racial tensions in the region discouraged white planters from doing business with black entrepreneurs. At the same time, the number of black landowners slowly increased after the war. Those black farmers would have been the likely patrons of the Jackson and Johnson establishment. While some blacks took advantage of the federal government's Southern Homestead Act of 1866, others relied upon their own resources to acquire farmland. As a result, African Americans in Georgia owned more that 350,000 acres of land by 1874.[24]

John M. Johnson's death during 1884 signaled an end to the business partnership, but not an end to the firm's success. Albert Jackson's announcement in the *Savannah Morning News* provided notice that while the firm of Johnson and Jackson had been dissolved with the death of Johnson on October 6, the business of the former firm would continue under Jackson's leadership.[25] The business assumed a family-oriented character as members of the Jackson family joined Albert in operating the firm and in filling the void left by Johnson's death. Mary worked alongside her husband, and their eldest son, Albert Jr., joined the business. By the mid-1890s, May and Sidney, the two youngest of the Jackson children, had joined the family enterprise.[26] May assumed more of a managerial role in the business as her parents aged. In an era when Victorian values dictated that middle-class white women remain domesticated and when their black counterparts, burdened by both race and gender biases, crusaded for women's rights and racial uplift, May Jackson eclipsed prevailing stereotypical roles to become a principal proprietor of the Johnson and Jackson firm and a leader in the business community.[27]

The Jackson couple became black community stalwarts in Savannah during the last three decades of the nineteenth century. By his involvement in a wide variety of organizations, charities, and civic projects, Albert Jackson distinguished himself as a community leader. He spearheaded an effort to create a black benevolent society that labored to assist victims of the 1876 yellow fever epidemic. In April 1884, Albert Jackson was one of eighteen men —and likely the only African American—selected that year to serve on a federal grand jury. Jackson, who worked as a bookkeeper in the early 1870s, joined fellow Savannah citizens—Thomas H. Cassels, a white bookkeeper; Alex McNulty, a white advertising clerk at the local newspaper; and Andrew Gilbert, another white clerk—to review evidence on several maritime-related cases involving seamen's wages.[28]

Albert Jackson died in 1901, and his will left evidence of his intelligence and wisdom. Years of shrewd real estate and financial investments combined with the sound management of his cotton brokerage firm provided the Jackson family with a very comfortable lifestyle. Albert left his youngest son, Sidney, a gold watch and chain, and he directed his will executors to give five hundred dollars to his sister Maria. His widow, Mary, and their four children received the remainder of his real and personal property. Besides the family residence on Charlton Street, Albert's estate included several other houses as well as a variety of securities. Albert instructed his executors to exhaust all the proceeds of his life insurance policy as well as the money in his bank accounts to provide a monthly allowance of twenty dollars each for his wife and daughter. Secondly, Albert wanted his executors to reinvest the income from his investments into real estate as a means to enhance the long-term financial security of his family.[29]

Albert Jackson's will contained provisions for the education of his two youngest children. When the elder Jackson drafted and signed his last will and testament at the end of March 1900, Sidney had already enrolled in college, and, thus, the will bequest guaranteed that the young man would have sufficient funds to complete his education. According to the provision, "[a]lso if my son Sidney should not have graduated my estate shall furnish the means to finish his college course." Sidney had several choices for his college studies. Because his aunt Maria Jackson, Albert Sr.'s younger sister, worked as an instructor at the local Georgia State Industrial Institute in Savannah, Sidney might have stayed in his home city and received his college education. For another option, Sidney might have followed in the footsteps of older brother Albert Jr., who earned his undergraduate degree at Hampton Institute in Virginia. Instead, Sidney attended Johnson C. Smith College in Charlotte, North Carolina.[30] Sidney and Albert Jr. were not the only children of Albert and Mary Jackson to receive an education. Albert made a specific bequest for the education of his daughter Cecilia May, known as May. May was already working in her father's firm and presumably well on her way toward a career in the cotton brokerage business when Jackson instructed his executors to have his daughter, "properly and usefully educated, having in view some useful employment by which she may earn a livelihood."[31]

Aspasia Mirault would have been pleased if she had witnessed the postwar family unity that existed among her descendants. As the most financially secure of all of Aspasia's heirs, Mary and Albert Jackson were especially generous with their time and resources in assisting other family members. When she purchased a Savannah lot in 1842, Aspasia gave her children and grandchildren a model for emulation. To be sure, Aspasia's granddaughter Mary and her husband recognized the value of landownership. The couple had already acquired several pieces of real estate by the early 1870s, and they helped other relatives buy property. In 1875, Albert held joint ownership of lot 20 in Bartow Ward with Robert Low, Albert's former brother-in-law and a fellow Confederate bandsman of Robert Oliver. Low was the half-brother of Albert's deceased first wife, Jeannette Bulloch Jackson. Low was also related to Mary Jackson through marriage. Josephine Mirault, Low and Jeannette's mother, was related to Aspasia's husband, Samuel Mirault. Many decades earlier Aspasia had employed Josephine in her bakery shop on Broughton and Bull Streets. Concerning the joint real estate venture between Albert and Low, it is likely that Low, as a first-time buyer, needed Albert's financial assistance to purchase the Bartow property. According to Chatham County records, Low held title to the southern portion of the lot while Albert owned the northern portion.[32]

Extending a helping hand and wise counsel to Louisa Williams Burton, Mary's little sister, probably gave the Jackson couple considerable satisfaction. Louisa and her husband, Tillman Burton, had enjoyed nine years of married life when Tillman died on March 30, 1881.[33] Two months after Burton's funeral, Louisa completed her application for a Widow's Year Support at the Chatham County Courthouse. It is not surprising that the Court of the Ordinary appointed Albert, Louisa's brother-in-law, together with two family friends and relations through marriage, Cyrus Campfield and Richard J. Artson, to serve as the administrators and appraisers for the Burton estate. Campfield, a jeweler, and Artson, a carpenter, were brothers-in-law and the husbands of Simon Mirault's daughters, Laura and Rose. These two African American artisans practiced their respective trades at 41 Whitaker Street. Under Georgia law, widows, such as Louisa, were entitled to money from their deceased husband's assets. The Widow's Year Support provision ensured that widows had an adequate amount of financial support over the period of time—usually one year—that it might take to settle the deceased's estate.[34]

Not long after Louisa's application for the widow's support had been approved, Albert and the others notified the court that Burton's lot, labeled as Letter E in Mercer Ward and valued at $500, should be set aside to provide Louisa with twelve months of maintenance and support. Four years later, in 1885, the appraisers informed the court that their initial work contained an error. Albert amended the record to reflect the correct location as the northeast triangle of lot 70 in Mercer Ward and the southeast triangle of Fraction B of Garden lot 58.[35] In the meantime, Louisa had begun making changes in her life that she likely deemed to be more suitable to her status as a widow. She moved from the Hall Street home that she had shared for nearly a decade with her late husband to the Charlton Street residence with her sister, brother-in-law, and their children. She maintained her career as a seamstress at the new residence.[36]

The circle of family and friends shared many joyous occasions as well as sorrowful occasions. Cyrus Campfield and his wife, Laura Mirault Campfield, provided encouragement and support to Louisa Williams when her husband died; in turn Louisa and other members of Aspasia Mirault's family were among the invited guests who joined the Campfield couple to celebrate the wedding of their daughter Lucy. With the Reverend J. J. Andrew of St. Stephen's Episcopal Church officiating, Lucy became the bride of George O. Price. The wedding took place on Tuesday evening, December 29, 1889, at the Campfield's residence on Jones Street. A few years later, another wedding brought the family members together in celebration. Mary L. Scott, the daughter of Mary A. Scott Jackson and the stepdaughter of Albert Jackson, wed James F. W. Moore, a Savannah barber. According to the *Savannah Tribune* reporter who covered the event, "the bride was most charmingly attired in cream crepe de chine en train, trimmed in chiffon lace and lilies of the valley." Joseph L. Mirault, a cousin of the bride's mother, served as the groomsman. For her attendants, the bride selected a friend, Lizzie Erwin, and her little sister May, the latter being the maid of honor. Both the wedding and reception took place at the Jackson residence on Charlton Street.[37]

Charles B. Stiles, who remained close to his two half-sisters, Mary and Louisa, probably attended the festive nuptials for his niece Mary. Besides their close relationship that extended throughout their lives, Charles had something in common with his siblings. Like Louisa and Mary, Charles too had lost his spouse through death. Jessie L. Stiles, died in 1874, around the same time that Charles and other family members were filing court documents to reclaim Aspasia's Whitaker Street property.[38] Because of his strong ties to his grandmother's house that had been his home since childhood, Charles must have been determined to preserve both the family inheritance and Aspasia's legacy. Both during and after his involvement in the *Oliver v. Swoll* litigation, Charles continued to practice his trade as a bricklayer.[39]

Charles was a Savannah resident all of his life. Throughout the 1878 trial and the appeal when his presence was required in Judge Tompkins's courtroom, he traveled to the Chatham County Court from his home on Southville Street.[40] During the course of the family's litigation, Charles remarried. His new bride was Annie B. Smith. Sometime after the litigation had been concluded, Charles moved to a house on St. James Street, near Habersham, where he and Annie raised Camille, his daughter by his first wife. Charles and Annie would have five children of their own, including two boys, Charles Jr. and Howard, and three girls, Geneva, Theodosia, and Annie. By the early 1890s, Charles had relocated his growing family to a residence at 404 First East Street.[41] There was standing room only on the afternoon of Wednesday, July 10, 1898, when two cousins, Geneva Letitia, Charles's daughter, and May, the daughter of Mary and Albert Jackson, performed in a piano recital. Geneva and May were two of the five budding pianists and music students of Alice M. Ellis, a music teacher who taught children to play the piano at her home on

East McDonough Street. May performed "Gallop" in a duet with her teacher. One of Geneva's solo selections was entitled "Missionary Ridge."[42]

Charles Sr., the master brick mason and grandson of Aspasia Mirault, died in 1905, but he lived to see his children grow to adulthood. In 1900, daughter Camille was working as seamstress, while her brother Charles Jr. had followed in his father's footsteps to become a brick mason. That same year, their three younger sisters were students in the local school, and their older brother Howard had learned the wheelwright trade.[43] Likely having grown dissatisfied with making wheels, Howard switched occupations four years later and began a career as a letter carrier delivering mail for the city of Savannah. A secure government job and the exercise of his citizenship rights characterized the life and times of Howard, who like his two cousins, Sidney Jackson and Robert Low, signed the voter registration roster for District 4 in 1904.[44]

The post-Mirault trial life of lead petitioner Robert Oliver is difficult to trace. Did Aspasia's son die or move away from the city of his birth in the years following the litigation? The extant record leaves few clues as to his whereabouts. While several of his relatives, including all three of the other Mirault family litigants, left records of property tax payments or were listed in the annually published Savannah city directory, no such records have survived for Robert Oliver. The single entry for Robert was a listing in the 1870 city directory, a full eight years before the Mirault trial began. According to that listing, Robert resided in a house on the corner of East Broad and South Broad Lane and was laboring as a bricklayer.[45]

For Oliver, it is likely that the post-trial appeal may have been a particularly troubling episode that weighed heavily on the mind of Aspasia's only surviving son. He may have pinned his hopes on the judicial system's ability to deliver a victory for his family. When the Supreme Court of Georgia reversed the favorable jury verdict, this turn of events may have constituted a crushing blow for Robert. He may have decided to abandon his Savannah roots and move his wife and children to another city. Alternatively, the occasion of his death may be the correct scenario to explain his sudden disappearance from the historical record.

While Robert's post-litigation activities remain a mystery, there is surviving evidence pointing to a change in residence for one of his children. The 1880 census lists a twenty-four-year-old Robert Oliver living in the nearby city of Augusta, Georgia. The age of this Augusta resident makes him a prime candidate to have been Robert Ward Oliver, Robert's son, Aspasia's grandson, and the godson of the former Savannah mayor John Ward. Eschewing the brick masonry trade of his father, the younger Robert lived on Ellis Street in Augusta and supported his wife, Alice, and their two young children, Edward and Amey, with his work as a shoemaker.[46]

If the elder Robert Oliver died soon after the court battle waged to reclaim Aspasia's property, then his epitaph would have been a tribute to a well-lived life, one that included a number of notable accomplishments. Having mastered a musical instrument as a teenager, Robert put that talent to good use years later when he secured successive positions in two Confederate army band units. Following the Civil War, Robert returned home to his wife and children, and he resumed his occupation as a skilled brick mason. When the Mirault family members discovered that a resort to the judicial system was necessary, Robert rallied the family unit, hired an attorney, and filed court documents to reclaim their valuable inheritance.

Those noteworthy deeds would not be forgotten. In fact, Robert's activities likely served as a source of pride and inspiration to succeeding generations. Five decades later, one of Robert's descendants, a W. H. Oliver who was at the time residing in Macon, Georgia, penned a letter to the Department of Confederate Pensions and Records in Atlanta, requesting a certified copy of Robert's Confederate army service record. State officials acknowledged the inquiry and honored Oliver's request in a letter postmarked December 15, 1936.[47]

A descendant's request for information about a service record corresponds with the historical search for information about black people and the Confederacy. Robert Oliver's service as a musician in the Confederate army and the labors of his cousins, Simon Mirault Jr., Robert Low, and others who volunteered to build military fortifications, provide an additional footnote to Civil War history. The wartime experiences of Aspasia's family members and other African Americans who lived in Savannah open a window for inquiry about the nature of their lives under Confederate rule.

As in the case of black Confederates who remain obscure so too are the untold story of blacks who asserted their citizenship rights during the postbellum decades. After the war, many African Americans tested their newfound freedoms. Having recently acquired their citizenship and the franchise under the Fourteenth and Fifteenth Amendments to the U.S. Constitution, black people, including the Mirault family members, took bold steps to exercise those rights and privileges previously enjoyed by whites. Blacks voted, entered places of public accommodation, sought seats on jury panels, and turned to the judicial system to rectify injustices.[48] The recounting of individual attempts to assert citizenship rights enhances our knowledge of black ambition during the postbellum era. Those times were ripe for making changes in race relations and for dispensing justice. Seeking a portion of that justice, Aspasia's family entered the judicial arena. When they filed their lawsuit against George Cally in 1874, Aspasia's relatives took their places among the thousands of other African Americans who tested their rights in court. The recounting of the *Oliver v. Swoll* litigation chronicles one African American family's experiences in opposing race-based conventions that postponed the creation of a new social order.

Lastly, the story of Aspasia Cruvellier Mirault constitutes a small segment in an unfolding account of free women of color in the antebellum South. The lives of many black women have been lost to history. Far too many of these women have precious few surviving private papers to illuminate their experiences. Yet, through the recounting of their lives, Aspasia and others like her allow us to bridge the knowledge gap about black southern womanhood. As a free woman of color living in a society designed for only two groups, free whites and black slaves, Aspasia managed to define her own destiny and through it all she achieved a degree of notoriety, especially among her descendants. Mary Scott Jackson, Aspasia's granddaughter, was known for her culinary skills. The Jackson descendants have always attributed Mary's skills to Aspasia, and they have passed down the information that Mary's family owned the best French bakery in Savannah. That bakery belonged to Aspasia.[49] When death deprived her first of one and then a second male partner, Aspasia persevered. She raised her children, established a bakery business, and constructed a home. Deftly, she cultivated important relationships across racial lines and among her own racial group. Emulating her example, Aspasia's children and grandchildren achieved varying degrees of financial independence and civic engagement. As a strong matriarch and as a notable contributor to her community, Aspasia's story and the stories of others like her provide new perspectives on black female experiences and achievements in antebellum America and beyond.

Appendix

Members of the *Oliver v. Swoll* Jury, 1878:

Frank Campbell (William F. Campbell), tinner, residence Bryan near Farm.

D. Lopez Cohen, carpenter and builder on Drayton and Harris, a boarder at 103 Macon.

Joseph M. Foreman, clerk 124 Bay, boarder at 19 Broughton, selected as foreman of the jury.

James P. H. Garrett, conductor, Savannah Skidway & Seaboard Railroad.

John D. Hill, clerk, residence 64 Bryan.

George S. Marshall, shipbrokers and commissioners (Theodore B. Marshall & Brothers, 107 Bay), residence 170 Liberty.

D. F. Maxwell, clerk 88 Bay, residence 108 Taylor.

George J. Mills, money broker at Planters Bank Building, residence on Hall Street and corner of Abercorn.

William G. Morrell, rice brokers (Pritchard & Morrell [G. B. Pritchard]), residence 124 James Street.

Florence Joseph J. Morris, retail grocery, business and residence 4 Price Street.

Frank Winter, clerk at H. Bryan establishment, residence 158 Liberty Street.

Thomas B. Turner, piano tuner, 134 State, boarder at 108 S. Broad Street.

Sources: *Savannah City Directories*, 1876 and 1877.

Notes

Prologue

1. Carol Ruth Berkin and Mary Beth Norton, *Women of America, A History* (Boston: Houghton Mifflin Company, 1979), 38, 139; Paula Giddings, *When and Where I Enter: The Impact of Black Women on Race and Sex in America* (New York: Bantam Books, 1984), 46–47.

2. Darlene Clark Hine, *The African-American Odyssey* (Upper Saddle River, NJ: Prentice-Hall, 2003), 151–53; John Hope Franklin, *From Slavery to Freedom: A History of Negro Americans* (New York: Alfred A. Knopf, 1988), 138–43.

Chapter One: The Cruvelliers in Savannah

1. F. D. Lee and J. L. Agnew, *Historical Record of the City of Savannah* (Savannah, GA: J. H. Estill, Morning News Steam Power Press, 1869), 132. Throughout the month of March in 1842, Savannah newspapers carried advertisements by local merchants selling spring and summer clothing. For example, see an advertisement placed by James J. Webb & Company in the *Daily Georgian*, March 20, 1842. The various historical records used in the research provided numerous spellings for Aspasia's surnames. Alternate spellings for Cruvellier included Crouvellier, Crevellier, Crivelier, and Cuvillier. Mirault was spelled Mero, Mirat, and Merault.

2. Pursuant to a city ordinance, section 37, passed on March 14, 1839, lots in Pulaski Ward were laid out and numbered in sequence from lot number seventeen to thirty-eight, inclusive. *The Savannah City Code: Comprising the Statutes and Ordinances relating to the City of Savannah* (Savannah, GA: George B. Clarke, 1871), 103–5.

3. The 1818 Georgia property statute appears in Lucius Q. C. Lamar, ed., *A Compilation of the Laws of the State of Georgia, 1810–1819* (Augusta, GA: W. S. Hannon, 1821), 815. Whittington B. Johnson, *Black Savannah, 1788–1864* (Fayetteville: University of Arkansas Press, 1996), 37–40.

4. Ira Berlin, *Slaves without Masters: The Free Negro in the Antebellum South* (New York: Pantheon Books, 1974), 8, 90, 91.

5. Ibid., 285–86; Kenneth Coleman, ed., *A History of Georgia* (Athens: University of Georgia Press, 1977), 185–86.

6. Details of the dilemma Aspasia Mirault faced in 1842 are set forth in the lawsuit brought by her son and grandchildren in 1878 to reclaim the property. See *Swoll et al. v. Oliver et al.*, 61 Ga. 248 (1878).

7. It was not unusual for white guardians to aid their black wards in the purchase of land. This happened in the case of one of Aspasia's contemporaries, Henry

Cunningham. James Morrison, Cunningham's guardian, purchased property and deeded it to him. See Johnson, *Black Savannah*, 76.

8. Berlin, *Slaves without Masters*, 33, 93–96.

9. Ibid., 190–91, 316–18.

10. Oliver H. Prince, ed., *A Digest of Laws of the State of Georgia* (Milledgeville, GA: Grantland & Orme, 1822), 458.

11. Prince, *Digest of the Laws of Georgia*, 456–57.

12. Ibid., 465.

13. Lamar, *Compilation of the Laws of Georgia*, 804–5; W. McDowell Rogers, "Free Negro Legislation in Georgia before 1865," *Georgia Historical Quarterly* 16 (March 1932): 27–28; Johnson, *Black Savannah*, 50–51.

14. Winthrop D. Jordon, *White over Black: American Attitudes toward the Negro, 1550–1812* (Baltimore: Penguin Books, 1969), 382–83.

15. Ibid., 382–84; Berlin, *Slaves without Masters*, 35–36; Thomas Gamble Jr., *A History of the City Government of Savannah, Georgia from 1790–1900* (Savannah: Georgia Historical Society, 1900), 59.

16. Thomas Paul Thigpen, "Aristocracy of the Heart: Catholic Lay Leadership in Savannah, 1820–1870" (Ph.D. diss., Emory University, 1995), 569; Charles Lwanga Hoskins, *Yet with a Steady Beat: Biographies of Early Black Savannah* (Savannah, GA: Gullah Press, 2001), 61.

17. By 1810, the free black population, then numbering 108,000 persons, was the fastest growing group within the southern region. Georgia and South Carolina experienced tremendous growth in their free black populations. See Berlin, *Slaves without Masters*, 49, 93–94.

18. Ibid., 215.

19. Prince, *Digest of the Laws of Georgia*, 458–59.

20. Loren Schweninger, *Black Property Owners in the South, 1790–1915* (Chicago: University of Illinois Press, 1990), 88.

21. Thigpen, "Aristocracy of the Heart," 247; Berlin, *Slaves without Masters*, 214–15.

22. Registers of the Free Persons of Color for the City of Savannah, Chatham County, Ga., 1817–1829, 1828–1835, 1828–1847, 1837–1849, and 1860–1864 (hereafter Register of Free Persons of Color), Georgia Historical Society (hereafter GHS). The Registers list James Morrison as the guardian for Francis, Hagar, Peter, and Aspasia Cruvellier from 1817 through the mid-1820s. Lewis D. D'Lyon is listed as Justine Cruvellier's guardian. Beginning in 1828, the Register lists James B. Gaudry as Aspasia Mirault's guardian and James Morrison for Hagar Cruvellier. See Chatham County Tax Digest, 1850. The Tax Digest for 1850 lists John Ward as Aspasia Mirault's guardian.

23. See John D. Cushing, ed., *The First Laws of the State of Georgia, Part I* (Wilmington, DE: Michael Glazier, Inc., 1981), 119–20; Edward F. Sweat, "The Free Negro in Antebellum Georgia" (Ph.D. diss., Indiana University, 1957), 111. The 1765 act for the establishment and regulating patrol conscripted white men and women "for preventing the many dangers and inconveniences . . . from the disorderly and unlawful meetings of [N]egroes and other slaves."

24. The statute mandating public work for free blacks appears in 97. Section VII of the December 18, 1818, law. See Prince, *Digest of the Laws of Georgia*, 467;

Johnson, *Black Savannah*, 40–41; Walter J. Fraser Jr., *Savannah in the Old South* (Athens: University of Georgia Press, 2003), 282.

25. See Lee, *Historical Record of the City of Savannah*, 77. The historian Whittington B. Johnson suggests that an epidemic probably motivated city officials to enact the work requirement law for free black residents. See Johnson, *Black Savannah*, 40–41.

26. Julie Winch, *Philadelphia's Black Elite: Activism, Accommodation, and the Struggle for Autonomy*, 1787–1848 (Philadelphia: Temple University Press, 1988), 15–16.

27. Prince, *Digest of the Laws of Georgia*, 466–67. Section V of the 1818 laws set forth the registration requirement. The court clerk published a list of all the registrants in the newspaper with notice that certificates would be issued if there were no objections from the public; Johnson, *Black Savannah*, 41.

28. Schweninger, *Black Property Owners*, 65.

29. Lamar, *Compilation of the Laws of Georgia*, 315.

30. *Journal of the Senate of the State of Georgia*, 1818 (Milledgeville, GA: S. & F. Grantland, 1819), 32. State senator Alfred Cuthbert, representing Chatham County, introduced the bill on November 19, 1818. It was entitled "an act supplementary to and more effectively to enforce an act prescribing the mode of manumitting slaves in the state, to prevent the emigration of free persons of color thereto, to regulate such free persons of color as now reside therein and for other purposes." Sweat, "Free Negro in Georgia," 112.

31. Thigpen, "Aristocracy of the Heart," 570.

32. Whittington B. Johnson, "Free African American Women in Savannah, 1800–1860," *Georgia Historical Quarterly* 76 (summer 1992): 262; Johnson, *Black Savannah*, 108.

33. Berlin, *Slaves without Masters*, 55.

34. According to the Register of Free Persons of Color, 1828–1835, Aspasia arrived in Savannah in 1800. For determining Aspasia's date of birth and the birth of her children and grandchildren, the U.S. Census for 1850 seems to be the most reliable. According to the census, she was fifty years old in 1850. Thus, she would have been an infant in 1800 when she arrived in Savannah with the other members of her family. For information on the black émigrés from Santo Domingo, see Johnson, *Black Savannah*, 109–11, and Berlin, *Slaves without Masters*, 35–36.

35. Hubert Herring, *A History of Latin America from the Beginnings to the Present* (New York: Alfred A. Knopf, 1972), 243–44: For a discussion of the Haitian Revolution, see Franklin, *From Slavery to Freedom*, 83–85.

36. *Columbia Museum and Savannah Advertiser*, January 21, 1800.

37. Berlin, *Slaves without Masters*, 86–90.

38. Chatham County Tax Digest, 1816; Johnson, *Black Savannah*, 79.

39. *Georgia Gazette*, November 6, 1800.

40. Chatham County Tax Digest, 1819; Thigpen, "Aristocracy of the Heart," 243. According to Thigpen, the Luis Mirault home was located in close proximity to those residences of other white leaders in the Catholic church.

41. Johnson, *Black Savannah*, 9–10.

42. Thigpen, "Aristocracy of the Heart," 216–17, 219. For information on the early history of the Catholic community in Savannah, see Mary Jane BeVard, ed.,

One Faith, One Family: The Dioceses of Savannah, 1850–2000 (Syracuse, NY: Signature Publication, 2000).

43. Thigpen, "Aristocracy of the Heart," 17, 112–13.

44. Johnson, *Black Savannah*, 109–10.

45. Thigpen, "Aristocracy of the Heart," 219–20. In his study of nineteenth-century Catholic leadership in Savannah, Thigpen documents the formation of a leadership group from several family groupings. The Miraults are named as the leading black family at St. John's Church. Family patriarch Louis Mirault sponsored numerous baptisms for black children. On July 17, 1803, he served as the godfather for the son of an enslaved woman. See Parish Register of the Church of St. John the Baptist, 1796–1816 (microfilm, GDAH (hereafter Parish Register of St. John, GDAH). The Parish Registers of the Church of St. John the Baptist for 1796–1816 and 1816–1838 are housed within the sacramental records of the archives of the Catholic dioceses of Savannah (hereafter Parish Register of St. John, courtesy Diocesan Archives).

46. Parish Register of St. John, GDAH.

47. Ibid.

48. See ibid. for the following entries: February 12, 1803, March 6, 1803, October 23, 1804, and June 4, 1807.

49. Ibid., July 17, 1803.

50. Ibid., April 4, 1812, April 11, 1814, January 21, 1815. The history of St. John's Church and the succession of priests who officiated at the church are detailed in BeVard, *One Faith, One Family*, 265.

51. Parish Register of St. John, 1816–1838, courtesy Diocesan Archives. The Reverend Joseph Stokes, an Irish priest who officiated at the marriage of Peter Cruvellier and Betsy Reding in 1818, was stationed in several Catholic missions in the United States. He went to Savannah around 1827 where he ministered until about 1832. He was later stationed in New England, and it was reported that he died a few years before the Civil War. See J. J. O'Connell, *Catholicity in the Carolinas and Georgia, Leaves of its History* (New York: D. & J. Sadlier & Company, 1878), 130–31, 231, 430.

52. Savannah newspapers printed the names of postal customers, both whites and blacks. See *Daily Georgian*, November 2, 1832. Louis Mirault received notice of a letter on February 10, 1822; his son, Simon Mirault, received a notice on May 2, 1841; Aspasia Mirault received notice of a letter, see *Daily Georgian*, December 3, 1840; Johnson, *Black Savannah*, 130.

53. *Daily Georgian*, December 3, 1819; *Daily Georgian*, December 9, 1839.

54. Johnson, *Black Savannah*, 43–44. See Chatham County Tax Digests, 1809–1831.

55. See Chatham County Tax Digest, 1810; Register of Free People of Color, 1828–1834; Johnson, *Black Savannah*, 62; Charles Lwanga Hoskins, *Out of Yamacraw and Beyond: Discovering Black Savannah* (Savannah, GA: Gullah Press, 2002), 112.

56. Johnson, "Free African American Women in Savannah," 265; Register of Free Persons of Color, 1817–1829 and 1828–1835.

57. For a discussion of African American occupations during the antebellum era, see Berlin, *Slaves without Masters*, 218–21, and Johnson, "Free African American Women in Savannah," 264–65. Register of the Free Persons of Color, 1828–1835.

58. Berlin, *Slaves without Masters*, 244–45; Loren Schweninger, *Black Property Owners*, 65–67.
59. Chatham County Tax Digest, 1816.
60. Chatham County Tax Digest, 1809–1810 and 1811.
61. Register of Free Persons of Color, 1817–1829 and 1828–1835.
62. Chatham County Tax Digests, 1819, 1820.
63. Johnson, "Free African American Women in Savannah," 266–67. For information on James Oliver's holdings, see Register of Free Persons of Color, 1828–1835.
64. Lee and Agnew, *Historical Record of the City of Savannah*, 77.
65. *Daily Georgian*, January 17, 1820.
66. William Harden, *A History of Savannah and South Georgia* (New York: Lewis Publishing Company, 1913), 288–89; *Daily Georgian*, January 17, 1820.
67. *Daily Georgian*, January 17, 1820. Philip Brasch is listed in the Chatham County Tax Digest for 1820. That year he paid a total of $4.25 in taxes of which $2.25 was paid for his three slaves and a poll tax of $2.00.
68. *Daily Georgian*, January 18, 1820.
69. Francis and Peter Cruvellier first appear on the Tax Digest rolls in 1809. Their names last appear on the rolls in 1821. See Chatham County Tax Digests.
70. Lee and Agnew, *Historical Record of the City of Savannah*, 77. On September 5, 1820, a vessel arrived from the West Indies with the yellow fever disease on board. The sickness spread until early November when it was checked.
71. Register of the Free Persons of Color, 1817–1829. Although the fate of her siblings is not indicated in the historical record, Dorrie Cruvellier continued to live in Savannah well into her adult years. During the 1850s she had become the head of her household, raising a family of three children, Oliver, Joseph, and Chevelier. See U.S. Census records for Chatham County, Ga., 1850.
72. Register of the Free Persons of Color, 1828–1835.
73. Chatham County Tax Digests, 1826, 1831.
74. Register of the Free Persons of Color, 1828–1835.
75. Ibid.
76. Record of Baptism provided courtesy of the Archives, Catholic Dioceses, Savannah, Georgia. On November 20, 1841, Louisa (Mirault) Nyall and Joseph Deberger sponsored the baptism of Jeannette Mirault, the daughter of Simon and Mary Jane Mirault. Simon was the son of Louis Mirault.
77. William Harden, *Recollections of a Long and Satisfactory Life* (New York: Negro Universities Press, 1968; reprint, William Harden, 1934), 77–78.
78. Mirault Property Case Transcript, Oliver, *Bill of Complaint*, filed in the Superior Court of Chatham County, GA., October 12, 1874, *William Swoll v. Robert Oliver* (1878), Records of the Georgia Supreme Court, Box 131, Location 111–08, case number 10161, RC 92–1–1, GDAH (hereafter Mirault Property Case Transcript). In his court documents, Robert Oliver, Aspasia's son, detailed the agreement between his mother and George Cally to purchase the lot.

Chapter Two: A Secret Trust Agreement

1. Mirault Property Case Transcript, Cally's Deed, April 29, 1842, Oliver, *Bill of Complaint*, and Oliver, *Bill of Exceptions*, filed June 26, 1878. Cally's name was also spelled "Calley" in some of the historical records used in this study.

2. Johnson, *Black Savannah*, 148.

3. U.S. Census records for Chatham County, Ga., 1850.

4. Prince, *Digest of Laws of Georgia*, 458–59.

5. Mirault Property Case Transcript, Depositions of J. J. Maurice and James S. Bowen.

6. U.S. Census records for Chatham County, Ga., 1850 and 1860.

7. Mirault Property Case Transcript, Deposition of Edward Lovell.

8. Johnson, *Black Savannah*, 42, 53.

9. See the Commercial Directory of the City of Savannah, 1848; Joseph Bancroft, *Census of the City of Savannah, relating to the trade, commerce, and mechanical arts* (Savannah, GA: Edward C. Council, printer, 1848).

10. Johnson, *Black Savannah*, 56.

11. Ibid., 56–57.

12. Commercial Directory of the City of Savannah, 1848; Harden, *Recollections*, 34.

13. Harden, *Recollections*, 34–35, 77–78; Johnson, *Black Savannah*, 56–57; Commercial Directory of the City of Savannah, 1848.

14. BeVard, *One Faith, One Family*, 265; see Parish Register of St. John, GDAH; Johnson, *Black Savannah*, 21–23.

15. Commercial Directory of the City of Savannah, 1848; City Directory for Savannah, 1858. Information about black Episcopalians in Savannah can be found in Charles Lwanga Hoskins, *Saints Stephen, Augustine and Matthew: 150 Years of Struggle, Hardship and Success* (Savannah, GA: Gullah Press, 2005), 1–2.

16. Johnson, *Black Savannah*, 8–10; Harden, *Recollections*, 26–33, 38; Commercial Directory of the City of Savannah, 1848.

17. Harden, *Recollections*, 17–20.

18. Ibid., 15, 16, 17–18.

19. Ibid., 9–10; Johnson, *Black Savannah*, 59; Commercial Directory of the City of Savannah, 1848.

20. Johnson, *Black Savannah*, 140–41; Harden, *Recollections*, 32; Commercial Directory for the City of Savannah, 1848.

21. *Daily Georgian*, March 23, 1841, to March 30, 1841. The italics appear in the advertisement.

22. Ibid.

23. Schweninger, *Black Property Owners*, 131.

24. Advertisers in the *Daily Georgian* paid $.75 or the first day and $.50 for each consecutive entry. See the *Daily Georgian*, March 30, 1841, containing the last entry of Aspasia's advertisement.

25. Harden, *Recollections*, 48–49.

26. U.S. Census records for Chatham County, Ga., 1850; Harden, *Recollections*, 49.

27. Register of Free Persons of Color, 1826 to 1835. For details about Simon Mirault's bakery establishment, see Thomas Paul Thigpen, "Aristocracy of the Heart," 247–48.

28. Simon Mirault's advertisement appeared in the *Savannah Morning News*, January 2, 1854. Charles Hardee, who resided in Savannah from 1835 and for the remainder of his life, recalled purchasing ice from the Wittberger ice house. According to Hardee, ice was cut from New England lakes and shipped to Savannah by sailing vessels. See Charles Seton Henry Hardee, *Reminiscences and Recollections of Old Savannah* (Savannah, GA: 1926), 78.

29. Schweninger, *Black Property Owners*, 131–33.
30. *Savannah Morning News*, January 31, 1854.
31. Ibid.
32. Johnson, *Black Savannah*, 80–81; Johnson, "Free African American Women in Savannah," 275.
33. Prince, *Digest of Laws of Georgia*, 456–57; see also U.S. Census records for Chatham County, Ga., 1820.
34. Schweninger, *Black Property Owners*, 104.
35. U.S. Census records for Chatham County, Ga., 1830.
36. Chatham County Tax Digests, 1835, 1836, and 1837.
37. *Daily Georgian*, July 18, 1839.
38. U.S. Census records for Chatham County, Ga., 1830; see also the Board of Health Minute Book, 1834–1839, GHS.
39. U.S. Census records for Chatham County, Ga., 1830 and 1840.
40. Aspasia had two daughters, Louisa Mirault (Nayle) and Letitia Mirault (Davis). Louisa was her oldest daughter. The extant records contain several spellings of Louisa's married name. She was listed as Louisa Mirault Nayle, and Neil, and Nayll. Letitia's married name was Davis.
41. Register of Free Persons of Color, 1828–1835; Chatham County Tax Digest, 1833.
42. Account of Robert Oliver, #1391, Registers of Signatures of Depositors in Branches of the Freedmen's Bureau Savings and Trust Company, National Archives, Washington, DC (unless otherwise indicated, the accounts referenced are contained in the Register of Signatures and Depositors); Register of Free Persons of Color, 1828–1835.
43. Johnson, *Black Savannah*, 110; Account of Charlotte Reed, #2717.
44. See the Register of Free Persons of Color, 1828–1847. James Oliver registered from 1828 through 1834. Oliver is later listed as deceased, providing a good indication that he died in 1835 or 1836.

Chapter Three: Hurricanes, Presidents, and the Death of a Matriarch

1. Mirault Property Case Transcript, Deed of George Cally, dated April 29, 1842. The deed for lot number 22 in Pulaski Ward details the lot's dimensions.
2. See Savannah, Ga., City Directory, 1858.
3. Mirault Property Case Transcript, Deposition Summary of George H. Ash.
4. Ibid. In his deposition summary, contractor George H. Ash stated that once he had completed Aspasia Mirault's home, George Cally moved into the residence with the Mirault family. See Mirault Property Case Transcript, Deposition Summary of W. H. May, where he stated that he knew Cally and the Mirault family well, and from May's observations of their interactions, he (May) assumed that Cally lived with the Miraults.
5. Mirault Property Case Transcript, Deposition Summaries of George H. Ash, J. J. Maurice, and James S. Barrow.
6. Marriage records courtesy of the Archives, Catholic Dioceses, Savannah, Georgia.
7. C. Vann Woodward, *The Strange Career of Jim Crow* (New York: Oxford University Press, 1966), 14. According to Woodward, racial segregation was neither

uniform nor complete in antebellum southern cities although blacks, slave and free, were typically excluded from most public facilities, including hotels and restaurants and public grounds.

8. Harden, *Recollections*, 80.

9. A photograph of the Forsyth Park fountain, taken by George N. Barnard in 1861, appears in Anne J. Bailey and Walter J. Fraser Jr., *Portraits of Conflict: A Photographic History of Georgia in the Civil War* (Fayetteville: University of Arkansas Press, 1996), 25.

10. Linton Weeks, *St. John's Centennial Program* (Savannah, GA: St. John's Episcopal Church in Savannah, 1985), 26.

11. Mirault Property Case Transcript, Deposition of J. J. Maurice.

12. Ibid.

13. Weeks, *St. John's Centennial Program*, 26.

14. Mirault Property Case, *Final Decree of Judge Henry Tompkins* (hereafter *Final Decree*) and Deposition Summaries of Hill Gowdy and J. J. Maurice. In Gowdy's deposition, he stated that when he asked Cally if he wanted to sell the property, Cally was residing in the Mirault home on Whitaker Street with the Mirault Family. Also see Savannah, Ga., City Directory, 1858. The directory for 1858 contains a listing for Gowdy and lists Cally as residing at the southwest corner of Whitaker and Macon Streets, which was the address of Aspasia Mirault's home.

15. Chatham County Tax Digest, 1849.

16. Ibid., 1853.

17. Ibid., 1855

18. Ibid., 1856.

19. Business Directory for the City of Savannah, Georgia, 1859.

20. Chatham County Tax Digests for 1855, 1856, 1858.

21. Savannah, Ga., City Directory, 1858.

22. Ibid.

23. U.S. Census records for Chatham County, Ga., 1860; Mirault Property Case Transcript, Deposition Summary of James Lovell.

24. Harden, *Recollections*, 19–20.

25. Schweninger, *Black Property Owners*, 133–34.

26. Harden, *Recollections*, 19–20.

27. *Savannah Morning News*, May 29, 1854; Harden, *Recollections*, 19–20.

28. *Savannah Morning News*, May 26, 1855; Edward F. Sweat, "The Free Negro in Antebellum Georgia," 128–29.

29. *Savannah Morning News*, April 22, 1854.

30. *Report of John E. Ward, Mayor of the City of Savannah for the Year Ending 31st October 1854 to which is added the Treasurer's Annual Report* (Savannah, GA: Purse Printing, 1854) (hereafter Report of John Ward).

31. Ibid.; Harden, *Recollections*, 78.

32. *Report of John E. Ward.*

33. William Elliot Griffin, *Millard Fillmore: Constructive Statesman, Defender of the Constitution, President of the United States* (Ithaca, NY: Andrus & Church, 1915), 148.

34. *Savannah Daily Morning News*, April 22, 1854.

35. *Savannah Daily Morning News*, April 22, 1854, and April 24, 1854; Elbert B.

Smith, *The Presidencies of Zachary Taylor and Millard Fillmore* (Lawrence: University of Kansas Press, 1988), 44. According to the historian C. Vann Woodward, blacks during the antebellum era were not permitted to patronize hotels and restaurants in most southern cities. See Woodward, *The Strange Career of Jim Crow*, 14.

36. Record of Baptism provided courtesy of the Archives, Catholic Dioceses, Savannah, Georgia. Although the infant Robert Ward Oliver was not the first-born child of Robert and Dinah Oliver, he was the first to survive. Two years earlier, in late January 1855, Diana gave birth to a son named Joseph. Named for his father's brother, the infant lived only one week before succumbing to a severe case of spasms. See *Laurel Grove Cemetery Records, 1852–1861*, vol. 1 (Savannah: Georgia Historical Society, 1993).

37. Harden, *Recollections*, 62–63. According to Harden, Ward, who was born in Liberty County, Georgia, practiced law in Savannah and later in New York City. His law partners in both cities were Colonel Charles Colcock Jones and General Henry R. Jackson. Ward's diplomatic career occurred during the Buchanan administration. Ward served as the nation's first minister to China until he was replaced by an Abraham Lincoln appointee.

38. John E. Ward, *Address delivered before the Wesleyan Female College at Macon, Georgia, July 15, 1857* (Savannah, GA: N. Nicholas Printer, 1957).

39. *Laurel Grove Cemetery Records*, vol. 1.

40. *Savannah Morning News*, June 6, 1915.

41. Thigpen, "Aristocracy of the Heart," 570–72, 575.

42. Letitia is listed as a confectioner at the Mirault residence on Whitaker in the Savannah, Ga., City Directory, 1859.

43. U.S. Census records for Chatham County, Ga., 1860.

44. See Savannah, Ga., City Directory, 1859. *Laurel Grove Cemetery Records*, vol. 1. See Chatham County Tax Digests, 1857, 1858, 1859, and 1860.

45. Letitia Davis's death was recorded in the *Laurel Grove Cemetery Record Book*, vol. 1.

46. The Oliver infant died on February 1, 1855. See *Laurel Grove Cemetery Records*, vol. 1.

47. Account of Robert Ward Oliver, #2677; Record of Baptism for Aspasia Matilda Oliver provided courtesy of the Archives of the Catholic Dioceses of Savannah, Georgia.

48. See Record of Baptismal for Aspasia Matilda Mirault, Courtesy of the Archives, Catholic Diocese, Savannah, Georgia. See *The Roster of the Confederate Soldiers of Georgia, 1861–1865*, vol. 3 and 5.

49. Account of Robert Ward Oliver, #2677 and Account of Aspasia Matilda Oliver, #4133 Aspasia Matilda Oliver; see also the *Laurel Grove Cemetery Records*. Alternate spellings for Truchelet included "Touchelet" and "Trechlin."

50. Baptismal record courtesy of the Archives of the Catholic Dioceses, Savannah, Georgia.

Chapter Four: Black Confederates

1. U.S. Census for Chatham County, 1850; Janet B. Hewett, ed., *The Roster of Confederate Soldiers, 1861–1865*, vol. 12 (Wilmington, DE: Broadfoot Publishing Company, 1996), 41, 42.

2. Franklin, *From Slavery to Freedom*, 195–96.

3. Leon F. Litwack, *Been in the Storm So Long: The Aftermath of Slavery* (New York: Alfred A. Knopf, 1979), 66–67; Franklin, *From Slavery to Freedom*, 182, 194; Hine, *African-American Odyssey*, 281–82; Jack D. Foner, *Blacks and the Military in American History* (New York: Praeger Publishers, 1974), 45–48.

4. Hine, *African-American Odyssey*, 270–71; Franklin, *From Slavery to Freedom*, 195–96.

5. Litwack, *Been in the Storm So Long*, 68, 92, 170; Franklin, *From Slavery to Freedom*, 196, 197–99. Also see Foner, *Blacks and the Military*, 34–38.

6. Franklin, *From Slavery to Freedom*, 192; John B. Boles, *Black Southerners, 1619–1869* (Lexington: University Press of Kentucky, 1984), 134–37.

7. *Savannah Morning News*, July 3, 1861.

8. Foner, *Blacks and the Military*, 48–50; Also see Charles H. Wesley, "The Employment of Negroes as Soldiers in the Confederate Army," *Journal of Negro History* (July 1919): 249–50.

9. The portion of Lee's letter is quoted in Foner, *Blacks in the Military*, 49–50.

10. Charles Kelly Barrow, J. H. Segars, and R. B. Rosenburg, *Forgotten Confederates: An Anthology about Black Southerners* contained in the *Journal of Confederate History Series*, vol. 14 (Atlanta, GA: Southern Heritage Press, 1995), 46–47.

11. See Bell Irvin Wiley, *Southern Negroes, 1861–1865* (New York: Rinehart & Company, 1938), 136 n. 11; Hoskins, *Yet with a Steady Beat*, 16.

12. *Savannah Morning News*, June 19, 1861. The same announcement appeared daily from June 19, 1861, through August 14, 1861.

13. Foner, *Blacks and the Military*, 37.

14. The U.S. Census records for Chatham County, Ga., 1830, list Aspasia Mirault as a slaveholder. See also the Chatham County Tax Digests for 1835, 1836, and 1837. Justine Cruvellier's ad for her runaway bondswoman appears in the *Daily Georgian*, July 18, 1839. Her name was spelled Jestine Crevillier in the advertisement.

15. Wesley, "The Employment of Negroes," 243–44.

16. See Robert Oliver's military service records contained in Military Service Records for the Twenty-fifth Regiment Infantry, microfilm-Roll 256, Box 54, and Roll 257, Box 45, GDAH (hereafter Military Service Records). Oliver's name also appears as a bandsman in Hewett, *The Roster of Confederate Soldiers*, vol. 12 (Hapeville, GA: Longino & Porter, 1960), 41, 42. Although Oliver's pay allotment is not included in his service records, the allotment amount is listed for his band colleague, Robert Woodson. Woodson collected his final pay allotment on September 16, 1863. He received twenty-four dollars for services rendered from July 1 to August 31, 1863. See Robert Woodson Service Records, Forty-seventh Georgia Infantry, Drawer 257, Boxes 44–46, GDAH; the roster of bandsmen for the Forty-seventh Infantry appears in Lillian Henderson, *Roster of the Confederate Soldiers of Georgia, 1861–1865*, vol. 5 (Hapeville, GA: Longino & Porter, 1960), 1–3.

17. See Henderson, *Roster of the Confederate Soldiers*, vol. 3, 91. According to oral and written accounts from his great-granddaughter Ruth Rivers, John Joseph Millen (1849–1884) was the son of Elizabeth Faro, who was the second wife of Simon Mirault. Family records suggest that Millen was a musician who played the cornet

for Confederate as well as Union bands. After the Civil War, Millen worked for the *Savannah Morning News* as a bookbinder.

18. Military Service Records for Robert Low, contained in Service Records for the Twenty-fifth Regiment Infantry, Drawer 256, Boxes 52, 53, and 56.

19. Henderson, *Roster of the Confederate Soldiers*, vol. 3, 89–91.

20. Ibid., vol. 5, 3.

21. *Rules for the Government of Savannah Artillery* contained in the Claudius Charles Wilson Papers, Collection 874, Folder 4, GHS; Clement Eaton, *A History of the Southern Confederacy* (New York: Macmillan Company, 1954), 228. Eaton lists a number of popular Confederate tunes as well as the writers and publishing houses of the era. Also see Barrow, *Forgotten Confederates*, 46.

22. Harden, *Recollections*, 88, 89; Coleman, *History of Georgia*, 197. General A. R. Lawton's Special Order No. 336 that is addressed to Colonel C. C. Wilson, November 9, 1861, is contained in the Claudius Charles Wilson Manuscript Papers, Box 1, Folder 5, Item 87, GHS.

23. Coleman, *History of Georgia*, 198.

24. Joseph H. Crute Jr., *Units of the Confederate States Army* (reprinted by Gaithersburg, MD: Olde Soldier Books, 1987), 101, 110.

25. Bailey and Fraser, *Portraits of Conflict*, 182–83.

26. Coleman, *History of Georgia*, 203.

27. Harden, *Recollections*, 117.

28. Ibid., 117–18; Coleman, *History of Georgia*, 203.

29. *St. John's Centennial Program*, 32–33; Harden, *Recollections*, 26–27.

30. *St. John's Centennial Program*, 32–33.

31. Coleman, *History of Georgia*, 223–27.

32. Adele Logan Alexander, *Ambiguous Lives: Free Women of Color in Rural Georgia*, 1789–1879 (Fayetteville: University of Arkansas Press, 1991), 142–44; Robert E. Perdue, *The Negro in Savannah, 1865–1900* (New York: Exposition Press, 1973), 3–5; Boles, *Black Southerners*, 199–202.

33. R. J. M. Blackett, ed., *Thomas Morris Chester: Black Civil War Correspondent, His Dispatches from the Virginia Front* (Baton Rouge: Louisiana State University Press, 1989), 303–4.

34. Joel Williamson, *The Crucible of Race: Black-White Relations in the American South since Emancipation* (New York: Oxford University Press, 1984), 44–45, 49; Robert E. Perdue, *The Negro in Savannah*, 10–12.

35. Edmond L. Drago, *Black Politicians and Reconstruction in Georgia, a Splendid Failure* (Athens: University of Georgia Press, 1992), 86–87.

36. *Colored Tribune*, December 4, 1875.

Chapter Five: Post–Civil War Savannah

1. See David Irwin, *The Code of the State of Georgia* (Atlanta, GA: Franklin Steam Printing House, 1867).

2. Donald L. Grant, *The Way It Was in the South: The Black Experience in Georgia* (New York: Carol Publishing Group, 1993), 215–16, 218.

3. Perdue, *Negro in Savannah*, 28.

4. Ibid., 7, 11–12, 15, 18.

5. Mirault Property Case Transcript, Oliver Bill of Complaint, October 8, 1874.

6. Register of the Free Persons of Color, 1860–1864.

7. Account of Diana Oliver, #487; Account of Robert S. Oliver, #1391; Account of Robert Ward Oliver, #2677; and Account of Aspasia Matilda Oliver, #4133. Eight-year-old Aspasia Oliver is listed as Aspassy in the U.S. Census records for Chatham County, Ga., 1870.

8. George Washington Williams, *History of the Negro Race in America from 1619 to 1880* (New York: G. P. Putnam's Sons, 1882), 410.

9. See Account of Diana Oliver, #487; Savannah, Ga., City Directories, 1866 and 1867; U.S. Census records for Chatham County, Ga., 1870.

10. U.S. Census records for Chatham County, Ga., 1860; Savannah, Ga., City Directories, 1866 and 1867.

11. Account of Diana Oliver, #487, and Account of Robert S. Oliver, #1391; U.S. Census records for Chatham County, Ga., 1870; Charles L. Hoskins, *African American Episcopalians in Savannah, Strife, Struggle, and Salvation, 1750–1995* (Savannah: St. Matthew's Episcopal Church, 1995), 46–47.

12. U.S. Census records for Chatham County, Ga., 1850.

13. Ibid., 1860; Letitia Davis died on December 5, 1860. See *Laurel Grove Cemetery Records*, vol. 1.

14. Hoskins, *African American Episcopalians*, 94–95.

15. *Marriage Records of Chatham County, Georgia, 1852–1877*, vol. 2 (Savannah: Georgia Historical Society, 1992); U.S. Census records for Chatham County, Ga., 1850, 1860, and 1870; Account of Jessie L. Stiles, #1356.

16. Hoskins, *African American Episcopalians*, 104.

17. Administration Records for the Estate of Justine L. Stiles, filed April 6, 1874, in the Court of the Ordinary, Chatham County Superior Court Records Department, Savannah, Georgia.

18. Louisa Nayle is listed as a seamstress in the Register of Free Persons of Color, 1837–1849; Charlotte Reed is also listed as a seamstress in the Register of Free Persons of Color, 1860–1864.

19. Chatham County Tax Digest, 1869; Account of Thomas R. Scott, #2400.

20. U.S. Census records for Chatham County, Ga., 1850, lists a Janet Bulloch who was five years old. See *Marriage Records of Chatham County, GA, 1852–1877*, vol. 2. According to the U.S. Census records for Chatham County, Ga., 1870, John W. (Wesley) Jackson was seven months old in June 1870. See the Administration Records of the Estate of Josephine Mirault, 1882, Probate Court of Chatham County Superior Court Records Department, Savannah. Albert Jackson Sr. was appointed the administrator for his ex-mother-in-law's estate. Albert Jackson Jr. received an equal portion of his grandmother's estate. See Randal K. Burkett, Nancy Hall Burkett, and Henry Louis Gates Jr., eds., *Black Biography, 1790–1980, A Cumulative Index* (Alexandria: Chadsyck-Healey, 1991), 248.

21. See Chatham County Tax Digests for 1874 through 1882; Savannah, Ga., City Directories for 1874 and 1875; *Marriages of Chatham County, 1852–1877*, vol. 2.

22. See Savannah, Ga., City Directories for the 1870s.

23. *Savannah Morning News*, November 11, 1874.

24. *Savannah Tribune*, September 9, 1876, and September 16, 1876.

25. *Savannah Morning News*, September 13, 1876; *Savannah Morning News*, September 18, 1876; *Savannah Morning News*, October 4, 1876; *Savannah Tribune*, September 16, 1876, lists the names of the association's directors.

26. U.S. Census records for Chatham County, Ga., 1850; Record of Baptism, October 26, 1862, provided courtesy of the Archives, Catholic Dioceses, Savannah, Georgia.

27. See Savannah, Ga., City Directories for 1877 and 1880; *Marriages of Chatham County, 1852–1877*, vol. 2; see *Petition of Louisa Tillman for Widow's Year of Support*, filed June 13, 1881, Probate Court, Superior Court of Chatham County Records Department, Savannah.

28. Williamson, *The Crucible of Race*, 49, 50; Litwack, *Been in the Storm So Long*, 261–63; Clark Hine, *African American Odyssey*, 274, 277–78, 295–96.

29. Perdue, *Negro in Savannah*, 29, 37–38.

30. Ibid., 7, 15, 20–21; Williamson, *The Crucible of Race*, 50.

31. Williamson, *The Crucible of Race*, 288–91.

32. Perdue, *Negro in Savannah*, 26–27.

33. Johnson, *Black Savannah*, 26–27; Perdue, *Negro in Savannah*, 46–47.

34. Litwack, *Been in the Storm So Long*, 471, 537–38; Perdue, *Negro in Savannah*, 25–29, 52–53. For a discussion of the Charleston, South Carolina, post–Civil War black community, see Wilbert L. Jenkins, *Seizing the New Day: African Americans in Post–Civil-War Charleston* (Bloomington: Indiana University Press, 1998), 65–67.

35. Account of the Bricklayers' Union Association of Savannah, #7118; Account of the Ladies' Bricklaying Union, #11168; Account of the Wagoneers' Union Association, 5477 and 8056; Account of the Friendly Association of Savannah, #12747 and #12940; Account of the Colored Enterprise Association, #1531.

36. Account of the Ladies' Mutual Aid Association, #12653.

37. See *Savannah Tribune*, May 14, 1898. See also the *Savannah Tribune* for June 25, 1898. The newspaper carried an article about McKane's graduation ceremony. The two graduates from the nurses training department of the hospital were Mrs. S. Louise Ward and Mrs. Lenora E. Wayring.

38. Account of the Girls and Ladies' Friendly Club, #9823; Account of the Social Love and Goodwill Society, #8986; Account of the Star Lights of Bethlehem, #10203; Account of the United Daughters of Lincoln, #10937; Account of the Sons of Africa Society, #10887; and Account of the Grand Lodge of the Free and Accomplished Masons of Georgia, #7656.

39. Johnson, *Black Savannah*, 180.

40. Ibid.; Account of the Ladies' Branch of the Pulaski Circle, #104971; see John W. Blassingame, *Black New Orleans, 1860–1880* (Chicago: University of Chicago Press, 1973), 151, 153–55, 157–58. According to Blassingame, many mulattoes in New Orleans considered themselves the natural leaders in the postbellum African American community and acted paternalistic toward the freedmen. Blassingame does reference evidence that blacks from different social groups tried to work together on occasion.

41. See *Mayor's Annual Report*, January 13, 1873 (Savannah, GA: Steam Power Press, 1877), 4–5, Municipal Research Library, City Hall, Savannah, Ga.

42. Ibid., 10.

43. Perdue, *Negro in Savannah*, 48–50; Hoskins, *Out of Yamacraw*, 117; Charles

Lwanga Hoskins, "Black Episcopalians in Savannah" (Savannah, GA: Self-Published Pamphlet, 1983), 23, Savannah State University Archives.

44. Perdue, *Negro in Savannah*, 4, 11.

45. Gamble, A *History of the City Government of Savannah, Georgia*, 285–86.

46. Ibid.

47. Hine, *African-American Odyssey*, 316–17; Thomas R. Frazier, ed., *Readings in African-American History*, 3d ed. (Belmont, CA: Wadsworth/Thomson Learning, 2001), 147.

48. *Savannah Morning News*, November 11, 1874, contains the list of all registered voters in Savannah.

49. Ibid., November 4, 1874.

50. Ibid., November 5, 1874; Litwack, *Been in the Storm So Long*, 64–65, 546–47. Prior to his political activities in Savannah, Georgia, Turner had served as chaplain of Company C of the First South Carolina Volunteers and the pastor of the Israel Bethel Church in Washington, DC.

51. *Savannah Morning News*, December 4, 1874; see also Hine, *African American Odyssey*, 344; Perdue, *Negro in Savannah*, 44–45.

52. Edwin S. Redkey, "Bishop Turner's African Dream," *Journal of American History* 54 (1967): 274, 294.

53. See Account of Diana Oliver, #487; Account of Robert S. Oliver, #1391; Account of Robert Ward Oliver, #2677; and Account of Aspasia Matilda Oliver, #4133; Franklin, *From Slavery to Freedom*, 219, 257.

54. Account of Jessie L. Stiles, #1356; Account of Thomas R. Scott, #2400; Accounts of Duncan S. Scott, #362 and #6367.

55. Robert E. Perdue, *Negro in Savannah*, 58; see Account of the Reverend Henry M. Turner, #12790, Index to Depositor's Ledgers, Freedmen's Savings and Trust Company, National Archives, Washington, DC.

Chapter Six: Betrayal and Litigation

1. Mirault Property Case Transcript, Oliver, *Bill of Complaint*. In their documents filed with the court, the Mirault heirs disclosed how they had trusted Cally over many years. They conceded that before his betrayal of the trust agreement, he had collected rents and paid the taxes on the property.

2. Mirault Property Case Transcript, Deposition of John R. Johnson.

3. Ibid.; Mirault Property Case Transcript, *Plea of the Defendant George Cally*, filed June 21, 1875.

4. Mirault Property Case Transcript, Deposition of John R. Johnson.

5. Mirault Property Case Transcript, Deposition of George Cornwell.

6. Ibid. At the time of the trial, George Cornwell provided deposition testimony in which he stated that he had been a resident of Savannah all of his fifty-five years. He recounted that the city's method for reentering property for payment of taxes had always been the same. Cornwell remembered from his boyhood that the city marshal posted a notice at the property and advertised that the property would be sold.

7. *Savannah Morning News*, February 5, 1872.

8. Harden, *Recollections*, 13–14; Mirault Property Case Transcript, Cally,

Complaint and Bill for Equitable Relief. Cally estimated the property was worth $6,000. In their *Bill of Complaint*, the heirs valued the property at $5,000.

9. Mirault Property Case Transcript, Deposition of William Swoll and *Petition of Receiver to make Repairs*, June 1, 1878. The court documents outlined the expenses incurred by Swoll in title and deed to the property. He paid $380 at the auction. Subsequently, he paid a total of $806.08 in the following amounts: $227.89—ground rent in arrears; $280.89—city taxes; $147.30—county and state taxes; and $150.00—insurance on the buildings.

10. Minutes of Council Meeting for the City of Savannah, Finance Committee Petitions, 1871–1872, Municipal Research Library, City Hall, Savannah, Georgia.

11. Minutes of Council, Record Book, 1872–1877, Municipal Research Library, City Hall, Savannah, Georgia; J. J. Waring is mentioned in Perdue, *Negro in Savannah*, 11.

12. Chatham County Tax Digests for 1855, 1856, 1858, 1866, 1867, 1870. In their *Complaint*, the heirs alleged that Cally had collected rent on lot 22 until 1872.

13. See *George Cally v. Max Meyer*, filed December 25, 1866 (J11439), contained in the Chatham County Superior Court Records, Savannah, Georgia. Cally alleged that Meyer owed him a total of $13,940 for two separate accounts of $3,970 and $9,970. Meyer countered that Cally owned him $3,524 for rent on building and for clothing and dry goods furnished to Cally by Meyer.

14. Mirault Property Case Transcript, Deposition of George Cornwell.

15. Mirault Property Case Transcript, *Final Decree*. In his *Final Decree* document, Judge Tompkins stated that the 1818 law had been repealed in conjunction with the new Georgia Constitution of 1865.

16. Chatham County Tax Digest, 1842.

17. Ibid., 1843.

18. Ibid., 1844 and 1845.

19. Ibid., 1844 through 1870.

20. Ibid., 1852, 1856, 1857, and 1858.

21. Savannah, Ga., City Directory, 1858.

22. Mirault Property Case Transcript, Cally, *Complaint and Bill for Equitable Relief*.

23. Mirault Property Case Transcript, Oliver, *Bill of Complaint*, filed October 8, 1874.

24. Ibid.

25. Mirault Property Case Transcript, Cally, Plea of Defendant, George Cally.

26. George Cally was involved as the plaintiff in three separate lawsuits, including his dispute with Max S. Meyer. According to the *Savannah Morning News* for December 10, 1875, a judgment for Cally was entered in the amount of $496.90, including interest from January 1, 1867. Cally also sued the operators of the Savannah Ogeechee Canal. That case was concluded with a favorable decision in Cally's favor in 1877. See *Savannah Morning News*, May 15, 1877.

27. Mirault Property Case Transcript, Cronk, *Answer on behalf of the Estate of George Cally*, filed February 14, 1878.

28. Mirault Property Case Transcript, *Demurrers* by Defendant William Swoll, April 3, 1875; Swoll filed both *Demurrers* on the same day.

29. Ibid.

30. Mirault Property Case Transcript, Oliver, *Bill of Complaint*.

31. Mirault Property Case Transcript, *Answer of Defendant William Swoll to the Complainant's Complaint*," August 3, 1877.

32. Ibid.

33. Perdue, *Negro in Savannah*, 37, 42–43. Perdue argues that early in the Reconstruction era, black Republican politicians in Savannah had high expectations about progress for the black community and for their inclusion in the decision making circles of the city and the state. The onset of the Redeemer governments prevented blacks from gaining any lasting power. See also Boles, *Black Southerners*, 203–4.

34. *Colored Tribune*, June 2, 1876. The name was later changed to the *Savannah Tribune*.

35. Savannah, Ga., City Directory for 1858; U.S. Census record for Chatham County, Ga., 1860.

36. Harden, *Recollections*, 13; The *Savannah Morning News* reported on July 2, 1873, that Swoll had contracted to sell a lot with 4 one-story wooden buildings in the Gaston Ward of the city to John H. Stegin for the sum of $1,300.

37. See Savannah, Ga., City Directories; *Savannah Morning News*, February 25, 1873; *Savannah Morning News*, May 23, 1873.

38. See Savannah, Ga., City Directories.

39. Perdue, *Negro in Savannah*, 38, 42. See also the *Savannah Morning News*, January 19, 1875.

40. Perdue, *Negro in Savannah*, 42. According the local newspaper, Rufus E. Lester successfully ran for Savannah mayor during the late 1880s. See the *Savannah Tribune*, February 22, 1887.

41. Edmund L. Drago, *Black Politicians and Reconstruction in Georgia*, 48–49, 95. See Drago's appendix for biographical information on the forty-nine black members of the Georgia Legislature. Lester's anti-Negro speech appeared in the *Savannah Morning News*, October 27, 1868.

42. Lester to Swoll, May 11, 1880, and June 18, 1880, Lester S. Revel Letter Book, contained in the Thomas Porcher Ravel Papers, GHS.

43. Perdue, *Negro in Savannah*, 130. According to Perdue's research, in addition to attorney Kinckle, the other black lawyers who practiced in Savannah from the end of the Civil War to around 1900 were G. H. Miller and Abraham L. Tucker. The *Savannah Tribune* reported that Tucker was admitted to the bar and two months later formed a law partnership with Kinckle. The Kinckle and Tucker firm occupied offices at 110 Bryan Street. See *Savannah Tribune*, July 23, 1898, and *Savannah Tribune*, August 6, 1898.

44. Savannah, Ga., City Directories, 1876 and 1877–1878.

45. U.S. Census records for Chatham County, 1860; Savannah, Ga., City Directory, 1877–1878.

46. See Judge Thomas M. Norwood, "Address on the Negro, On Retiring from the Bench," December 31, 1907, Savannah, GHS. According to the Savannah, Ga., City Directory, 1899, Norwood's annual judicial salary was $3,000.

Chapter Seven: A Trial Indeed

1. U.S. Census records for Chatham County, Ga., 1850, lists Robert Oliver and his brother, Joseph, as teenage musicians living in their mother's home; Mirault

Property Case Transcript, Oliver, *Bill of Complaint*, October 8, 1874. See Military Service Records for Robert Oliver.

2. For a discussion of African American litigants and the Reconstruction-era judicial system, see Janice Sumler-Edmond, "The Quest for Justice: African American Women Litigants, 1867–1890," in *African American Women and the Vote, 1838–1965*, ed. Ann D. Gordon (Amherst: University of Massachusetts Press, 1997), 114–18. For details about Reconstruction-era racial tensions in Georgia, see Coleman, *History of Georgia*, 246–50. Perdue also details Savannah's racial strife during the 1860s and 1870s in his work. See Perdue, *Negro in Savannah*, 18–22.

3. Mirault Property Case Transcript, Cally, *Complaint and Bill for Equitable Relief*, and Tompkins, *Final Decree*, May 13, 1878; *Savannah Morning News*, November 14, 1875.

4. Mirault Property Case Transcript, Oliver, *Bill of Complaint*. Cally, *Complaint and Bill for Equitable Relief*, and Judge Henry B. Tompkins, *Order*, February 14, 1878.

5. Gordon B. Smith, GBS Notebook, "Judge Henry Bethune Tompkins, 1844–1903," GHS.

6. Henry B. Tompkins File, Container 160, Location #1783, GDAH, hereinafter cited as Tompkins File. The *Savannah Morning News* reported the results of a case in which Tompkins represented the publishers of the *Daily Republic* in a libel action brought by P. Geibehouse. The plaintiff asked for damages in the amount of $10,000, but won a verdict for only $50 when they could not prove malice had motivated the defendants. See *Savannah Morning News*, March 5, 1874.

7. Tompkins File; Coleman, *History of Georgia*, 217; Smith won reelection in 1872 by some 60,000 votes out of the 145,000 cast to defeat his challenger Dawson Walker from Whitfield County; James F. Cook, *The Governors of Georgia, 1754–1995* (Macon, GA: Mercer University Press, 1995), 156–58; Keith Hulett, "James M. Smith," *The New Georgia Encyclopedia* (Athens: Georgia Humanities Council and the University of Georgia, on-line, 2006).

8. Tompkins to Governor Smith, July 7, 1874, Tompkins File.

9. Tompkins File. For notice of Tompkins's appointment to the Superior Court bench, see *Savannah Morning News*, January 2, 1875. A handful of black politicians remained active in Georgia politics at the end of the nineteenth century. By 1876, the prominent black elected officials had left government. See Drago, *Black Politicians and Reconstruction*, 157–59, 160–62.

10. The *Colored Tribune*, June 3, 1876, included an editorial complaining about the failure of the city and county to call any black jurors to hear and decide cases.

11. Savannah, Ga., City Directories, 1876 and 1877.

12. See Mirault Property Case Transcript, documents detail the opening of court on February 14, 1878, with the selection of jurors, and procedural orders and instructions issued by Judge Tompkins.

13. Savannah, Ga., City Directory, 1877, lists Albert Jackson as a partner in the cotton brokerage firm of Johnson & Jackson, located at 84 Bay Street in Savannah. That year there were ten other such firms in the city. Johnson & Jackson was the only black-owned firm. The same city directory lists Tillman Burton as a cotton sampler. He may have worked in his brother-in-law's firm. Charles B. Stiles was listed as a brick mason who resided on Southville Street in Savannah. Robert Ward Oliver and his sister Aspasia Matilda Oliver opened accounts in the Savannah branch of the Freedmen's Bank, located on Bryan Street near Drayton. See

Account of Robert Ward Oliver, #2677, and Account of Aspasia Matilda Oliver, #4133.

14. George Cally's death is recorded in the *Laurel Grove Cemetery Index to the Keeper's Record Book, 1852–1938*, vol. 1, compiled by the WPA (Savannah, GA: 1939). See #411 Administration of George Cally's Estate, 1876, Court of the Ordinary, Chatham County Superior Court Records Department, Savannah, Georgia, hereafter Administration of the Estate of George Cally. While working for the city, William Swoll purchased numerous pieces of Savannah real estate. See Harden, *Recollections*, 13–14.

15. Savannah, Ga., City Directory, 1877. *Savannah Morning News*, February 15, 16, 18, 1878; Mirault Property Case Transcript, Deposition Summary of John R. Johnson.

16. U.S. Census records for Chatham County, 1860; Savannah, Ga., City Directory, 1877; Mirault Property Case Transcript, Deposition Summary of Edward Lovell; Aspasia Mirault's bakery establishment is mentioned in William Harden's *Recollections*, 48–49.

17. Mirault Property Case Transcript, Lovell Summary of Deposition.

18. Ibid.

19. Savannah, Ga., City Directory, 1858; U.S. Census records for Chatham County, 1860; Mirault Property Case Transcript, Deposition Summary of George H. Ash.

20. Ibid.

21. Savannah, Ga., City Directory, 1877; Mirault Property Case Transcript, Deposition Summary of J. J. Maurice.

22. Mirault Property Case Transcript, Deposition Summary of W. H. May.

23. Ibid.

24. Mirault Property Case Transcript, Deposition Summary of James Russell.

25. Savannah, Ga., City Directory, 1858. Mirault Property Case Transcript, Deposition Hill Gowdy; Aspasia Mirault's death is recorded in the *Laurel Grove Cemetery Records, Volume I, 1852–1861*.

26. U.S. Census records for Chatham County, 1860; Mirault Property Case Transcript, Hill Gowdy Deposition.

27. *Savannah Morning News*, February 16 and 18, 1878.

28. *Savannah Morning News*, February 15, 16, and 18, 1878. Mirault Property Case Transcript, *Verdict* of the Jury. For a summary of the jury's findings, see *Swoll et al. v. Oliver et al.*, 61 Georgia Reports 248 (1878), hereafter *Swoll v. Oliver.*

29. See *Swoll v. Oliver.* The findings of the jury were restated in *Swoll v. Oliver* on page 250.

30. Ibid.,

31. Ibid.

32. Mirault Property Case Transcript, Deposition of Hill Gowdy; *Swoll v. Oliver.*

33. *Swoll v. Oliver;* Administration of the Estate of George Cally.

34. Mirault Property Case Transcript, *Final Decree* of Judge Tompkins.

35. Robert Oliver listed his address when he opened his account at the Freedmen's Bank. See Account of Robert Oliver, #1391.

36. U.S. Census records for Chatham County, 1860; Mirault Property Case Transcript, Deposition Summary of Henry Roggenstein. There were a variety of

spellings found for the tenant's name. The Savannah, Ga., City Directory, 1859, used Roggentin. Later directories and the various court documents used Roggensteine.

37. U.S. Census records for Chatham County, 1860.

38. Mirault Property Case Transcript, Roggenstein Deposition.

39. Mirault Property Case Transcript, Oliver, *Bill of Complaint* and Roggenstein Deposition; Savannah, Ga., City Directory, 1877.

40. Mirault Property Case Transcript, *Petition of Receiver John C. Rowland*, March 24, 1876, and *Orders* issued by Judge H. B. Tompkins, March 24, 1876, and April 8, 1876; *Savannah Morning News*, April 10, 1876. Roggenstein testified that he paid $350 annually for the first seven years of his tenancy and $400 thereafter until his attorney advised him to withhold rent until the dispute between Swoll and Cally had been resolved. See Roggenstein Deposition.

41. Mirault Property Case Transcript, *Petition of Receiver John C. Rowland*, June 1, 1878, Minutes. The Mirault heirs joined Receiver Rowland in his second Petition to Judge Tompkins. Alfred B. Smith, counsel for the heirs, signed the Petition. See *Savannah Telegram*, June 2, 1878.

42. Mirault Property Case Transcript, *Judgment and Decree of Judge Henry Tompkins on Rowland Petition*, June 1, 1878.

43. Mirault Property Case Transcript, *Order* issued by Judge H. B. Tompkins, February 26, 1879.

Chapter Eight: Reversal of Fortune

1. Mirault Property Case Transcript, Tompkins, *Final Decree*.

2. Ibid.

3. Ibid.

4. Ibid.

5. The two U.S. Supreme Court cases cited by Tompkins were *Clarke v. Bazadone*, 5 Cranch 212, 281 (1803) and *Church v. Hubbart* 6 Cranch 187 (1804).

6. Mirault Property Case Transcript, Tompkins, *Final Decree*.

7. Franklin, *From Slavery to Freedom*, 216–17. Coleman, *History of Georgia*, 208–11.

8. Mirault Property Case Transcript, Tompkins, *Final Decree*.

9. Ibid.

10. Ibid.

11. Ibid. Also see *the Savannah Morning News*, May 14, 1874, announcing details of Tompkins's *Final Decree* document.

12. Mirault Property Case Transcript, Tompkins, *Final Decree*.

13. Mirault Property Case Transcript, Tompkins, *Order to Deny Defendants' Motions for a New Trial*, on June 10, 1878.

14. Mirault Property Case Transcript, court document dated January 7, 1879, Z. D. Harrison, clerk of the Georgia Supreme Court, entered the Court's *Judgment* in the *Oliver v. Swoll* matter. Harrison's minutes of the court's proceedings referenced that R. E. Lester, Esq. paid the Bill of Costs.

15. See "Memorial of the Life and Character of the Honorable Hiram Warner," contained in 68 *Georgia Reporter* 845 (1882) appendix, 845–47.

16. "Memorial of Hon. James Jackson," contained in 78 *Georgia Reporter* 897 (1888) appendix 807–11.
17. "Memorial of Hon. Logan E. Bleckley," contained in 128 *Georgia Reporter* 849 (1907): 849–53.
18. Mirault Property Case Transcript, Tompkins, *Final Decree*.
19. *Swoll v. Oliver*, 252.
20. Ibid.
21. Ibid., 253.
22. Mirault Property Case Transcript, Tompkins, *Order* issued on January 13, 1879.
23. The *Savannah Morning News*, March 29, 1879, reported the concluding proceedings of the Mirault property case.
24. Franklin, *From Slavery to Freedom*, 238, 246.
25. Mirault Property Case Transcript, Tompkins, *Final Decree*.
26. *The Planters' Loan and Savings Bank v. Johnson et al.*, 70 *Georgia Reports* 302 (1882).
27. *Planters' v. Johnson*.
28. Ibid.
29. *Beatty et al. v. Benton, Executrix*, 73 *Georgia Reports* 187 (1884).
30. Ibid.
31. Ibid.

Epilogue

1. Swoll paid $380 for the lot at the public auction in 1872. He subsequently was required to pay another $806.88 for back taxes, ground rent, and insurance. See Superior Court Minutes, GDAH. Details of the sale to Adam and Anna Kessel are contained in the Chatham County, Georgia, Grantor-Grantee Records, Box 4-Z, pages 106–8, Chatham County Courthouse, Savannah, hereafter referred to as Grantor-Grantee Records.
2. Ibid.
3. Ibid. See Savannah, Ga., City Directory, 1898.
4. *Savannah Morning News*, April 16, 1879.
5. Ibid., August 5, 1876; August 8, 1876.
6. Ibid., August 22, 1874, page 3, col. 3.
7. Ibid., January 9, 1876, page 3, col. 2.
8. *Indenture and Settlement* between Maria Swoll, widow of William Swoll, and her children, January 11, 1888, Court of the Ordinary, Chatham County Superior Court Records Department, Savannah, Georgia.
9. Administration records for the Estate of Maria Swoll, May 2, 1902, Court of the Ordinary, Chatham County Superior Court Records Department, Savannah, Georgia.
10. Coleman, *The History of Georgia*, 221.
11. There was considerable fanfare connected to Tompkins's appointment to the bench in January 1875. The local newspaper praised his reputation and predicted that although he was probably the youngest judge in the state at the time, he "will prove himself a credit and honor to the bench, as he has to the bar." See *Savannah Morning News*, January 2, 1875, page 3, col. 2.

12. See *Report of the 2nd Annual Meeting of the Georgia Bar Association* (Macon, GA: J. W. Burke & Co., 1886).

13. Ibid.; Coleman, *History of Georgia*, 305–6; Thomas Gamble Jr., *A History of the City Government*, 8.

14. *Report of the 2nd Annual Meeting of the Georgia Bar Association*, 80.

15. Ibid., 48.

16. See *Reports of the Annual Georgia Bar Association* meetings 1888, 1889, 1890, and 1891.

17. *Savannah Morning News*, May 14, 1878.

18. Savannah, Ga., City Directories for 1877 and 1882.

19. Will of Albert Jackson, 1901, Will #640, Court of the Ordinary, Superior Court of Chatham County Records Department, Savannah, Georgia.

20. Account of John M. Johnson, #53; Johnson opened his account at the Freedmen's Bank on January 26, 1865; see U.S. Census records for Chatham County, 1870; see also Savannah, Ga., City Directories for 1870, 1871–1872.

21. See Savannah, Ga., City Directories for 1874–1875. According to the Chatham County Tax Digest for 1869 and 1879, Deas was a Savannah landowner. In 1869, Deas paid a total of $19.50 on lot 22 in Oglethorpe Ward. The lot and improvements were valued at $1,300 that year. In 1870, Deas paid $21.00 and the value of his property had increased by $100. See Savannah, Ga., City Directory for 1871–1872.

22. See Savannah, Ga., City Directories, 1882 and 1883.

23. Michael Perman, *The Road to Redemption: Southern Politics, 1869–1879* (Chapel Hill: University of North Carolina Press, 1984), 242, 245–46, 255–56.

24. Franklin, *From Slavery to Freedom*, 214.

25. See *Savannah Morning News* for October 8 and 14, 1884. According to the local newspaper, Johnson's funeral was held on October 8, at 9:00 A.M. at St. Phillip's Church on New Street.

26. See Savannah, Ga., City Directories for the period of the 1880s and 1890s. Following Johnson's death, the directories published listings for Jackson and Sons.

27. See Savannah, Ga., City Directories for 1884, 1885, 1886, 1891, and 1899. May C. Jackson is listed as the primary proprietor of the firm in the Savannah City Directory for 1899. For a discussion of the crusade of black women who demanded respect and worked for racial uplift at the end of the nineteenth century, see Paula Giddings, *When and Where I Enter*, 97–98.

28. *Savannah Morning News*, April 24, 1884; Savannah, Ga., City Directory for 1884; the U.S. Census records for Chatham County, Ga., 1870, list Albert Jackson as a twenty-six year old bookkeeper.

29. Will of Albert Jackson.

30. *Hampton Institute Bulletin*, 1894, Hampton University's Archival and Museum Collection. Sidney M. Jackson attended Johnson C. Smith College. Oral account from Richard Jarvis, Burke, Va., grandson of Sidney Jackson and great grandson of Albert and Mary Jackson. Albert Jackson's will contains two spellings for the first name of his youngest son. The two spellings are Sidney and Sydney.

31. Will of Albert Jackson; Albert Jackson Jr. attended Hampton Institute in Virginia from 1888 to 1894, earning a diploma. From 1898 through 1900, he studied medicine at Howard University's Medical College and resided at 1834 Eleventh

Street, NW, Washington, DC. See *Hampton Graduates, 1871–1899*, May 1899, Courtesy of Hampton University Archives; Howard University Medical Department, *A Historical, Biographical and Statistical Souvenir of the Medical Faculty of Howard University* (Washington, DC: R. Beneford, 1900), reference contained in Burkett, *Black Biography*, 248.

32. Chatham County Tax Digest, 1875 and 1876. Albert Jackson married Jeannette Bulloch on January 6, 1869. See *Marriage Records of Chatham County, Ga., Volume II, 1852–1877*; Jeannette Bulloch Jackson died on September 25, 1872, according to the Laurel Grove Cemetery Records, Savannah.

33. *Marriage Records of Chatham County, Ga., Volume II, 1852–1877*.

34. *In Re Estate of Tillman Burton, Application of Widow for Year's Support*, June 13, 1881, Court of the Ordinary, Superior Court of Chatham County Records Department, Savannah, Ga. Cyrus Campfield and R. J. Artson placed business advertisements in the local newspaper. See *Savannah Tribune*, February 12, 1887.

35. *In Re Estate of Tillman Burton, Application of Widow for Year's Support*.

36. Savannah, Ga., City Directories, 1883 and 1884.

37. *Savannah Tribune*, February 2, 1889; *Savannah Tribune*, February 27, 1892. According to the family history, Mary Louisa Moore died of complications giving birth to twins. Mary and both infants died. Oral account from Richard Jarvis.

38. The U.S. Census records for 1850 lists nine-year-old Charles Stiles as a resident in his grandmother's home. Charles's sister, three-year-old Louisa Williams, was also residing there at the time.

39. Savannah, Ga., City Directory, 1877.

40. Ibid. See *Renunciation and Application for Administration of the Estate of Justine L. Stiles*, 1874, Superior Court of Chatham County Records Department, Savannah, Ga.

41. See Savannah, Georgia City Directories, 1882, 1883, 1884, 1885, 1886, and 1889.

42. *Savannah Tribune*, July 13, 1898.

43. U.S. Census records for Chatham County, 1880 and 1900.

44. Voter Registration and Voter Oaths Books, Record Numbers, GHS.

45. Savannah, Ga., City Directory, 1870.

46. U.S. Census records for Chatham County, 1880.

47. Georgia Confederate Pensions and Records Department, Alphabetical card file, microfilm, drawer 253, roll 47, GDAH.

48. Monroe Berger, *Equality by Statute: The Revolution in Civil Rights* (Garden City, NY: Doubleday, 1967), 4–8; A. Leon Higginbotham Jr., *Shades of Freedom: Racial Politics and Presumptions of the American Legal Process* (New York: Oxford University Press, 1996), 172–73.

49. Oral account from Richard Jarvis.

Selected Bibliography

Manuscript Collections

Administrations, wills, and trial documents, Probate Court and Superior Court, Chatham County, Georgia.
Confederate military records, Georgia Department of Archives and History, Atlanta.
Freedmen's Bureau Savings and Trust Company, National Archives, Washington, DC.
Photographs and rare books, Georgia Room of the Savannah Public Library, Savannah.
Photographs and rare books, Hampton University Archives, Hampton, Virginia.
Photographs and rare books, Manuscript, Archives, Rare Book Library, Emory University, Atlanta.
Photographs and rare books, Savannah State University Archives, Savannah.
Sacramental papers, Diocesan Archives, Savannah.
Supreme Court of Georgia Records, Georgia Department of Archives and History, Atlanta.
Claudius Charles Wilson Papers, John E. Ward Papers, rare books and photographs, Georgia Historical Society, Savannah.

Newspapers

Colored Tribune, later the *Savannah Tribune*
Columbia Museum and Savannah Advertiser
Daily Georgian
Georgian Gazette
Savannah Morning News

Published Sources

Alexander, Adele Logan. *Ambiguous Lives: Free Women of Color in Rural Georgia, 1789–1879*. Fayetteville: University of Arkansas Press, 1991.

Berlin, Ira. *Slaves without Masters: The Free Negro in the Antebellum South*. New York: Pantheon Books, 1974.

BeVard, Mary Jane, ed. *One Faith, One Family: The Dioceses of Savannah, 1850–2000*. Comp. Gillian Brown, Father Douglas K. Clark, David T. Gleeson, and Sister Mary Faith McKean. Syracuse, NY: Signature Publications, 2000.

Blackett, R. J. M., ed. *Thomas Morris Chester: Black Civil War Correspondent, His Dispatches from the Virginia Front*. Baton Rouge: Louisiana State University Press, 1989.

Cook, James F. *The Governors of Georgia, 1754–1995*. Macon, GA: Mercer University Press, 1995.

Drago, Edmond L. *Black Politicians and Reconstruction in Georgia, a Splendid Failure*. Athens: University of Georgia Press, 1992.

Henderson, Alexa B. *Atlanta Life Insurance Company, Guardian of Black Economic Dignity*. Tuscaloosa: University of Alabama Press, 1990.

Horton, James Oliver. *Free People of Color, Inside the African American Community*. Washington, DC: Smithsonian Institution Press, 1993.

Hoskins, Charles Lwanga. *Yet with a Steady Beat: Biographies of Early Black Savannah*. Savannah, GA: Gullah Press, 2001.

Johnson, Walter. *Soul by Soul: Life inside the Antebellum Slave Market*. Boston: Harvard University Press, 2001.

Litwack, Leon. *Been in the Storm So Long: The Aftermath of Slavery*. New York: Alfred A. Knopf, 1979.

Merritt, Carole. *The Herndons, an Atlanta Family*. Athens: University of Georgia Press, 2002.

Purdue, Robert E. *The Negro in Savannah, 1865–1900*. New York: Exposition Press, 1973.

Schweninger, Loren. *Black Property Owners in the South, 1790–1915*. Chicago: University of Illinois Press, 1990.

Terborg-Penn, Rosalyn. *African American Women in the Struggle for the Vote, 1850–1920*. Bloomington: Indiana University Press, 1998.

Whittington B. Johnson. *Black Savannah, 1788–1864*. Fayetteville: University of Arkansas Press, 1996.

Index

JANICE L. SUMLER-EDMOND is professor of history and chair of the Department of Humanities and Fine Arts and director of the W.E.B. Dubois Honors Program at Huston-Tillotson University in Austin, Texas. She is also an attorney and coeditor of two previous books: *Freedom's Odyssey: African American History Essays from Phylon* and *Black Women's History at the Intersection of Knowledge and Power: ABWH's Twentieth Anniversary Anthology*.